WORLD PREHISTORY

Ivory carving of head of an Advanced Palaeolithic woman from
Brassempouy, France

WORLD PREHISTORY

AN OUTLINE

BY

GRAHAME CLARK

*Fellow of Peterhouse and Disney Professor of Archaeology
in the University of Cambridge*

CAMBRIDGE

AT THE UNIVERSITY PRESS

1961

PUBLISHED BY

THE SYNDICS OF THE CAMBRIDGE UNIVERSITY PRESS

Bentley House, 200 Euston Road, London, N.W. 1
American Branch: 32 East 57th Street, New York 22, N.Y.
West African Office: P.O. Box 33, Ibadan, Nigeria

CAMBRIDGE UNIVERSITY PRESS

1961

Printed in Great Britain at the University Press, Cambridge
(Brooke Crutchley, University Printer)

IN MEMORIAM

V. G. CHILDE
O. G. S. CRAWFORD

CONTENTS

CONTENTS

ix

LIST OF PLATES

SOURCES: Cambridge University Press (IX); University Museum of Archaeology and Ethnology, Cambridge (I, XI, XII); Museum of Classical Archaeology, Cambridge (VI); Oriental Institute, Chicago (III); National Museum, Copenhagen (VII); Egypt Exploration Society (IV); Jos Museum, Nigeria (V); Dr K. M. Kenyon (II); Museum of National Antiquities, St Germain (courtesy Messrs Thames and Hudson, Ltd) (Frontispiece); State Historical Museum, Stockholm (VIII); Messrs Thames and Hudson, Ltd (X).

LIST OF MAPS

PREFACE

The object of this book is to present a brief outline of man's prehistoric past. The varying intensity of archaeological research in different parts of the world, the author's unequal reading and the insistent progress of knowledge, which modifies conclusions almost before they can be set down, all help to distort the picture. Yet, as a teacher, the author is aware that even an imperfect text may have its uses, more especially to those prepared to adventure more widely in the literature of the subject.

In a volume of this scope and size an author has no choice but to state conclusions without being able to argue his case in any detail or even, save on occasion, to specify alternatives or do more than indicate the very extensive areas of uncertainty which envelope his subject. The present author trusts that where his interpretation differs without explanation from that of some authorities cited at the end of this volume, the nature and limitations of his book will be remembered. One of the pleasures of preparing it has been the stimulus to read more widely, and the author acknowledges the benefits he has received in this way.

In seeing the book into print the author has received valuable help and criticism from members of the staff of the University Press.

Permission to publish photographs has been kindly given by the following: the University Museum of Archaeology and Ethnology and the Museum of Classical Archaeology at Cambridge; the Cambridge University Press; Messrs Thames and Hudson; Dr K. M. Kenyon; the Museum of National Antiquities, St Germain; the Oriental Institute, Chicago; the Museum, Jos, Nigeria; the National Museum, Copenhagen; and the State Historical Museum, Stockholm.

Finally, the author would like to acknowledge the skill and understanding with which Mrs Ruth Daniel has drawn the maps.

PETERHOUSE, CAMBRIDGE GRAHAME CLARK
August 1960

INTRODUCTION

The idea that human history began when the first hominids pro-
claimed their humanity by making tools according to socially
transmitted patterns is one that has only taken shape during the
hundred years or so since Darwin published *The Origin of Species*.
It had of course been realized much earlier that something could
be learned about times before the earliest written records by
diligent study of monuments and other material traces, though to
begin with antiquarians were mainly concerned with traces of
classical or medieval civilization. By the end of the eighteenth
century archaeology had already begun to be applied systemati-
cally to a study of the prehistoric, as well as the historic, ages of
man. A close relationship can indeed be observed between the
development of men's ideas about the biological world and about
their own earliest history, and it may be said that scientific enquiry
killed the idea that history was limited to the span of literate
tradition as surely as it did the dogma of the fixity of species.

The first systematic attempts to classify archaeological data
were both evolutionary in conception and show very clearly the
impact on the study of human history of ideas that had been
stirring in the realm of biology since the days of Buffon. C. J.
Thompsen's Three Age System (1836) was based on the succession
of stone, bronze and iron as the leading raw materials for tools and
weapons; and Sven Nilsson's (1838–43) classification was based
on a supposed progression from a hunter-fisher mode of life to
that of literate civilization by way of herding and cultivation.
These and later attempts to grade prehistoric societies in terms of
evolutionary development owed much to the observation of
modern primitive peoples. In much the same way, it was the
opportunities for studying nature at work gained on Darwin's
journey with the *Beagle* and Wallace's travels in the Malay

archipelago that led to the theory of evolution by natural selection. The publication of Darwin's book, and above all perhaps its championing by Thomas Huxley in relation to man's place in nature, proved a real turning point. Acceptance of the geological antiquity and zoological relationships of man served to emphasize the immensity and significance of his prehistory. The need to bridge the gap between what was known about man from traditional sources and what was implied by the new hypotheses of natural science in relation to his origins was now manifest.

It was to fill this gap that prehistory as we understand it came into being as a recognized field of study. The use of this term to designate the history of preliterate societies in contradistinction to that of literate ones may be thought to be illogical and to run counter to the basic continuity and unity of history. Yet there is a strong case for recognizing the distinction between the two disciplines, so long as it is remembered that there is in fact no break in the phenomena they seek to study. The kind of information about the prehistoric past to be won by archaeology is very different from that obtainable from written documents, so that whereas the historian is able to delve down into the motives and choices of individuals, the prehistorian must as a rule be content with the fate of communities or classes, and must concern himself with trends more often than with events. Again, although it is true that the methods perfected by prehistorians can generally be applied to elucidating the historic past, the skills and techniques most frequently used by the historian and by the prehistorian differ widely, as do their relations with other branches of knowledge.

If prehistory originated from a philosophical need brought into existence by the progress of biology, the more general applications of modern science have recently added urgency both to the prosecution and the dissemination of prehistory. It is not difficult to detect among lay public and professional historians alike a sense of the inadequacy of traditional history at the present juncture of human affairs. Whatever may be thought about his philosophy or scheme of history, it is a merit in Professor Toynbee to have emphasized the deficiencies in our age of supersonic aircraft and nuclear fission of the kind of history appropriate to the age of the horse and buggy or even of the railway. Anomalies frequently have their comical aspect, but equally they are liable to be dangerous; and this property is likely to be particularly marked when something so deeply charged with emotion as men's view of the past is involved. What is above all needed is surely a view of history capable of reconciling the requirements of national societies with those of a world order. Yet, if Toynbee's case against identifying general history with the history of western civilization is accepted, his insistence on the autonomy of the major literate civilizations runs the danger of substituting cultural for national rivalries. It is surely the prehistoric past, largely overlooked by Toynbee, that provides the only common source of all civilizations and so of all literate history.

The aim of this book is to survey in barest outline the history of mankind from the first dawn of culture down to the time when successive societies attained literacy. Since, once they had emerged as such, literate, civilized peoples tended to exert influence over those still living under prehistoric conditions, it will be necessary to sketch in the outlines of their subsequent histories at least down to the time when they were drawn into the range of younger dominant civilizations. In an outline of this kind it is hardly practicable to incorporate or even to summarize the kind of evidence, archaeological and natural-scientific, on which the reconstruction of prehistory depends. Our concern is not with the bricks and mortar so much as with the building, and attention will only be directed here and there to the kind of details needed to convey a vivid impression of texture and substance. It is nevertheless important to remind the reader that the account presented here rests on fragmentary but concrete evidence, most of it excavated from the soil and all of it subjected to the kind of scrutiny practised by experts in the field of criminal detection.

Since the reader is asked to take so much for granted, he is entitled to be made aware of some of the main areas of uncertainty and entreated to remember that the intensity with which prehistoric research has been carried on varies widely in different parts of the world. Yet, during the hundred years since the publication of *The Origin of Species*, enough has been learned to make possible a reasonably valid outline of what happened in prehistory.

A main difficulty is to ensure a proper balance. It is important to avoid European or other regional bias, yet it would be pointless to try and achieve a kind of time-space parity for its own sake; every period of time and parcel of territory has not contributed on equal terms to the early story of mankind any more than it has to contemporary history. Since by and large the tempo of change has quickened with each advance in culture, it will be necessary to treat the much shorter closing phases of prehistory on equivalent terms to the lengthier ones that preceded them; yet we must guard against paying the younger periods undue attention merely because of the bulk and diversity of the archaelogical material that survives from them, and we must seek all the while to weigh the relative importance of each main episode in the total history of mankind. Again, it has to be recognized that the focus of human progress has shifted within wide geographical limits in the course of time, so that first one region and then another has the chief claim on our attention. It is inevitable therefore, and indeed desirable, that whereas wide territories over long periods of time will receive hardly more than a passing mention, quite brief episodes will be given proportionately fuller treatment. The aim is not to produce a chronicle, a kind of Bayeux tapestry worked flatly on a roll of fabric, but something more like a history, painted in depth on a canvas of fixed dimensions. The main difficulty is to create a unity, to give the illusion of unfolding a complete panorama and yet at the same time to highlight significant groupings and reveal telling details. Fully to realize this calls for exceptional powers, and the writer will be content if he helps his readers in some measure to view the histories of their own cultures in the broad perspective of world prehistory.

An obvious precondition of this is a chronological framework of world-wide application. So long as one confines oneself to the prehistory of a single region, one can often piece together an outline story by analysing changes of fashion, the association in finds of one period of miscellaneous artifacts and the sequence of deposits on archaeological sites; moreover, events in different regions can often be synchronized if trade relations existed between them. So soon, however, as the field of study is enlarged beyond the range of prehistoric trade and extended backwards in time and outwards in space, the need for a more universal system or chronology becomes apparent. Episodes in the spheres of climate, geography and animal and plant life during the Pleistocene era of geological time provide a rough framework for prehistoric chronology, but a much finer grid is needed for the later stages of the story when the tempo of change grew so much more rapid. The ideal is clearly a system of absolute chronology in years, world-wide in validity and capable of being applied readily to archaeological sites. Dates founded on recorded history are of limited use: they can only be applied to comparatively recent prehistoric communities within territories bordering on the ancient centres of civilization; and even so are generally subject to considerable margins of error, due both to uncertainties in the earliest historical chronologies themselves and to the difficulty in effecting certain correlations between these and the prehistoric sequence. Systems based on minute fluctuations of climate as expressed by variations in the thickness of sediments deposited in glacial melt water or in the amount of growth made by trees in certain habitats will often provide a useful yardstick; yet it is only locally and exceptionally that these can be applied to measuring the progress of human prehistory. It is easy to see why the radio-carbon method devised by Dr W. F. Libby in 1949 holds so much promise, for here we have a technique yielding dates in terms of years and capable of being applied to archaeological sites all over the world. The method depends on the fact that when organisms die their radio-activity runs down at a known rate, so that by measuring accurately their remaining supply of C^{14} it is possible to estimate the time since death. It is very important to know that the method has plenty of limitations: apart from the possibility of contamination, which cannot be avoided even by the greatest care in collecting the sample and may involve troublesome pre-treatment, there is at present a limitation in range of around 50,000 years; and, most important of all, there is an inherent element of statistical uncertainty due to the random disintegration of atoms, which means not merely that C^{14} dates have to be expressed with a standard deviation of error, but that, even so, only a proportion of correct dates can be expected to fall within the given range, a consideration often ignored by critics of the method who fail to understand what it claims to do. Yet, though no reliance can be placed on individual analyses, a general pattern, based on a growing number of analyses and backed by intensive research into sources of error, is beginning to emerge wherever the method has been applied, a pattern which allows us for the first time to view the achievements of something like 2000 generations of men in historical perspective. Since this book is intended as an outline for wide use, isolated C^{14} dates will in general be avoided and the chronology adopted will be that generally accepted by prehistorians, taking account of the radiocarbon, as of other, geochronological methods, and utilizing where possible dates extrapolated from the earliest historical sources.

CHAPTER I

MAN'S PLACE IN NATURE

A major paradox to be faced when we consider our own origins is that man, who through the power of his mind has come near to complete mastery over the forces of external nature as they confront him on this planet, and who is even now engaged in extending his dominion into outer space, is himself an animal. In common with all other animals he forms part of the nexus of living things and individually is subject to the same processes of growth, maturity and death. Like them, also, he lives within the framework of a physical environment. If therefore we are to interpret correctly the material traces of his culture recovered by archaeology, it is important to begin by considering at least in broad outline the evolution of his geographical setting during Pleistocene and later times. Equally, since he owes his power in the first instance to the physical and mental endowment acquired from his forebears in the course of evolution, it is essential to consider, if only in bald outline, the main steps in the recent history of his emergence as a biological entity.

PHYSICAL ENVIRONMENT

The Pleistocene era, which witnessed both the biological and cultural evolution of the earliest men, was one of profound environmental change. It was marked above all by a succession of climatic fluctuations of sufficient magnitude to produce major shifts of animals and plants as well as changes in the disposition of land and water sufficient to alter, sometimes drastically, the possibilities of human migration and settlement. The existence of these repeated fluctuations in the conditions under which the

7

earliest men lived is significant for two reasons: it affords some insight into the kinds of challenge encountered by our forebears, both as biological organisms and as builders of culture; and it provides a broad framework of natural chronology for the main stages of his early prehistory.

Glacial and pluvial periods

In the existing temperate zone and in the tropics at high altitudes the most dramatic feature of the Pleistocene was the extension and contraction of ice-sheets. Sheets of boulder-clay of the type laid down by glaciers and trains of boulders marking their passage, as well as more prominent topographic features, like the moraines deposited by ice-sheets withdrawing from their former margins, show that great ice-sheets covered extensive parts of North America and Europe which now enjoy temperate conditions. In periglacial zones immediately beyond the margin of the ice, great sheets of loess, a fine dust blown out of exposed frost-soils by winds issuing from glaciated territories, blanketed the landscape, and during temperate episodes between glacial phases their surfaces weathered, leaving a clear record of climatic fluctuations. The direct effects of the Pleistocene glaciations on early man through their denial of areas for settlement and through the barriers they interposed against human migration, though locally considerable, were less widespread than those of the geographical and biological changes associated with them. For instance the locking up of water in ice-sheets had a profound influence on sea-levels: calculations show that the excess over what is contained in the existing ice-caps would have been sufficient to reduce sea-levels by around 100 metres (c. 325 feet) and geological evidence points to a lowering of sea-levels during Pleistocene times of just this order of magnitude. Where thick, immensely heavy ice-sheets were formed, the earth's crust might locally be temporarily depressed, only to recover again when the ice melted, an effect known as isostasy; in areas subject to heavy glaciation, therefore, the onset of a glacial period might entail a depression of the land in relation to the sea. Nevertheless, apart from areas under or immediately contiguous to ice-sheets, glaciations were marked by falls and interglacial periods by rises of sea-level, producing what are known as eustatic changes—enough to form or intersect land-bridges of cardinal importance to human migration. Over the extensive tropical and subtropical territories, which played so important a part both in the early genesis of man and in his culture, as well as in the development of farming and urban life, climatic change expressed itself in pronounced and prolonged periods of heavier rainfall—so-called pluvial periods— interrupted by interpluvial ones with lower rainfall, marked respectively by such phenomena as rises and falls of lake-levels and the activity and inactivity of springs.

No less profound were the biological consequences of the changes of climate of which glaciations and pluvials and subsidiary episodes were merely local expressions. What was in effect happening with each major cycle was a shifting back and forth of climatic zones: when ice-sheets expanded into temperate zones, rain-belts encroached on subtropical ones and the tropics themselves contracted; conversely, when ice-sheets retreated, temperate conditions began to reassert themselves over territories formerly covered by ice and deserts to reclaim regions temporarily revived by temperate conditions. Apart from their direct impact, climatic changes influenced the conditions of human life profoundly through the plants and animals on which mankind depended for food as well as for many of the substances required for his material culture. Widespread transformations in vegetation were an inevitable accompaniment of climatic cycles of sufficient magnitude to bring about large-scale glaciations: tundra, coniferous, deciduous and evergreen forests, desert and tropical rain-forests all shifted in response to changes of precipitation and temperature. Equally, since they depended directly on vegetation, the herbivorous animals with which man was principally concerned reacted

9

in similar fashion to the onset and retreat of each climatic cycle, so that a forest fauna might in any particular locality be replaced by one adapted to steppe or tundra conditions and vice versa.

The cumulative effect on human societies of these major fluctuations in the character of the external environment must have been all the greater in view of the pitifully small cultural capital available during prehistoric times. When it is remembered that they were repeated at frequent intervals during the million years or so of the Pleistocene—no less than fifteen times if the evidence of ocean cores is to be relied upon—it is hard to resist the idea that some causative link must have existed between them and the process of change involved in man's biological and cultural evolution. Environmental change was a potent agent of biological mutation, just as it stimulated migration and emphasized isolation. On the cultural side anthropological studies suggest that at any given moment of time an apparent equilibrium exists between any human society and the habitat (soil and climate) and biome (vegetation and animal life) of the ecosystem (total natural setting) in which it subsists and of which in a sense it forms an integral part: any change in habitat or biome must of necessity call for readjustments in human society of a kind involving cultural change, migration, or both, the outcome of which is the establishment of a new and likewise temporary equilibrium. It is in this continuous process of challenge and response—to use Toynbee's vivid phrase—enriched and complicated by interaction between rival societies and increasingly by contending classes—that we may surely see some explanation for the mechanics of human progress, even if it brings us no nearer an ultimate explanation of prehistory.

The Pleistocene period that witnessed the unfolding of human prehistory probably began about a million years ago. It was marked in the fossil record by the appearance of true elephants, horses and oxen, but during its Early stage elements of the old

Tertiary fauna survived in the Villafranchian beds, including such forms as *Dinotherium*, *Stylohipparion* and *Sivatherium*. As we have seen the period as a whole was marked by frequent and sometimes pronounced climatic changes, which assumed different guises in various parts of the world. Among the most dramatic were the repeated advances and withdrawals of ice-sheets in the present temperate zone. On dry land the geological record of these is incomplete or at least damaged by more recent episodes. Yet, both on the north European plain and in the Alpine area it has been possible to map fairly closely the moraines of four major glaciations, which are here named after localities in the Alps where they were first recognized. The indications are particularly clear for the Late Pleistocene, which embraced the last or Würm glaciation and its preceding interglacial phase. The Middle Pleistocene, which owes its special interest to the fact that deposits of this age have yielded the earliest certain traces of human industry, was marked by two major glaciations (Mindel and Riss) and a prolonged Mindel–Riss interglacial. On the other hand the evidence for the Early Pleistocene is much less well preserved, even though this phase apparently lasted longer than the two later ones combined; indeed, geologists have only been able to recover abundant signs of one glaciation, that of Günz, though traces of at least three earlier ones have been detected. Recent studies of deep-sea cores drilled from the beds of the Caribbean and Pacific suggest that in all there were fifteen main glaciations, as against less than half that number established by ground survey in the Alps. This only goes to show how little is known about the history of the Early Pleistocene period, which must on the other hand have witnessed vital stages in the emergence of humanity.

The most recent glacial deposits are as a rule better preserved and allow finer divisions to be made, so that in the following Table A three phases can already be distinguished in the period of the Würm glaciation.

TABLE A. *Major sub-divisions of the Pleistocene period in central Europe and East Africa*

Geological time	Radio-carbon dates B.C.	Glacial episodes (central Europe)	Pluvial episodes (East Africa)
	12,000–8,000	Late Würm	
Upper	29,000–12,000	Middle Würm	Gamblian
Pleistocene	70,000–29,000	Early Würm	
	100,000–70,000	Riss–Würm inter-glacial	Interpluvial
Middle Pleistocene		Riss	Kanjeran
		Mindel–Riss inter-glacial	Interpluvial
		Mindel	Kamasian
Early Pleistocene		Günz–Mindel inter-glacial	Interpluvial
(Villafranchian fauna)		Günz	Kageran
c. 1,000,000		Sequence of numerous earlier glaciations	—

The younger episodes of the Late Würm are naturally those which have so far been most closely dated. The results set out in Table B are those obtained from a limited part of north-western Europe, but both the Allerød oscillation and the somewhat abrupt close of the Late Pleistocene around ten thousand years ago have left records over extensive zones of the northern temperate zone.

TABLE B. *Minor sub-divisions of the Late Würm in north-western Europe*

Radio-carbon dates B.C.	Climatic stages	Forest history zones
8,850–8,000	Younger Dryas	III
10,000–8,850	Allerød oscillation	II
10,500–10,000	Older Dryas	Ic
11,500–10,500	Bølling oscillation	Ib
12,000–11,500	Oldest Dryas	Ia

Outside the glaciated territories, in lands where subtropical and tropical climates now prevail, fluctuations of climate occurred of comparable magnitude, taking the form of pluvial phases of markedly greater rainfall, interrupted by arid, interpluvial ones. In Table A the pluvial periods of Africa and Asia are shown for convenience marching alongside the glacial ones of Europe and North America, but it needs to be emphasized that it is quite unknown whether or how closely they were in fact synchronous. For this we must await the development and application of techniques that make it possible to assign absolute dates far enough back in both areas.

The value of sequences of this kind for providing a chronological framework, even for periods for which no absolute dates are yet available, hardly needs stressing. What is hardly less true is the importance of climatic changes of the magnitude and frequency known to have occurred during Pleistocene times to a proper appreciation of the geographical conditions under which early man developed both as an organism and as a cultured being. Thus variations in precipitation and temperature, quite apart from their direct effects, altered radically the conditions for gaining a livelihood through their influence on vegetation and animals. Similarly, the changes of land and sea-levels which resulted from the growth and retreat of ice-sheets (see pp. 8f.) must have influenced the pattern of settlement and above all, in an age before sea-going craft had come into use, have had a profound effect on the possibilities of migration. Knowledge of the precise coast-line is of particular importance for the Late Glacial and early Neothermal period, during which widespread migrations occurred. Deep borings in the Pontine Marshes of Italy and elsewhere have fortunately made it possible to measure with some accuracy the displacement of sea-level during the last glaciation and this, in turn, allows one to form a good impression of the extent of the land-connections that, for example, linked Britain with the European mainland, Alaska with Siberia, south-east Asia with Indonesia as far as the Makassar Strait and Australia with New Guinea and Tasmania.

Neothermal climate

Although in a broad sense the Pleistocene or Quaternary period lasted down to the present day, it has been found useful to designate the time since the last major fluctuation by a distinct term. Workers in the present temperate zone understandably began by referring to the Recent or Holocene period as Postglacial, but in the context of world prehistory the more modern term Neothermal is preferable, since the passing of glacial conditions was only one of several local effects of a world-wide phenomenon. Radiocarbon analyses agree with counts of the varved or finely layered sediments deposited annually in the melt-waters of the contracting Scandinavian ice-sheet to indicate that the Neothermal period, which witnessed the gradual emergence of existing physical environments and an immense acceleration in the process of social evolution, began some ten thousand years ago. Since the deposits are both more accessible and better preserved, it is hardly surprising that we know the history of the Neothermal period in far greater detail than we do that of any previous geological era. In the temperate zone in particular it has been possible through a statistical analysis of the fossil pollen incorporated in successive layers to zone deposits belonging to this period in terms of their vegetational history: to begin with, only trees capable of living under relatively cold conditions were able to colonize the landscape freed by the contraction of ice-sheets; only gradually and progressively did an increase in warmth-demanding trees reflect the rise of temperature to a maximum noticeably above that now prevailing in the temperate zones at the time of what in these territories constituted the Neothermal climatic optimum; and during the concluding phases vegetational change reflected above all a decline from the climatic optimum and the transformation of the landscape under the influence of farming and industrial activity.

Rather less has yet been discovered about minor environmental changes in the existing tropical and more particularly in the present subtropical zones that played so crucial a part in the origins of farming and the early development of civilization. The most complete sequence is that worked out for East Africa, where two minor periods of increased rainfall (Makalian and Nakuran) have been distinguished for Neothermal times. Detailed study of the fauna from the upper levels of the Mount Carmel caves has confirmed the existence in Palestine of an initial dry phase followed by a wet one that presumably corresponds with the Makalian, and there is some evidence that this latter extended over a broad zone of northern Africa.

TABLE C. *Sequence of climatic stages during the last 10,000 years*

Dates B.C.	North-west Europe Forest zones	North-west Europe Postglacial	North America Neothermal	East Africa Epipleistocene
0	IX	Sub-atlantic	Medithermal	Nakuran
2000	VIII	Sub-boreal		Dry
		Optimum		
4000	VII	Atlantic	Altithermal	Makalian
6000	VI V	Boreal	Anathermal	Dry
8000	IV	Pre-boreal		

Fluctuations of sea-level

Corresponding to the broad climatic changes of Neothermal times were fluctuations of sea-level resembling, though on a much reduced scale, those of the Pleistocene. Leaving aside isostatic movements, which, however pronounced, were local in their effects, the main change was the eustatic rise of sea-level due to the melting of ice-sheets. Radio-carbon analyses of samples from deposits submerged off the coasts of north-west Europe, North America and New Zealand indicate that in areas unaffected by crustal movements sea-levels rose at a rate of approximately three feet a century between *c.* 12,000 and 4000 B.C. Close study of ancient strand-lines has further shown that at the peak of the Neothermal climatic optimum sea-levels rose a certain height above modern sea-level from which they have since receded.

BIOLOGICAL EVOLUTION

The Primates

The physical similarities between men and anthropoid apes are so close as to leave no reasonable doubt of their near zoological affinities: this is so whether one considers the general structure of the skeleton, the muscular anatomy or the disposition of the visceral organs, or whether one takes account of the evidence of metabolic processes or serological reactions; even the human brain has recently been stated by a leading authority to be 'in its morphology...little more than a magnified model of the brain of an anthropoid ape'. Indeed, one might almost go so far as to classify both apes (Pongidae) and hominids (Hominidae) (the latter comprising all varieties of living men together with fossils of all the forms to appear since the anthropoid apes diverged from the parent stem) as falling within the same family *Hominoidea*, a family which is comprised, together with that of the catarrhine monkeys (Cercopithecidae), in the order Primates. Yet the general weight of opinion, impressed by the notably larger size of the brain in relation to body-weight in man and by significant differences in dentition and in linear proportions of the limbs, inclines to rate the Pongidae and Hominidae as separate families alongside the Cercopithecidae.

From an evolutionary point of view the most significant step in the emergence of the hominids seems to have been the assumption of an erect posture. It was this which released the hands from locomotion, making them available for tool-making and the securing and preparation of food, and in due time led to the head being balanced on top of the spinal column rather than suspended from its upper extremity. No doubt the changes in dentition, characteristic of the hominids, were to some degree linked to the growing importance of the forelimbs and in turn affected the architecture of the cranium, more particularly of the brow-ridges. What is reasonably certain is that our remote hominid ancestors attained a more or less erect posture before their brains had notably exceeded the range of the great apes.

The Australopithecines

It would seem that, whereas the great apes were adapted to life in the forest and so specialized in a brachiating mode of locomotion (that is, one in which they still made considerable use of their arms) the hominids developed in more open country and early adopted an erect, bipedal carriage. Three main genera may be distinguished in the family Hominidae. The first to appear in the course of evolution were the Australopithecinae; the second *Pithecanthropus*; and the third *Homo*. The original discovery of *Pithecanthropus erectus* revealed a creature that combined an erect habit with a brain not much bigger than that of a large ape. The more recent revelation of the Australopithecines has confirmed beyond doubt that in the evolution of the hominids bipedal locomotion preceded the enlargement of the brain. The majority of the Australopithecine fossils have been recovered from Early Pleistocene deposits in South and East Africa and this strongly suggests that these territories must have been the main centres of hominid evolution at this time: indeed, the only find so far made from south-east Asia, that of *Palaeojavanensis* (cf. *Maganthropus*), came from Djetis beds of Sangiran in Java now generally assigned to an early stage of the Middle Pleistocene (Map 1). The South African Australopithecine fossils belong to two main groups, each of sub-generic status and dating from successive stages of a late phase of the Lower Pleistocene. The earlier sub-genus *Australopithecus*, which dates from the last dry interstadial and the onset of the final wet phase of the Kageran pluvial, comprises two main species, *A. africanus* from Taungs and Makapan and *A. transvaalensis* (cf. *Plesianthropus*) from Sterkfontein. The younger sub-genus *Paranthropus*, including *P. robustus* from Kromdrai and *P. crassidens* from Swartkrans, dates from the last Kageran wet phase. Two important finds from East Africa can be classified within this framework: the so-called *Meganthropus africanus* from

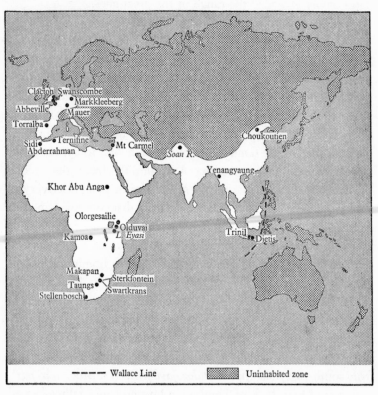

1. The prehistoric world to the end of the Middle Pleistocene

near Lake Eyasi in Tanganyika falls into *A. transvaalensis*; and the recently discovered *Zinjanthropus boisei* from the lowest bed in the lacustrine series at Olduvai in the same land fits quite well into *P. crassidens*.

Morphologically, and particularly in the general structure of the skull, notably its height above the orbit, the contour of the forehead and upper facial area, and the mastoid process, as well as in the pattern of the dentition with its evenly curved parabolic arcade, small teeth, spatulate canines and absence of the diastemic intervals or gaps either side of the canines, the fossil remains of the Australopithecines reveal clear hominid affinities, even though the cubic capacity of the brain ranged only from 450 to 700 c.c. compared with 685 c.c. for the largest known cranium of a gorilla. The character of the limb and pelvic bones makes it reasonably certain that these small-brained, but nevertheless basically hominid Australopithecines had adopted an upright posture. Their general evolutionary significance is thus clear: they provide just the antecedents one might have expected for the Pithecanthropians of the succeeding Middle Pleistocene era. Yet it would be wise to recognize that in the existing state of knowledge the precise status of the Australopithecines in hominid evolution is far from being agreed by expert opinion. In particular it is sometimes argued that *Australopithecus* and *Paranthropus* mark culminations of side-branches from the main line of hominid evolution leading to Pithecanthropus rather than standing on the main stem; and great significance has been attached to a fossil jaw from the *Paranthropus* deposit at Swartkrans. Yet until more complete fossils of *Telanthropus*, as it has been termed, are available there seems no prospect of deciding whether this form is entitled to a separate status, still less whether it stood closer to the main line of evolution than *Paranthropus*.

The Pithecanthropians

Since the original discovery of remains of *Pithecanthropus erectus* in the Trinil beds of Java, several more finds have been made on the island and there seems no doubt that hominids of this genus were living there in Middle Pleistocene times. A much larger assemblage of upwards of forty individuals has been re-covered from North China in the Middle Pleistocene filling of rock-fissures at Choukoutien near Peking (Pl. I). At first these remains were given the status of a distinct genus, *Sinanthropus*, but later studies have shown that they belong to the genus *Pithecanthropus*; indeed it is doubtful whether they ought to be accorded even the specific designation *pekinensis*, since the flattening (*platymeria*) of the shaft of the thigh-bone, on which the distinction from *P. erectus* has been held to rest, could so easily result from nutritional factors. More recently traces of the same genus (needlessly termed *Atlanthropus mauritanicus*), in the form of two mandibles and part of the cranium of a younger subject, have come to light in Early Pleistocene deposits exposed in a sand-pit at Ternifine near Palikao, Algeria; and the old find of a mandible from Mauer near Heidleberg suggests that the Pithecanthropians were also present in Europe during Middle Pleistocene times. In general character they represent an advance from forms akin to the Australopithecines and in particular they show a notable increase in brain capacity: thus the mean of three crania from Java was 860 c.c. and that of four from Peking was 1075 c.c., placing them in this respect more or less intermediate between *Australopithecus* (400–700 c.c.) and *Homo sapiens* (c. 1350 c.c.); the fact that the Chinese group is well to the fore accords with its wholly Middle Pleistocene age.

Although they illustrate at least the beginning of the second main advance in hominid evolution, the growth of the brain following the attainment of an upright posture, the Pithecanthropians display a number of features which mark them off from more evolved forms. Thus the skull has a low vault with frontal flattening, a marked ridge at the junction of the two main side bones and thick walls; the mastoid process is small; the palate is enormous and there is marked alveolar prognathism, the lower part of the face projecting forward noticeably; the mandible is massive and, in the case of the Java form, the teeth, though hominid in their general arrangement, show tendencies for the upper canines to overlap the lower ones and for a diastemic gap to appear between the incisors and canines; and the weight of the mandible is matched by a correspondingly massive development of the supraorbital and occipital brow-ridges, which, together with the flattened forehead, would probably strike us most forcibly were we to encounter one in the flesh. Yet the Chinese variety was quite certainly manufacturing tools and using fire.

TABLE D. *Simplified classification of the Hominidae*

Geological time	Genus	Sub-genus	Species
Late Pleistocene	*Homo*		*H. sapiens* *H. neanderthalensis* *H. soloensis* *H. rhodesiensis*
Middle Pleistocene	*Pithecan-* *thropus*		*P. heidelbergensis* (cf. *H.h.*) *P. africanus* (cf. *Atlan-* *thropus*) *P. pekinensis* (cf. *Sinan-* *thropus* *P. javanensis* (cf. *P.* *erectus*)
Early Pleistocene (Villafranchian)	Australo- pithecinae	*Telanthropus?* *Paranthropus* *Australopithecus*	*P. javanensis* (cf. *Palaeojavanensis*) *P. robustus* *P. crassidens* *A. africanus* *A. transvaalensis* (cf. *Plesianthropus*)

It was from this Pithecanthropian stock that the primitive forerunners of *Homo sapiens* must have developed. The rarity and fragmentary character of well-documented fossils makes it difficult to know what these were like. The surviving bones of the Swanscombe skull obtained from Mindel–Riss gravels in the Lower Thames basin, together with hand-axes of the type first recognized at Saint-Acheul, near Amiens in North France, show no characteristics which enable them to be distinguished clearly from skulls of *Homo sapiens* in his modern form. On the other hand the frontal bone is missing and it is precisely this that, in the case of the comparable skull from an interstadial deposit of the Riss glaciation at Steinheim in South Germany, shows primitive characteristics in the form of the massive brow-ridges that commonly went with large teeth and heavy jaws. It seems most likely that the Middle Pleistocene inhabitants of Europe and probably of Africa, while retaining certain Pithecanthropian features in modified form, had a moderately well-developed frontal region, a relatively high cranial vault and a face of only moderate size.

Neanderthal and Neanderthaloid men

By early Late Pleistocene times the picture is more complex. Now for the first time we have evidence for a truly modern type, lacking massive brow-ridges, in the two fragmentary skulls from the cave of Fontéchevade in the Dordogne, France. This find is all the more striking in that it was overlaid by a deposit containing Mousterian flints (of the kind found at Le Moustier in the Dordogne and elsewhere) with remains of Neanderthal man, a variety named after the discovery of a brain-case in the Neanderthal in the German Rhineland, and since exemplified by a number of others from Europe dating from the first phase of the last or Würm glaciation. The limb bones of this kind of man are thick-walled, heavy and unduly short, especially in the forearm and calf, in relation to his trunk. Again, his skull, although having a cranial capacity well up to modern average, displays a number of aberrant features: for instance the cranial vault is flattened, the face is large and the foramen magnum, the hole at the base of the skull through which the spinal cord passes to the brain, is set slightly backward; the supraorbital ridge or torus is prominent and continuous, and with this is associated a chinless jaw of massive proportions; and, finally, the molar teeth exhibit the condition of taurodontism much more often than is usual among modern man. It may be significant that this extreme form appears to be confined to a marginal territory of the palaeolithic world; perhaps, as has been suggested, it represents an aberration in response to extreme climatic conditions, under which the chance of genetic variation was likely to have been at a maximum precisely when opportunities for migration were reduced.

In many ways it is unfortunate that the earliest finds which have created our image of the 'classic' Neanderthal type should have been made in this marginal territory. Analogous finds from regions that enjoyed more temperate conditions, for example those from the Palestinian caves of es-Skhūl and et-Tabun, Mount Carmel, the Shanidur cave in northern Iraq and the cave of Teshik-Tash in Uzbekistan, display Neanderthal characteristics to a much less pronounced degree. It has sometimes been argued that these Asiatic Neanderthaloids were the product of interbreeding between Neanderthal and Sapiens stocks, but a more likely view is that they stand closer to the main stem of human evolution and represent, or at least are closely related to, types intermediate between Swanscombe and Steinheim on the one hand and modern man on the other. One reason for thinking that this is so is that *Homo sapiens* almost certainly emerged somewhere in Eurasia and most probably in western Asia.

Homo sapiens *and modern races of man*

In any event the people identified with the Advanced Upper Palaeolithic hunting cultures that immediately succeeded the Mousterian in this region were essentially modern in type. The limb bones, relatively light and slender, suggest a fully upright posture, as does the position of the foramen magnum which faces directly downwards; the forehead is rounded and approximately vertical and the muscular ridges on the cranium are only lightly marked; the brow ridges are moderately developed and are never continuous; and the jaw has a well-defined chin, is light in build and has relatively small teeth. The overwhelming consensus of professional opinion is that the existing races of mankind are without exception variants of this single species, *Homo sapiens*.

When and where did the various races of man diverge? The first question is particularly difficult to answer, because so many of the leading criteria by which racial differences are distinguished, such as pigmentation and hair form, are such as can hardly be studied from skeletal material. Attempts have been made to read racial characteristics into some Upper Palaeolithic remains—for instance the type first recognized from the Grimaldi caves near Mentone has been variously interpreted as Negroid or primitive Mediterranean and that from the rock-shelter of Chancelade in the Dordogne has even been held to be Eskimo in type—but the dangers of drawing conclusions from such limited evidence are obviously very great and it is wisest to admit that we do not yet know when the existing races of *Homo sapiens* came into being. What seems most likely is that they arose as a result of gradual genetic diversification following on the widespread migrations and colonization of new territories that occurred some time during the final major glacial cycle. The degree to which the distribution of certain well-defined pigmentation types fits in with that of specific environments, after due allowance is made for the effect of migration since the period of characterization, is sufficiently close to suggest that differences of pigmentation must have been to some degree adaptive: thus in the Old World blonde fair-skinned people tend to go with a cool, cloudy habitat; brunettes with the strong sunlight and bright skies of climates like that of the Mediterranean area; the darkest skinned with the hottest, non-forested regions (for example, the savanna of Africa); and those with yellowish skin and crinkly hair with the tropical rain-forests of Africa and south-east Asia. Again, there are sound reasons for linking width of nasal aperture with climate, since it is a function of the nose to mitigate the temperature of the air before it is drawn into the lungs: it is therefore not at all surprising to observe the narrow nostrils of the Eskimo or even the North European, the medium ones of the Mediterranean or the broad ones of the Negro. Yet it would be quite wrong to suppose that all geographical variations were necessarily adaptive, since the isolation which must have increased as man extended his geographical range could well in itself have been sufficient to promote genetic variations.

A last point to make is that it was only during the final stages of the Pleistocene that man spread over the greater part of the earth. The early types of men were confined to the warmer parts of the Old World: their remains are found widely over Africa from Algeria to the Cape; in Europe as far north as lowland England and central Germany; in western Asia up to the mountains of northern Iran; in India, south-east Asia and Indonesia; and as far east as the Makassar Strait, coinciding with the great biological divide first recognized by Darwin's collaborator, A. R. Wallace. It was not until some time after he had emerged in his modern form that *Homo sapiens* occupied northern Eurasia and spread on the one hand into the New World and on the other into Australia and Tasmania and across Polynesia to New Zealand. The extension of human settlement over progressively wider territories is one of the major themes of the prehistory of Late Glacial and Neothermal times to be treated in later chapters of this book: it was made possible by the relatively unspecialized character of *Homo sapiens* as a biological species, but above all by the possession of culture, by means of which man has been able to adapt himself to the widest range of environments.

CHAPTER 2

LOWER PALAEOLITHIC CULTURES AND THEIR SURVIVALS

Criteria of culture

Although most palaeontologists agree that the assumption of an upright posture was sufficiently important to justify separating the hominids from the great apes, few would maintain that it is possible to distinguish on purely zoological grounds between those hominids that remained prehuman and those that had attained the status of man. To qualify as human, a hominid has, so to say, to justify himself by works: the criteria are no longer biological so much as cultural. Yet it remains true that a close interrelationship must exist between cultural achievement and biological endowment. The adoption of an erect posture, which may well have been a response to the thinning of forest and the consequent need to cross open country between one area of woodland and another, in itself facilitated the acquisition of culture; the freeing of the hands from locomotion made them available for tool-using and ultimately for tool-making; and these activities stimulated the development of the brain. At the same time they facilitated it by modifying the architecture of the skull: the diminishing role of the teeth for eating and manipulating had the effect of reducing their size, the weight of the jaw and the strength of the brow-ridges and muscular attachments. On the other hand the two-footed stance had its dangers, and ultimately only those hominids survived who made an intelligent use of tools and weapons. Indeed the ability to acquire culture was evidently of adaptive value in the sense that the strains most capable of doing so were those whose genotypes were propagated most abundantly in the course of natural selection. This may well explain why the increase in the size of the brain that permitted ever greater advances in culture developed so rapidly in the course of Pleistocene times. Even the biological evolution of the most advanced hominids was thus in large measure an outcome of developments in culture.

In many ways the most striking of these, and certainly the one most likely to find reflection in the archaeological record, is the ability to make tools. Here the distinction between tool-using and tool-making is one that needs stressing: it may be true that one has grown out of the other, but it is important to emphasize that it is as a fabricator that man stands out from his fellow primates. By the use of a tool is meant the active manipulation by an organism for the furtherance of its aims of some object taken from the external environment: thus, to quote Dr W. H. Thorpe's example, a Californian sea-otter bringing boulders up from the sea-bottom to crack molluscs is using a tool, whereas a gull dropping a mollusc on a rock to break it is not doing so. Tool-using in the true sense can be traced far back among quite lowly forms of life, but it does not of itself imply intelligence or insight. Even the great apes, though showing some dexterity in the manipulation of sticks and strings and in the stacking of boxes, reveal grave limitations in their behaviour. For instance, they show little understanding of statics, and in their handling of boxes rely almost entirely on blind improvisation rather than insight. Again—and this is even more significant—their activities are directed exclusively to securing visible objectives, so that even when some preparation is involved, such as sharpening the end of one stick to fit into a socket, the element of foresight and planning is really very slight. By contrast, tool-making and the building of structures, even among the most primitive human societies, are based on a precise knowledge of raw materials and, within the limits of the technology prevailing, of how most effectively to handle them. Moreover, it is characteristic of human beings that they have a much greater appreciation of the factor of time than the other primates: in their oral (and in due course literary) traditions they draw on memories of the past, which serve them as a kind of cultural capital; and by taking account of the future they gain the impetus needed to undertake operations which may in themselves be long-drawn out, and to meet contingencies not always precisely foreseeable.

Speech

Speech was almost certainly another cultural attribute of the earliest men. Students of the great apes are agreed that one of their greatest drawbacks is the lack of speech, which alone is sufficient to prevent them acquiring the elements of culture. It is true that chimpanzees have a wider 'register of emotional expression' than most humans and that they are able to communicate to one another not only their emotional states but also definite desires and urges; yet, as Köhler has emphasized, 'their gamut of phonetics is entirely "subjective", and can only express emotions, never designate or describe objects'. In this connection it is interesting that in their famous enterprise of bringing up the chimpanzee Viki from the age of three days to three years, Dr and Mrs Hayes found it possible to train her to certain commands, but failed after eighteen months of intensive tuition to get her 'to identify her nose, eyes, hands and feet'. Until hominids had developed words as symbols, the possibility of transmitting, and so accumulating, culture hardly existed. Again, as Thorpe has remarked, man's prelinguistic counting ability is only of about the same order as that of birds or squirrels: serious mathematics, with all the immense advances in control of the environment that it portends, first became possible with the development of symbols. Speech, involving the use of symbols, must have been one of the first indications of humanity. Its only drawback as a criterion for the prehistorian is that there is no hope of being able to verify its existence directly for the remotest ages of man. Despite suggestions to the contrary, the best palaeontological opinion is against the notion that articulate speech can be inferred either from the conformation of the mandible or from study of casts taken of the inner surfaces of skulls. Probably the best clue is the appearance of tools of standardized and recognizable form, since it is hard to see how these can have been popularized and transmitted without the use of verbal symbols.

The first fabricated tools

Without doubt the most palpable signs of the earliest culture are the tools made by prehistoric man. The oldest ones recognized by the pioneers of prehistory were hand-axes, flaked down from nodules or thick flakes on either face so as to form a well-defined working-edge. The occurrence of such tools side by side with remains of extinct animals in ancient river gravels and other diluvial deposits provided the earliest good evidence for the antiquity of man. Further evidence was obtained from rock-shelters and caves, the exploration of which had already begun more than a generation before Darwin published *The Origin of Species*, but which was resumed more intensively in 1858. By 1865 enough had been learnt for Sir John Lubbock to contrast the immensely long Old Stone or Palaeolithic Age, during which men lived by gathering and by hunting animals that included many species now extinct, with the New Stone or Neolithic Age, most fully revealed by the finds from the pile-settlements (not long since exposed by the shores of the Swiss lakes), which mirrored the lives of peasants living a more settled life based on farming and practising a variety of new crafts that included potting and sometimes weaving.

The transition from using whatever lay to hand to the fashioning of purposive tools must have been gradual and therefore difficult to detect in the archaeological record. We are indeed fortunate that early man made extensive use of relatively imperishable substances such as flint or stone, in addition to the organic materials that have vanished almost entirely from the earlier chapters of the story. Even so there are grave difficulties in recognizing man's first essays in the working of flint and stone, since not only might a very slight amount of trimming suffice to adapt a fragment detached by frost or some other natural agency, but nature herself is capable of simulating artificial flaking of quite a high order. Assuming that there must have been a more primitive stage in the working of flint and stone than that represented by the Palaeolithic hand-axes from diluvial deposits, certain prehistorians of the opening decades of this century addressed themselves to what they took to be industries from the dawn of the Stone Age. Many of the so-called eoliths (Eos, Greek goddess of dawn) were in themselves reasonably convincing (even if the product of intensive selection), but the very zeal of the eolith hunters proved their undoing: it was not merely the numbers in which they found them that aroused scepticism, but even more the increasing age of the deposits in which they occurred. Specimens from the Pliocene seemed permissible, but when they were found in deposits of successively earlier phases of the Tertiary era, from Miocene, Oligocene and even early Eocene deposits, it became evident—since after all man-sized apes first appeared in the fossil record from the Miocene—that something was amiss. Prehistorians also became aware that similar forms occurred in much younger deposits containing well-made palaeolithic tools and this helped to stimulate research into the natural agencies that might have been responsible. In due course assemblages of chipped flints and stones were found under conditions which showed them to have been the indubitable products of nature. From a study of these it is now possible to attribute to specific natural agencies many of the earlier 'industries': for instance the so-called 'Cromerian' flints were products of quite recent storm wave action on the foreshore; the Kentish 'eoliths' were made by the friction of one flint against another in the course of soil-creep; the 'eoliths' from Eocene deposits at Clermont in the French department of Oise were produced by pressure and movement caused by solution of the calcareous formation underlying the flint-bearing strata, and many 'Kafuan' 'implements' from Uganda were apparently the work of waterfalls and rapids in steep gorges.

The oldest certain indications of industrial activity date from the transition from Early to Middle Pleistocene times and present indications suggest that they were made by people of advanced Pithecanthropian type. The possibility exists that certain Australopithecines were tool-makers. Three Australopithecine teeth were recovered from a breccia of Sterkfontein which yielded flakes and cores of comparatively advanced workmanship, and Australopithecine skeletal remains have recently been found on more than one floor in bed I at Olduvai, Tanganyika, associated with animal remains and flaked stone tools. Whether the tools were in fact made by the Australopithecines or by their hypothetical hunter (*Telanthropus?*) can hardly be determined from the evidence yet available; the absence of tools from the Australopithecine sites in the dolomite areas of South Africa has been explained by the suggestion that these were the dens of carnivores rather than living-sites, but such an argument is somewhat double-edged, since if the Australopithecines had really been tool-makers it seems hard to credit that they can have been such ready victims, especially when we consider the achievements of Peking man with similar or even inferior tools. A point to be emphasized is that the brains of the Australopithecines never exceed in capacity that of modern gorillas (max. 685 c.c.), whereas there is no proof that even *Pithecanthropus javanesis* of Java, with an average skull capacity of 900 c.c., made tools. Tools have never yet been found either in the Djetis beds, which yielded part of the skull of a young individual, or in lower levels of the subsequent Trinil beds from which the main body of hominid fossils came: the earliest lithic industry yet recognized in the Sangiran area is that from the upper levels of the Trinil beds, though it should be emphasized that lithic tools of very primitive character could easily escape detection, especially on open sites without recognizable fire-places.

The culture of Peking man

If the status of the Java Pithecanthropians with regard to tool-making must remain an open question, there is no doubt that the earliest industries of the Far East and of North Africa alike were associated with hominid remains of the same general category. There are signs that *Sinanthropus*, to use the original but now generally discredited term for *Pithecanthropus pekinensis*, was geologically slightly later and anatomically rather more advanced than the Java forms; in particular the Peking people, with a cranial capacity averaging 1000 c.c., had noticeably larger brains. There can be no question but that they possessed a culture, even though a rudimentary one. The earliest deposits (locus 13) at Chou-koutien, dating from the earlier part of the Middle Pleistocene, yielded a typical chopping tool made by alternate flaking from a chert pebble, giving a sinuous working-edge. The main fissure (locus 1), dating from rather later in the Middle Pleistocene and the source of remains of upwards of forty representatives of Peking man, has produced a wealth of stone artifacts made from intractable materials like green-stone, coarse chert and quartz. It must be admitted that many of these were so crudely fashioned that they would hardly have been recognized as human if recovered from an ordinary geological deposit. Nevertheless the industry, much of the material of which was brought to the site and which was intimately associated with traces of fire and other human activity, has certain well-defined characteristics: there are no tools comparable to the hand axes of Africa and parts of Europe and south-west Asia; pebbles and flakes were employed as materials for tools and the flakes had sometimes been formed by crushing nodules between two boulders, resulting in signs of percussion at either end; secondary retouch was scarce and irregular; and the leading tools were intended for chopping and scraping, the former generally made from pebbles, from which a few flakes had been struck to form irregular working edges, and the latter by trimming lumps or flakes to form smooth edges. With this rudimentary stone equipment, supplemented by such tools as he was able to shape by its aid, Peking man succeeded in living largely on the flesh of his competitors in the animal world. In this he contrasted significantly with the great apes, who if not so averse to meat as is sometimes suggested had in practice to make do almost entirely on a vegetarian diet.

To judge from the animal remains associated with him, Peking man depended largely on venison, since two-thirds of them belong to two species of deer, namely *Euryceros pachyosteus* and *Pseudaxis grayi.* Yet he by no means restricted himself to this meat and his victims seem to have included elephants, two kinds of rhinoceros, bison, water-buffaloes, horses, camels, wild boars, roebucks, antelopes and sheep, not to mention such carnivores as sabre-toothed tigers, leopards, cave bears and a huge hyaena. How he managed to secure this varied selection of game we can only speculate. No specialized projectile-heads have survived in the archaeological record, but to judge from evidence from elsewhere he would have had available wooden spears with the tip hardened in fire and it seems likely in view of the character of some of his victims that he would have used primitive pit-traps. The meagreness of his material equipment only emphasizes the important part that team-work, based on articulate speech and on a conscious network of social relations, must have played even at this early stage of development, when groups were so small and so sparsely scattered. Equally we should recognize the immense courage of these primitive men, who in the face of powerful and largely unknown forces made their way—and our way—in the final resort by their prowess as hunters, by confronting and vanquishing animals larger, faster and stronger than themselves.

One of their most important aids was fire and it was in layers discoloured by burning and mixed with ash and charcoal that most of their discarded refuse was found. Fire would have been of value for keeping wild beasts at bay, for warming the cave, for hardening wooden weapons and of course for roasting meat. In addition to meat, wild animals provided skins and, in their bones, teeth and antlers, potential raw materials for making tools and weapons. There seems no doubt that Peking man utilized certain of these, though not to the extent that has sometimes been claimed. Deer antlers were certainly detached from their frontlets, the beams were sometimes cut into sections and the tines removed, no doubt for use. Again flakes, from the long bones of various animals have the appearance of having been used and even trimmed by flaking. On the other hand there is no sign that Peking man fabricated well-made artifacts from these materials.

Both the way in which the bones of Peking man himself occurred and their condition throw light on other aspects of his behaviour. There can have been no question of burial, since the remains were distributed in the cultural deposit in just the same way as animal bones. This, indeed, taken together with his primitive appearance, was enough to suggest to at least one eminent authority that Peking man was himself the victim of some more advanced human type. The fact remains that, despite the most careful search of thousands of cubic metres of deposit and the recovery of an impressive body of material relating to Peking man, no single trace of his supposed overlord has ever been found. If it be accepted that Peking man was himself the hunter—and this view is now unquestioned by leading authorities —then the condition of his bones argues strongly that he was a cannibal as well as an avid consumer of animal flesh: his long bones are normally split exactly as were those of wild animals to facilitate the extraction of marrow, and the aperture at the base of the skull has habitually been enlarged in just the same way as among the Melanesians of recent times who favoured human brain as a delicacy.

The evolution and spread of hand-axe industries

The stone industry from the Middle Pleistocene deposits at Choukoutien is not merely archaic in appearance, but in fact represents what historically speaking is the most primitive level of human culture certainly recognized. This does not mean that even the material from locus 13 at Choukoutien is the oldest in time. The question precisely where hominids first crossed the threshold of humanity has yet to be decided. Certainly this must have happened somewhere within the comparatively restricted territories to which Lower Palaeolithic cultures were confined. One reason for preferring east central Africa is that it seems to have been there that cultural evolution proceeded most rapidly during Middle Pleistocene times: above all it was there that the industrial advance, symbolized by the evolution from crude chopping-tools of hand axes flaked on both faces to form a progressively more regular working-edge, was achieved. By contrast, in regions outside those over which the hand-axe industries spread in the course of Middle Pleistocene times, the old chopping-tool and flake tradition persisted, in some localities even through Late Pleistocene and into Neothermal times. Industries of this general type have already been recovered from Pleistocene deposits between Ichang and Chungking in the Valley of the Yangtze in South China, in the Mei Fingnoi valley near Bhan-Kao in Thailand, from the Kota Tampan district in the Perak Valley of northern Malaya, from Yenangyaung and other sites in the Middle Irrawady in Burma and from the tributaries of the Indus in the Punjab, notably from the Soan Valley.

It was most probably in east central Africa that the great hand-axe tradition first arose. Assemblages of stone tools from successive levels in the Middle Pleistocene sediments exposed in the Olduvai gorge in Tanganyika (Map 1) display the gradual emergence from roughly made chopping-tools of hand-axes similar in form to those originally recognized at such European sites as Chelles, Abbeville and St Acheul in the north of France. The basal level (bed I) at Olduvai on the other hand yielded an assortment of tools in the old tradition flaked from water-worn pebbles or from irregular nodules of quartz, lava, chert or quartzite. These included choppers, ranging in size from ping-pong to croquet balls and formed by striking flakes from two directions; simpler tools made by striking flakes from one direction only; and flakes, many of which were struck in the production of chopping-tools. At Olduvai hand-axes proper first appeared in the lowest levels of bed II and in their first stage they were primitive in form, comparable to those from the French Abbe-villian, flaked only at the pointed end, either by being struck by stone hammers or by themselves being beaten against stone anvils, and having a markedly irregular working-edge; moreover they were accompanied by about the same number of primitive chopping-tools, the form from which they were evidently themselves derived. Thereafter in successive levels of beds II-IV ten more stages could be recognized, leading up to forms of more evolved Acheulean type requiring less and less raw material. Not all of these need be described here and it may be sufficient to say that hand-axes with a working-edge all the way round appeared for the first time in stage 4; that by stage 5 the technique had begun to come into use whereby thin flat flakes making possible a more even working-edge were struck off by a baton of wood or bone instead of by a stone hammer or against an anvil; and that from stage 6, if not before, cleavers, that is, tools with a straight working-edge as opposed to the more or less pointed business-end of the hand-axe or the irregular edge of the primitive chopping-tool, appeared alongside hand-axes.

Similar types of tool spread widely over much of Africa and contiguous parts of Europe and Asia during Middle Pleistocene times. In due course they covered the whole of Africa apart from the region of the Kalahari desert and a broad zone extending from the south-west Sudan across French North Africa, today occupied by savannah and by the southern fringe of the Sahara. From Kenya and Uganda they extended south through the Rhodesias and Mozambique to the Cape, where the site at Stellenbosch lends its name to the earlier stages of the local hand-axe industry, and west over the Zambezi–Congo watershed, where an outstanding factory site has been explored on the Kamoa stream, to Angola and the Congo basin proper. Northwards the current seems to have passed up the Great Rift, by-passing the Horn of Africa until the close of the Middle Pleistocene, into the Nile Valley, where it is represented by a rich site on the Khor Abu Anga, a left-bank tributary joining the main river immediately below the confluence of the Blue and the White Nile. From the Nile Valley it spread in two main directions. North-westwards the hand-axe people occupied, not merely the Gebel el Akhbar and the Maghreb, but the whole broad territory from the Nile to the Atlantic, including most of the Sahara, which in pluvial times supported a rich fauna resembling that of central Africa today. It was without doubt from north-west Africa that hand-axe users spread into south-west Europe as far as the Rhine and south-east England, and by way of the French Riviera into the Italian peninsula. Equally, Egypt was a bridgehead for Asia and hand-axe industries are found in Jordan, Palestine, Syria and Mesopotamia. No doubt it was a prolongation of this movement, presumably across what is now the head of the Persian Gulf and round the northern coast of the Arabian Sea, that brought hand-axe industries to India, where they occupied much of the peninsula south of the Narmada river. It will be noted that the Middle Pleistocene hand-axe users nowhere penetrated the mountain zone linking Anatolia, Iran, Afghanistan and the Himalaya; indeed, they never completely filled up the territories to the south, and though they penetrated north-west India they failed to displace the older flake and chopping-tool tradition represented by the stone industries of the Soan Valley.

This, and even more the northward limit on their spread into Europe, suggests that the real barrier to the spread of the hand-axe cultures was not the mountains as such but rather the ecological setting. There seems little doubt that these cultures were adapted specifically to a forest environment: there they originated and there their distribution was mainly if not entirely confined. It is doubtless in the light of this that one should interpret the appearance on the northern margins of the province, in south-east Britain, Belgium, North France and parts of Germany, of a counterpart to the Soan of Pakistan, namely the industries named after Clacton-on-Sea, England. In these industries, dating from the Mindel–Riss interglacial, flakes were removed by the same anvil technique employed by the early Abbevillian hand-axe makers. Frequently the flakes, which showed a characteristically prominent bulb and a high angle between the striking-platform and the main flake surface, were struck from the parent nodule in two directions, leaving chopper-like cores, resembling the chopping-tools of the Soan, Choukoutien and similar industries of the East. The idea, advanced by some earlier prehistorians, that the Clactonians relied exclusively on flakes in stark contrast with the Abbevillian hand-axe makers can hardly be reconciled with their chopping-tools or with the fact that Clactonian-like flakes were commonly produced in the course of making hand-axes by means of the anvil technique. What can legitimately be said is that the Clactonians laid greater stress on flake-tools than the hand-axe peoples. The most likely explanation of this is ecological, namely that they occupied territories, as did the Soans, on the northern fringe of the main forest zone.

The progressively more economical use of the raw material implied in the refinement of the hand-axe was carried a stage further with the development at the time of the Riss glaciation of industries which take their name from the site of Levallois near Paris. In these there can be no question that the prime object was the production of flake tools. The Levallois flint-workers, who like the Acheulian hand-axe makers used the baton or rod technique, began by preparing the nucleus or core which they trimmed into the shape of a tortoise, leaving the under face comparatively flat and making the upper one convex by striking flakes radially from different points on the circumference: only when this work had been completed did they strike off the main flake, which bore on its upper surface and on its faceted butt traces of the preparatory shaping of the parent core. Such Levallois flakes were tools in their own right fully capable of being used for many of the same purposes as the finer hand-axes with which they were often found.

Lakeside camping places

When we remember that they were first and foremost big-game hunters, it is hardly surprising that the Middle Pleistocene hunters should have settled in river valleys like the Thames or the Somme, the Nile, Vaal or Zambezi, the Soan or the Narmada, and the Mei Fingnoi or the Irrawaddy and by the shore of lakes, such as those of Olduvai and Olorgesailie in east central Africa, Karar in Algeria, Torralba in Spain or Hoxne in England. We saw from Choukoutien what an immense variety of animals they took, and very similar evidence is forthcoming from the settlements of hand-axe makers. The Olorgesailie people killed and ate giant baboon, giant pig, and a large kind of horse and hippopotamus; at Karar the animal remains included elephant, rhinoceros, hippopotamus, buffalo, zebra, giraffe, warthog and gazelle; and at Torralba straight-tusked elephant, rhinoceros, wild ox, stag and horse. Although, as in the case of the Choukoutien hunters, their methods of hunting must remain largely a matter of surmise, we have good evidence that primitive wooden spears of which the tip had been hardened in the fire were used; a fragment of one made from yew-wood was found at Clacton and a complete, though broken, specimen of the same material and nearly eight feet long was recovered from between the ribs of a straight-tusked elephant at Lehringen, near Verden in Lower Saxony, Germany: the first from an interglacial deposit of Mindel–Riss, the second from one of Riss–Würm age. It is interesting to note that the pygmies of the Cameroons have been accustomed to stalk elephant with a wooden spear not much more than six feet long, which they thrust into the animal's body with both hands; as the animal tries to escape the spear works in more deeply and the trail of blood allows the hunters to keep on his track. When a kill of a large beast is made among such people it is customary for folk to collect from far and near to feast off the meat. During the Stone Age, when implements were easily made and expendable, it is likely that these would often be worn out and discarded at the site of a kill and it seems easiest to explain in this way finds like that at site HK in bed IV at Olduvai, which yielded no less than 459 hand-axes and cleavers blunted by use and lying amid the disarticulated skeleton of a hippopotamus.

What kind of men were responsible for the hand-axe industries of the Middle Pleistocene is a difficult question to answer. The most likely reply at the moment is that while retaining certain features of Pithecanthropian ancestry, such as large face and teeth, heavy jaws and massive brow-ridges, they were beginning to show in the general conformation of the skull a trend towards *Homo sapiens*. This is a view consistent with the occurrence of hand-axes in North Africa in association with jaws of Pithecanthropian character and with the admittedly ambiguous Swanscombe find (see pp. 21 f.). At the present time there is no well-founded evidence to support the idea that a more advanced 'Presapiens' type had emerged at this stage of prehistory.

Decline of hand-axe industries

The close of the Middle Pleistocene was marked by the onset of desiccation in territories which by reason of their forested environment had been most favourable to the hand-axe industries. The onset of drier conditions transformed much of the Sahara from a rich hunting-ground to a vast desert and destroyed the large measure of homogeneity that had hitherto prevailed over the whole African continent and contiguous parts of Europe and Asia, reduced North Africa, deprived of its extensive hinterland, to an outlier of western Asia and converted the territories of the Congo and South Africa into provincial backwaters.

South of the Sahara the expiring hand-axe tradition left twin heirs during Late Pleistocene times, provincial cultures occupying mutually exclusive territories, namely the Sangoan, which maintained itself amid the forest country of the great river systems of the Congo and Angola, in the Zambezi Valley and in the region of the Great Lakes, and the Fauresmith, found near fresh springs on high ground in the Orange Free State, Bechuanaland and Kenya. Both agree in combining hand-axes and faceted flakes struck from prepared cores, but the Fauresmith hand-axes were generally smaller and the industry also included well-made cleavers; the Sangoan on the other hand had begun already in its middle stage to develop lanceolate hand-axes and lanceheads of quite specific character. Such changes as did occur were of essentially local significance. This was even more the case over the extensive territories in the east of the Old World, into which the hand-axe cultures never penetrated and where the old chopping-tool and flake traditions persisted, as they appear to have done in successive stages of the Soan culture of northern India, without contributing anything essential to the course of world prehistory.

Mousterian and Levalloiso-Mousterian cultures

It fell to the northern parts of the Lower Palaeolithic world to witness the genesis and rise of the Advanced Palaeolithic cultures on which the future development of mankind was largely to depend. The precise origins of these cultures, as of the fully developed *Homo sapiens* with which they were associated, remain among the prime objectives of prehistoric research. Recent discoveries in south-west Asia suggest that the lithic traditions of the Advanced Palaeolithic may go back to a period contemporary with the last Interglacial period in Europe. What is certain is that the industries prevailing at the outset of the last Glaciation were still essentially Lower Palaeolithic in character and were associated with men of Neanderthal and Neanderthaloid type. Over parts of western Europe, including in particular the territory between the Loire and the Pyrenees, the lithic industries were of the kind named after the rock-shelter of Le Moustier in the Dordogne: the tool-kit was still very restricted, comprising scrapers and points made from flakes trimmed on one or both edges by secondary flaking of a kind that left abrupt steps on the surface but also including small hand-axes of triangular or heart-shaped form. Further south, extending from the French riviera and Italy to central Europe and the regions bordering the north-east of the Black Sea, namely the Crimea, the Don–Donetz region and the coast of the west Caucasus, hand-axes were rarer or absent; but the industry was enriched by hand awls, points with a shallow flaking on the under surface and narrow strip flakes with steep secondary flaking down the working edge. Further south again, in Palestine, Syria, Iraq and south-west Iran, as well as in northern Africa, the industries of this time had a pronouncedly Levalloisian character.

Owing to their habit of occupying caves, we have reasonably full information about the animals on which the Neanderthal and Neanderthaloid peoples mainly depended for food, about the use they made of bone and related materials and the way in which they disposed of their dead. As hunters these people show no signs of having been in any way more advanced that their immediate predecessors. Where, as in certain of the Mount Carmel caves in Palestine, Levalloiso-Mousterian levels overlie ones dating from early stages of the Palaeolithic, there is no indication that an extended range of animals was hunted. Equally, there is no sign of any marked improvement in the methods of hunting; reliance evidently continued to be placed on proved methods like wooden spears, stone balls (probably used as bolas stones) and presumably on primitive pit traps; and there is a notable absence of specialized projectile-heads. Again, exceedingly limited use was made of bone and related materials, which, as we know from later practice by stone-age hunters, were capable of providing a variety of spear-, harpoon- and arrowheads, as well as fish-hooks and pointed fish-gorges, a variety of tools and many kinds of personal ornament: pieces of dense bone, including phalanges, or toe-bones, were used as anvils for working flint, but there is no evidence that bone or antler was worked to make well-defined implements or weapons of any description. Another and possibly more significant limitation is the absence of any indication of a developed aesthetic sense: Lower Palaeolithic man was capable of producing a limited range of tools with an astonishing economy of effort, and the perfection of form and degree of standardization that they achieved, often over great areas and despite wide variations in the qualities of the raw materials used, bear witness to firmness of intention and a definite sense of style; but as far as we know he practised no art—no sign of carving or engraving for example has been found among all the wealth of bone and antler from Mousterian and kindred sites; nor is there evidence of even so much as a single bored tooth to suggest that he fabricated ornaments to adorn his person.

In two significant ways however Neanderthal man made important advances. For one thing he extended the range of settlement well to the north of the frost-free zone to which earlier men had confined themselves and this at a time of glacial intensity. Precisely how far he reached has still to be settled in detail, but there are indications that he colonized parts of Siberia for the first time, though probably not as early as Würm I times, and even reached as far as China. The presence of well-made flint scrapers as an important element in his standard equipment suggests that he found it necessary in his northerly habitat to wear animal skins, at least out of doors. It was probably the cold conditions of Würm I times, also, that caused the Mousterian and Levalloiso-Mousterian people to occupy caves where these were available.

The other marked advance shown by Neanderthal man was in his treatment of the dead. Certain discoveries from the closing phase of the last Interglacial seem indeed to indicate the continuance of cannibalism, notably the Neanderthal skull from Monte Circeo, Italy, with the base broken open for the extraction of the brain, and the mass find at Krapina in Yugoslavia, where remains of upwards of a dozen individuals, male and female, young and old, were discovered mixed up in the cultural deposit with wild animal bones and treated in the same way, having been broken up for the extraction of marrow, partly burnt in the fire and so on. On the other hand the Mousterian deposit at La Chapelle-aux-Saints was found to overlie a grave, cut into the rock floor and containing the crouched skeleton of a Neanderthal man; similar burials have been found at La Ferrassie, likewise in the Dordogne, and also at Kiik-Koba in the Crimea. Even more significant evidence was uncovered at the Mugharet es-Skhūl, Mount Carmel, in the form of a veritable cemetery of ten graves with remains ranging from a girl of three and a boy of four to a man over fifty years of age. As at La Chapelle-aux-Saints the graves were only just big enough to accommodate bodies with the arms and legs flexed. No red ochre or personal ornaments were found, but the jaw-bones of a large wild boar were seen to be clasped in the arms of the old man. A more recent discovery of exceptional interest is that of a Neanderthaloid child in the cave of Teshik-Tash, Uzbekistan, the head surrounded by six pairs of horns of the Siberian mountain goat, which had evidently been stood upright in a circle while still attached to the frontal bones. Quite clearly men of the Neanderthaloid type had developed concepts well beyond what one might have expected from their lowly material culture.

There was a considerable range of variation in physical type among the makers of Mousterian and kindred industries. As we have seen (p. 22), the fragmentary skulls from Fontéchevade suggest that a comparatively modern form, lacking massive brow-ridges, had already emerged before the onset of the Würm glaciation, and to this period the extreme Neanderthal form, represented by the Chapelle-aux-Saints and other finds, belongs. This latter type is restricted to limited parts of Europe and is generally regarded as aberrant, the product of isolation on the margin of the Palaeolithic world and one which died out without contributing to the modern races of man. Of much wider distribution are finds of a Neanderthaloid type that combines such features as large teeth, heavy jaws and massive brow-ridges with varying degrees of advanced characteristics. It is worthy of note that these less specialized types occur widely distributed over the extensive territories of Eurasia, within which *Homo sapiens* in his modern form—and the Upper Palaeolithic blade and burin cultures of which he was the bearer—must have emerged. It seems highly probable that the Neanderthaloids associated with Levalloiso-Mousterian industries over a wide territory from Gibraltar to Italy, South Germany, Yugoslavia, the Crimea, Cyrenaica, Palestine, Iraq and Uzbekistan stood close to the main line of hominid evolution that culminated in modern *Homo sapiens*.

Survivals in Africa and South Asia

The Advanced Palaeolithic cultures (Chapter 3) which first appeared in a developed form between 30,000 and 40,000 years ago both in Europe and western Asia, were confined to the more northerly parts of the Old World. Over extensive territories to the south, among them the oldest centres of human prehistory, Lower Palaeolithic cultural traditions persisted, albeit with modifications, down to comparatively recent times. From the point of view of world history, most of Africa, India and southeast Asia were henceforward by-passed by the main currents of creative change throughout the remainder of prehistoric times. This does not of course mean that they did not undergo a certain evolution of importance to their own populations; but it is worthy of note that such evolution, for example in the direction of microlithic tools of flint or stone, often followed patterns set by Advanced Palaeolithic peoples or their Mesolithic successors who in Africa were restricted to parts of the Mediterranean zone with a dubious extension to Kenya. The industries with flint burins or graving-tools and blades blunted by steep flaking on one or more edges, often known as backed-blades, that appeared in Cyrenaica during the Late Pleistocene are presumed to have intruded from western Asia. Those of Algeria and Tunisia, including the Capsian (after Gafsa in Tunisia) once considered as a possible source of the Advanced Palaeolithic of Europe, have been shown by radio-carbon dating to be predominantly of Neothermal age. Equally, the industry from Kenya that has been compared with the Advanced Palaeolithic Aurignacian culture of Europe is almost certainly much too young.

One of the most conservative parts of Africa at this time was the Nile Valley, where traditions stemming from the Lower Palaeolithic Levalloisian persisted well into Neothermal times and give rise to industries of Epi-Levalloisian character. One such was the industry first noted at Sebil in Egypt and characterized by small crescents and trapeziform pieces shaped by a steep edge-flaking and evidently designed as insets for composite tools of the kind that first came into use among Advanced Palaeolithic people.

In other parts of Africa Levalloisian and Levalloiso–Mousterian traditions gave rise to industries marked above all by various types of projectile heads with bifacial retouch. Thus the Aterian (after the Tunisian site of Bir-el-Ater near Tebessa), based on the production of faceted flakes from tortoise cores, but featuring also barbed and tanged arrowheads, leaf-shaped points and tanged flakes with bifacially flaked tangs, extended in a belt across North Africa from west of the Nile to the Atlantic. The Still Bay culture (after a locality in Cape Province, South Africa), was characterized above all by leaf-shaped points made from faceted flakes by bifacial flaking and had an even wider geographical range stretching from the Sudan, Abyssinia and Somaliland, through Uganda, Kenya and Tanganyika to the Rhodesias and the Union of South Africa. The resemblance between the Aterian and Still

Bay cultures, separated though they were by the Nilotic province, has often been noted. One explanation would be that they represent expansions north and east from central equatorial Africa, where the Upper Sangoan (sometimes known as Djokocian) combines specialized forest tools like tranchet axes, of which the working edges are formed in the main by the intersection of two flake-surfaces, with lance heads made from faceted flakes by working on both faces; and in this connection there is an interesting resemblance between the tanged arrowheads of the Final Sangoan (or Lupemban) and those of the Aterian. An alternative possibility is that similar forms were developed in widely separated areas from a common cultural inheritance, possibly under the impulse of the notion, emanating from Advanced Palaeolithic sources, of hafted projectiles.

During Neothermal times the Still Bay tradition, like the Epi-Levalloisian, developed towards microlithic forms intended for insertion into composite tools and weapons. During the arid period (c. 8000–5500 B.C.) that followed the last Pluvial, the area of human settlement in East and South Africa seems somewhat to have contracted. Yet the Magosian culture that takes its name from Magosi in Uganda maintained a high degree of homogeneity over an extensive territory down to the Cape. Over this region we find industries with diminutive points of Still Bay type, associated with small blades removed from prepared cores by punches, and backed blades and lunates shaped rather like a thin section of a tangerine with the straight edge sharp and the curved one blunted by steep flaking. There seems little doubt that the Magosian, along with more or less parallel cultures like the Hargesian of Somaliland, was in its turn a source of the even more widespread microlithic industry, characterized by small double-ended scrapers and lunate insets for arrows and known after the South African locality of Wilton. This first appeared during the succeeding Makalian wet phase and at the extremities of its distribution lasted down to modern times. Other industries included in what South Africa prehistorians term their Late Stone Age are the variant of the Wilton named after the Nachikufu caves in north-east Rhodesia, found in the savannah woodland country north of the Zambezi and marked in its earliest stage by narrow pointed microliths; and the Smithfield of the Vaal and Upper Orange rivers, an industry with special forms of scraper, but lacking microliths, the general aspect of which is doubtless related to the nature of the raw material, a variety of indurated shale. In the course of their long history—there is a radio-carbon date of 4350± 250 B.C. for a low level in the Nachikufan cave—these industries underwent many changes and were enriched by contact with more advanced cultures (see pp. 113 ff.). In East Africa the art of potting was early acquired from neighbouring groups, but in the Union this was a more recent trait. Among other features that appeared only in the younger stages in South Africa may be mentioned stones bored from both faces to give an hour-glass perforation and polished stone axes and beads made from ostrich and mollusc shell. Both in the Horn of Africa and in the Union cultures of essentially Mesolithic type lasted down to the spread of iron-working, which first reached Rhodesia on its way south during the first millennium B.C.; indeed, microlithic industries in the Wilton tradition were still being made when European influence began to penetrate South Africa. It seems probable, though by no means proved, that the makers of the later Wilton industries were Bushmen. Although at present confined to the Kalahari desert, where certain groups have recently been the subject of intensive ethnographical research, these hunters formerly ranged over the whole of the eastern part of South Africa into which they came at an unknown period from the north. The Bushman's way of life is basically the same as that which archaeology leads one to infer for the Wilton people, and moreover, they make beads of eggshell, weight their digging-sticks with bored stones and use the bow and arrow for hunting; a main difference is that they now tip their arrows with bone or iron, but in times gone by arrows were armed with lunates set in resin with the sharp edges exposed.

The presence of more or less naturalistic rock-paintings over broad tracts from Tanganyika and Nyasaland, south through the Rhodesias to the eastern zones of the Transvaal and Orange Free State and on to the Cape and south-west Africa, has attracted widespread interest because of their supposed affinities to ones of Advanced Palaeolithic age in eastern Spain. A more sober view of the African paintings is now taken, for many of them were almost certainly executed during the last two or three hundred years by Bushmen; moreover, the East Spanish are now generally considered to be of Neothermal age. Yet there is little doubt that some of the African paintings are of prehistoric age and that they were executed by makers of Wilton industries. Again, it is generally accepted that the rock-engravings found in the interior of the Union were made by the Smithfield people within whose territory they are confined. The practice of this rock-art, like the wearing of personal ornaments and the use of bows with arrows inset with blunted-back microliths, shows that even peoples remote from the great centres of Advanced Palaeolithic development were to some degree, even if belatedly, quickened by impulses radiating from them.

Very little is yet certainly known about what was going forward in southern and south-east Asia during Late Pleistocene and early Neothermal times. One of the few general conclusions is that the trend of development in India seems to have been broadly analogous to that in much of Africa. Late Soan industries made by developed Levalloisian techniques can be traced down to Late Pleistocene times and the presumption is that it was these that gave rise to the microlithic industries with lunates found in large numbers in the Gujarat and more widely scattered over the Indian peninsula down to its southern extremity and in Ceylon.

CHAPTER 3

ADVANCED PALAEOLITHIC AND MESOLITHIC CULTURES

ADVANCED PALAEOLITHIC PEOPLES

New and more spacious prospects were opened up during the latter half of the Late Pleistocene era by men whose intellectual capacity and physique differed in no significant way from our own. It was somewhere between Atlantic Europe and Inner Asia that man seems first to have given signs of freeing himself from the narrow conceptual limits within which Lower Palaeolithic peoples had been confined. It was here in this heartland of Old World culture that around thirty-five thousand years ago he first achieved Advanced Palaeolithic status as a specialized hunter, using a variety of weapons, adorning his person and practising an art that testifies to an imaginative awareness and a creativity beyond anything of which he had previously given signs and in which we can detect a first promise of his later achievements.

The technology of Advanced Palaeolithic peoples was founded on lithic industries based on the production, by some kind of punch, of blades or flakes relatively narrow in proportion to their length and having more or less regular, parallel flake-scars. From such blades were made a variety of types adapted to different functions: knife blades and projectile points and barbs were made by a steep retouch which gave a rest to the finger or facilitated mounting in a handle or shaft; scrapers for dressing skins and probably for shaping other materials were formed by trimming blades to a convex edge; and burins, vitally important for working antler and bone as well as for engraving, were made by striking off flakes more or less counter to the main axis of the blade. The much greater use of antler and bone, facilitated by the flint burin, was another leading feature of Advanced Palaeolithic industry. Here again many different forms were produced, such as various patterns of lance- and harpoon-head, spear-throwers, perforated batons, leather-working tools, awls, and delicately eyed needles. All in all, the Advanced Palaeolithic industries give the impression of being far more diversified and highly specialized than those practised by Lower Palaeolithic peoples, whether of an earlier age or persisting down to Neothermal times over the extensive tracts of Africa and the Far East that remained outside the sphere of Advanced Palaeolithic culture.

Although modern research in eastern and central Europe and in western Asia has produced evidence vitally important for establishing the spread of the various Advanced Palaeolithic cultures, the sequence established in the caves and rock-shelters of south-western France and set out in Table E remains in some respects a key one.

TABLE E. *Simplified sequence of Advanced Palaeolithic cultures in south-western France*

Radio-carbon dates B.C.	Cultures
15,000–8,000	Magdalenian
18,000–15,000	Solutrean
22,000–18,000	Gravettian (Upper Perigordian)
28,500–22,000	Aurignacian
32,000–28,500	Châtelperronian (Lower Perigordian)

The first of these, the Châtelperronian, is of little general significance, being confined to south-west France: a substantial proportion of the flint tools from Châtelperronian levels is of Mousterian type and a likely explanation of the culture is that it represents a local development from the Mousterian in the same general direction as that taken by the more important Advanced Palaeolithic cultures that follow it in the French sequence.

4-2

Aurignacians and Gravettians

Among the earliest widely spread blade and burin industries two main varieties may be distinguished, each named after French localities, namely the Aurignacian, characterized by projectile heads of bone, flint scrapers with steep secondary flaking running up to a keel and flint burins of beaked form, and the Gravettian, characterized by flint knives and projectile tips and barbs with steep retouch. Industries of Aurignacian type are known to have extended from Northern Iraq and Afghanistan to Transcaucasia, the Crimea, Syria and Palestine and westward from Roumania to Hungary, Lower Austria, South Germany, France and Cantabrian Spain. The Gravettian zone is very different, extending from South Russia, where sites occur most abundantly on the banks of the Don and Dnieper and their tributaries, to central Europe and thence, by way of Italy and South Germany, to France and Spain.

Very little is yet certainly known about origins, but a Pre-Aurignacian flint industry of basic blade and burin type has more than once been recognized in Palestine and Syria, where it underlies Levalloiso–Mousterian deposits and is even associated with the 'Jabrudian', and industry of Late Acheulian affinities. Such would argue for an ultimately Asiatic rather than a European origin for the blade and burin industries. The Aurignacian and Gravettian may probably be thought of as divergent specializations from a Pre-Aurignacian base that may itself have occupied a fairly extensive territory in western Asia. To judge from existing radio-carbon dates it would seem that the Aurignacian was already established over a broad zone of western Asia as far east as Afghanistan by around 35,000 years B.C. On the other hand the Gravettian, which in central and parts of western Europe is found stratified above Aurignacian industries, seems already to have appeared in Austria around 28,000 B.C.

Whereas the Aurignacians lived mainly in caves and shelters, the Gravettians who extended their range into the loess-lands of South Russia often in such areas made artificial shelters, the earliest for which certain evidence is yet available. Basically these appear to have comprised skin tents, supported on a few sticks, weighted round the margin by heavy bones or tusks and covering irregularly-shaped floors that were often slightly hollowed out of the subsoil. The oval or more or less round houses identified at Gagarino in South Russia or Dolni-Věstonice in Czechoslovakia, which ranged from around four to seven metres in width, presumably housed single families, but the larger dwelling-areas, like those at Kostienki IV ranging up to twenty-eight or thirty-four metres in length, must surely have been intended to shelter larger groups. Yet the distinction is more apparent than real, since where extensive excavations have been made, as at Pavlov in Moravia, small dwellings have been found to occur in clusters and on the other hand the larger ones have been shown to have been divided into family units. The oblong dwelling-area at Puskari on the Desna with its three fire-places has for example been interpreted as due to the confluence of three conical skin tents. Again, the ones at the lower level at Kostienki IV, which it may be noted were never more than from five to six and a half metres across, are best regarded as rows of family units, such as are more plainly visible in the upper level of the same site with its rows of adjacent more or less circular huts, each having its own hearth. What seems clear enough is that as a rule the Gravettians of the South Russian and Czechoslovak loess-lands lived and moved about in bands made up of a number of primary households. Whether these were matriarchal clans, as claimed by Russian prehistorians, partly on account of the female figurines found at several of their settlements, can hardly be determined on the basis of existing evidence; but the fact that they operated as a group, rather than as mere biological families, is easily explained when one remembers the ineffectiveness of their armament and the fact that in these territories at any rate the Gravettians depended to a large degree on the mammoth, a beast that must have required teamwork both in hunting and dismembering.

The earliest art

One of the most characteristic and widespread traits of the Gravettian was the manufacture of female figurines in which the sexual characteristics are emphasized at the expense, for example, of the head and features. These figurines, which are found from France and Italy to the South Russian plain (Map 2), were most

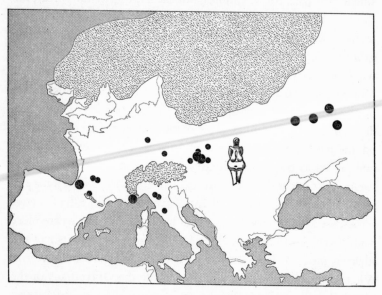

2. Europe in the Last Ice Age: the spread of naturalistic 'Venus' figurines (large dots indicate three or more; ice sheets are shown by stippling)

commonly made of mammoth ivory or of various kinds of stone, but at three Czechoslovak sites examples were also made from fired clay. The heads as a rule are represented by mere nobs: hair is rarely and features still more rarely indicated (Frontispiece). The figure is shown with full breasts and buttocks and is commonly pregnant; apart from a girdle at the back of one of those from Kostienki and a fringe at the rear of that from Lespugue, the figurines are unclothed. The arms are generally puny and may be folded across the breast and the legs taper from well-filled thighs, the feet, where these have not been broken off, being suggested rather than shown in detail. In two cases at least the figurines were coloured with red paint. The selective emphasis with which these figurines have been shaped suggests that they were connected in some way with a cult or at least with a body of ideas centering round fertility, and the fact that all those with a definite provenance came from settlements, whether from caves or artificial dwellings, argues for their domestic rather than public or ceremonial significance. In addition to the Venus figurines, as they have sometimes been called, the Gravettians carved and modelled figures of various animals in a more or less naturalistic style. Thus at Kostienki I, one of the most famous of the South Russian stations figures of mammoth were cut rather crudely from the same chalk material as two of the Venus figures, together with the heads of many kinds of animal including lion, bear, and wolf, some with partly human features. The Gravettians of Czechoslovakia were similarly fond of carving animals, and in addition modelled a considerable variety— mammoth, rhinoceros, cave bear, reindeer, bison, horse, lion or tiger, wolf and lynx—from clay which they hardened on the fire like pottery.

Engraving, on the other hand, was much rarer in eastern and central Europe than in the west. Objectives of personal adornment and various tools of bone and ivory were ornamented by incised fringes and simple criss-cross and linear chevron patterns and the South Russian mammoth-hunters sometimes built up conventional designs by means of small pits. Occasionally, as in the stylized engraving of female figures from Predmost, more ambitious engravings were attempted, but few engravings of more naturalistic type have been found and none of these is very convincing. Yet in the west the Gravettians and even the Aurignacians engraved lively outlines of wild animals on stone slabs and pieces of bone and, what is even more significant, on the walls of caves and rock shelters. Although the distribution of the two by no means coincides, it seems likely that the rise of vigorous schools of naturalistic engraving on small objects was connected in some way with the practice of cave art. This latter was restricted even within the territories of the blade and burin culture in which caves were naturally available: it was not practised for instance by those who inhabited the caves of western Asia and of central Europe and was in fact concentrated in the south-western parts of France and in Cantabria, with outliers in Old Castille and Andalusia and in South Italy and Sicily.

The basic drive behind the cave art, as seen for instance at Lascaux, was a sense of the hunter's dependence on the continued abundance of game and on his ability to secure victims. This is shown clearly enough by the preoccupation of the artists with game animals and to a minor degree with the beasts of prey that might threaten them, rather than with human beings; by their concern with individual beasts rather than with groups and scenes, apart only from the theme of male and female; and by the representation of weapons, wounds and medicine men. Yet such anxieties and tensions are, and no doubt were, resolved among many hunting communities by mime, dancing and the beginnings of dramatic representations—indeed, there are signs that the cave art itself grew from them, even if they are hardly in themselves sufficient to account for its practice. It must have been the caves themselves, with their dark recesses, that heightened mystery and suggestibility and led the hunters of certain territories well-provided with caves to develop the art of engraving and painting their walls, ceilings and on occasion their floors. In this connection it is interesting to note that the artists sometimes worked with the aid of lamps deep in the limestone rock; for instance at Niaux in the Dordogne the first traces of cave art that greet the intruder are some 510 metres (over 550 yards) from the mouth and those deepest from the mouth as much as 1114 metres, or well over two-thirds of a mile. Again, there is ample evidence that the prehistoric artists were stimulated by the natural irregularities of caves, such as bosses in the rock, stalagmitic columns, or drip-marks on the floor, which they were fond of improving or incorporating in the shapes of wild animals; or again by the muddy slime on the floors or the walls of caves, that led by way of ape-like doodling not only to meanders drawn by the fingers and, thus, ultimately to naturalistic outlines but also to plastic modelling.

During the first or Gravettian (later Perigordian) cycle of cave art, both engraving and painting were carried out. Engraving was done by flint graving tools or in the case of clay surfaces by the finger-tip; and painting by means of various ochres, oxide of manganese and carbon, ground on stone palettes and either applied in powdered form by being blown from the mouth or through a tube or mixed with animal grease and applied by means of brushes or soft stumps. The engravings of this first cycle comprised meandering lines made by fingers on clay and naturalistic engravings of animals, drawn in outline often with great vigour, though with stiff legs and commonly having the horns depicted full-face. Allied to these engravings were a number of low reliefs like the five figures from Laussel, one male and four female, one of the females carrying a bison's horn in the right hand. Paintings included red and yellow meanders drawn by several fingers; human hands, either positive red ones or negative ones silhouetted in various colours; crudely painted red animals and club-shaped signs; line drawings in red, yellow and black; wide blotted lines; flat washes; and the beginning of painting in two colours.

When the Gravettian hunters died they were given ceremonial burial dressed in their finery and scattered over with red ochre. From such finds and from discoveries made on dwelling sites it is evident that the Upper Palaeolithic hunters of western and central Europe were accustomed, unlike their Mousterian predecessors, to wear head-dresses and girdles of perforated snail-shells, bracelets, necklaces and anklets of ivory, perforated animal teeth and shells. Some of their bracelets in particular were elaborately decorated with geometric engravings.

Szeletian and Solutrean

The contrast between the makers of blade and burin industries, more particularly the Gravettians, and the Mousterians and Levalloiso-Mousterians was thus considerable, not only in the more versatile nature of their handwork and in the greater adaptability of their dwellings, but still more in their aesthetic awareness and above all in their capacity for cultural progress. Yet the fact that evolution occurred and that fruitful contact was sometimes made between the two ought to warn us against over-emphasizing the immediate differences between them and remind us that the essential contrast was one of potentialities. Thus, the Szeletian culture, named after the Hungarian locality of Szeleta, combined split-based bone points of Aurignacian type with bifacially flaked points of Mousterian ancestry, recalling those of the Aterian and Still Bay industries of Africa. Again, flint work from levels immediately overlying Gravettian deposits in South Russia shows a recrudescence of the bifacial technique that prevailed in the underlying ones and carried forward Mousterian traditions like those manifested at the Caucasian site of Ilskaya. Equally, in France, industries with bifacially-flaked points, named after the site of Solutre, Saône-et-Loire, directly succeeded the Gravettian. At first, under the impact of impulses that probably came from central Europe, plano-convex points were made with shallow pressure flaking encroaching on part of one face; these were followed by laurel-leaf points of characteristic shape; and, finally, by shouldered or tanged points which sometimes combine flat flaking with the steep edge retouch of the Gravettian. The best indication that, alongside impulses from a more archaic industrial source, substantial continuity was maintained with the blade and burin tradition is afforded by the naturalistic art which persisted both in France and Spain, to flower again in the closing phases of Upper Palaeolithic times.

Magdalenian and other specialized groups

In the south and east, in Spain, Italy, central Europe and South Russia, the heirs of the Gravettians maintained their traditions with only comparatively minor changes right down into Neo-thermal times. In north-western Europe and in south-west Asia on the other hand new, regionally differentiated cultures appeared. Of these the best endowed was the Magdalenian, which seems to have developed locally from Gravettian sources and to have flourished mainly in a limited territory extending from western and south-western Germany across France to Cantabria, with an extension for a time into eastern Spain. The Magdalenian is note-worthy for a marked development in the use of bone and above all of antler for the fabrication of a broad range of weapons, implements and objects of personal adornment, including barbed harpoon heads and eyed needles of a fineness unsurpassed by any other prehistoric people; and secondly for carrying cave art and the enrichment of smaller objects to a new peak of development. In the field of cave art the Solutreo-Magdalenian phase was marked by renewed attempts to suggest fullness. Figures might be thrown into apparent relief by cutting deeply into the sur-rounding limestone: good examples are the friezes of horses, oxen, ibex and the rest from the Solutrean and Early Magdalenian sites of the Dordogne and the even more splendid one at Angles-sur-Anglin to the north in Vienne which included representations of the waists and thighs of three women. An alternative method was to suggest relief by means of fine hatching such as can still be seen at Altamira or Marsoulas. Similarly in painting, after passing once again through the sequence of simple line to blotted and flat-wash work, the artists attained to polychrome representations outlined in black, as seen in some of the best work at Altamira and Font de Gaume, before relapsing at the close of the Pleistocene into small red drawings. Quite as remarkable in its way was the work of Magdalenian artists in bone and antler. This is particularly well displayed in the reindeer-antler spear-throwers characteristic of the middle phases of the culture: two kinds were made, weighted ones with figures carved in relief at the lower or hooked end and unweighted ones that might be carved all the way down the shaft, but in each case the artist showed admirable skill in the way in which he enriched an object of great functional importance by his renderings of horses, ibex, bison and other animals in full or partial relief. Altogether the art of this last phase of the Upper Palaeolithic in western Europe reflects the apogee of an advanced hunting culture operating in conditions that must have been highly congenial and productive of leisure.

In Palestine and Syria the Aurignacian was followed by a local derivative known as the Atlitian and this in turn was succeeded at the close of Upper Palaeolithic times by one of generalized and debased Gravettian affinities (the Kebaran or Nebekian) characterized by narrow micro-blades with blunted back, a few microliths of lunate and triangular shape of the type used to back and tip projectiles, and small burins and scrapers. A rather similar industry, though somewhat closer to the Gravettian, has been located in caves in the Zagros Mountains at Zarzi and elsewhere. Further north, on the South Russian plain, the Gravettian industries with traces of bifacial retouch were succeeded by ones of somewhat degenerate type with smaller implements in less variety like those from Gontzi and Timonovka. Meanwhile hunters especially adapted to hunting reindeer were beginning to colonize the North European plain as far west as northern Holland and southern England and more or less up to latitude 55° N.; for the most part they were compelled to live in the open and there are signs that, in North Germany at least, they occupied skin tents, though in Britain they took the opportunity of occupying caves where these were available. Although the antler harpoon-heads made by the Hamburgians recall in general terms those of a certain stage of the Magdalenian, the antler-work as a whole is unique in character and the flint-work reminds one of the flint industries of South Russia and central Europe rather than of western Europe, and there seems little doubt that the northern plain was colonized from the south or south-east. During the final cold spell of the Late Glacial period reindeer hunters had penetrated Denmark and the number of distinctive cultural groups (Ahrensburgian, Swiderian, Bromme, Tjonger) had continued to multiply.

Colonization of Siberia

Finally, it was during Late Glacial times that Siberia seems to have been first occupied by man. Although the total extent of the territory is so vast, the area open to human settlement was in fact limited in the north by the existence of a great zone of lake and marsh south of the northern glaciated zone, between the Urals and the Yenisei and on the south by the mountain zone of Inner Asia, much of the outer rim of which was glaciated. Traces of Upper Palaeolithic settlement have so far been found in the Upper Ob and Yenisei, the Angara and Selenga basins near Lake Baikal and the Upper Lena River up to latitude 61° N. To judge from the fauna, two phases of Late Glacial settlement appear to be represented— an earlier one by Mal'ta and Buret' in the Angara Valley and a later one by Afontova Gora near Krasnoyarsk in the upper Yenisei—and these were followed by one of Neothermal age well seen at Verkholenskaia Gora. The flint industries from Mal'ta and Afontova Gora are both basically Mousterian in tradition with typical tortoise cores, points and side-scrapers. On the other hand the presence of blades, burins and, at the latter site, of microlithic points with battered backs points clearly to a contribution from the Upper Palaeolithic blade and burin tradition, a contribution which is emphasized by the wealth of antler, bone and ivory artifacts (including eyed needles, slotted bone handles, perforated batons, and objects of personal adornment such as plaques and pendants decorated with pits as well as tubular and disc beads); and still more by the presence of female figurines. The easiest way to account for this apparent mixture is to suppose that Gravettians moving east from the South Russian Plain came in contact with descendants of the Mousterians spreading northward from Uzbekistan. The wealth of ornaments found with the ceremonial burial of a child at Mal'ta suggests that the early settlers of the Baikal region had come to satisfactory terms with their environment, which to judge from the fauna shared certain characteristics of steppe and tundra. One way in which they managed to survive the cold winters was to build semi-subterranean houses with entrance passages, a type which in its basic character still survives in the circumpolar zone. Another, testified by the fine-eyed needles and by a figurine from Buret' on the Angara river, carved from a mammoth tusk and apparently clothed in furs, was the use of sewed skin clothing, for which there is also good evidence at the other end of the Upper Palaeolithic world in the Magdalenian of western Europe.

One of the main interests of these early Siberian industries is that they provide an obvious source for those earliest intruders into North America who laid a basis for the prehistory of the New World as a whole. In this connection especial significance attaches to the presence already at Mal'ta of bifacially flaked points of a kind that emerged from similar antecedents in many parts of the Old World. Up to the present it is true that no sites of Late Glacial age have been encountered north of latitude 61°, but research in this remote part of the Soviet Union is still in its early days and it should not be overlooked that much of the low-lying plain to the north of the inhospitable mountainous interior of easternmost Siberia, a plain that once linked Alaska with the Lower Lena Valley, has been submerged by the rise of sea-levels during the Neothermal period.

MESOLITHIC COMMUNITIES

The onset of Neothermal conditions about ten thousand years ago exerted a profound influence on the course of prehistory. This applied particularly to the Advanced Upper Palaeolithic peoples occupying regions subject to Late Glacial or Pluvial climate. There the changes in ecological conditions were so great and so relatively sudden as to upset the balance of the human societies involved and so gave rise to major readjustments in the sphere of culture, which serve to define Mesolithic from Advanced Palaeolithic communities. Conversely, in intermediate territories like Italy and Spain, where no such marked or sudden change occurred in the natural environment, it is frequently difficult to distinguish on purely cultural grounds between the two stages, and Advanced Palaeolithic cultures grade almost imperceptibly into ones of Epi-Palaeolithic character.

Origins of domestication

As a generalization one might say that the Mesolithic peoples of the Old World bridged the transition from the old hunter-fisher mode of life to one based on the new economy of farming. They did this in several ways. To begin with, it was Mesolithic people who, early in Neothermal times and almost certainly somewhere in western Asia, initiated the domestication of animals and plants. This process, gradual and difficult to trace in its earliest stages, led in the course of a few centuries to the rise of economies in which hunting and fishing had sunk to roles altogether subsidiary to that of agriculture and stock-raising and which provided a firm basis for the earliest civilizations of the Old World. Equally it was Mesolithic people who carried on the old way of life throughout the very extensive regions over which farming spread, in the course of millennia, from the earliest centres to the outermost limits imposed by contemporary climate and vegetation. Moreover, it was these Mesolithic survivors who helped to diversify the provincial Neolithic cultures, which arose essentially by a process of acculturation.

It is a reasonable hypothesis that the domestication of animals and plants was carried out under stress of the arid conditions that followed immediately on the end of the last Pluvial period in parts of western Asia. The existence of these conditions has been demonstrated particularly clearly from the Neothermal levels of rock-shelters on Mount Carmel, Palestine, in which the preponderance of antelopes and specifically of gazelles over the woodland fallow deer was greater than during any previous period represented in the deposits. The change must not be over-emphasized, since we know from other sites that woodland and scrub must have survived in certain localities of Palestine, but from the point of view of early man it was certainly for the worse. The desiccation created a situation that could only be met by a reduction in population or by improvements in the means of subsistence.

Mesolithic groups in south-west Asia

The Mesolithic people about whom we know most in western Asia are the Natufians, so called after the Wady en-Natuf, where their traces were first recognized. They were centred on a strip of territory mostly within some forty miles of the East Mediterranean between Beirut in the north and the Judaean Desert in the south, with outliers in Syria and far away to the south-west at Heluan, some twenty miles south of Cairo. Over the greater part of their territory the Natufians occupied rock-shelters, though recent discoveries at Eynam and Jericho make it clear that already during an early stage in their history they had begun to live in the open. The dead were commonly buried at their place of settlement; for instance the Mugharet el-Wad produced a cemetery of 87 individuals, including 64 adults, most buried on the platform but a few in the interior, though it is fair to point out that not all of these were of one period. The earliest Natufians habitually buried more than one person in the same grave, though in such cases one individual was marked out from the rest by being accompanied by personal ornaments. The settlement of Eynam included a monumental circular tomb, sunk nearly a metre into the ground and having walls lined with plaster, which appears to have been used on more than one occasion. The Eynam tomb also yielded, above two layers of burials, a complete skull with two neck vertebrae, suggesting that it had been severed from the trunk while still clothed with flesh.

The material equipment of the Lower Natufians reflects an economy based primarily on hunting, but in which fishing, indicated by slender bone spearheads barbed on one edge and by plain fish-hooks, played locally an important part, and in which cereal grasses were harvested for the first time by reaping-knives formed by flint blades inset into slotted handles of bone (and presumably also of wood) and converted into meal by stone pestles and mortars. The production of blades and burins and the use of bone and antler on a considerable scale carried on Advanced Palaeolithic traditions; so did the vigorous art, in which animal forms were rendered in a more or less naturalistic style; and so did the wearing of personal ornaments, comprising head-dresses and thigh-bands made from Dentalium shells, necklaces made up of perforated ends of gazelle phalanges, bored teeth, and twin-pendants of carved bone separated by Dentalium spacers. On the other hand the abundance of microliths, though not unknown in certain Advanced Palaeolithic cultures, is more characteristic of Mesolithic ones. The lunate form that predominated in the Natufian was retouched on the convex back by flaking from two directions, producing the so-called ridge-back retouch, designed to make them, like the blades of reaping-knives, fit more snugly into grooves or slots when mounted in handles or the heads of projectiles. The use for reaping of narrow blades with ridge-back retouch, inset in bone handles, of which several more or less complete examples have been preserved, is indicated by the presence of diffuse lustre of the kind that results from friction with the silica in cereal stalks, but it is important to emphasize that as yet we have no biological evidence of the precise nature of the cereals reaped by the Natufians, nor above all of the extent to which these had been domesticated and improved by breeding. The fact that even the reaping-knives bore carved animal heads on their handles and that stone pestles were shaped in the form of animal hoofs suggests that hunting was still the main source of food and this is supported by the absence of bones of domestic animals from deposits certainly of Lower Natufian age; even the dog, which commonly precedes domestic food-animals, did not certainly appear before the Middle Natufian. On the other hand it has been argued that the mere fact that specialized reaping equipment had been developed points to the harvesting of cereals improved by breeding to a point at which they retained their seeds for a period after ripening instead of shedding them almost at once.

That the Mesolithic inhabitants of Palestine contributed vitally to the early development of settled life based on stable farming will become more apparent when we consider the sequence brought to light in the early levels at Jericho (p. 81, below). Yet the probability is that when more is known about the prehistory of the area extending from the Mediterranean to the Iranian plateau, over which the earliest settled communities made their appearance, it will be found that the process of readjustment to less friendly environmental conditions caused more than this one Mesolithic group to seek closer relations with selected species of animals and plants in a way that led ultimately to their domestication. Further, one has to remember that, even in remote prehistoric times, men and therefore knowledge crossed tribal boundaries and so were capable of influencing groups with quite distinct cultural traditions, provided that they stood at an appropriate technological level. The question 'who invented agriculture?' is one that is hardly worth asking, since there is no prospect, certainly in the foreseeable future, of its receiving a convincing answer. Meanwhile hints that the earliest farmers in different parts of western Asia preserved traces of Mesolithic ancestry emphasize the essentially transitional character of the Mesolithic peoples: thus, the pre-pottery farmers of Jarmo in Iraq used microliths and the formally Neolithic, if not Chalcolithic (that is using some copper alongside flint and stone), inhabitants of Sialk in Persia made reaping-knives by setting flint blades into slotted bone handles carved at one end with animal heads. How far this implies that any particular group shared in the original transition from hunting and gathering to farming and how far that they merely adopted the new way of life from more advanced neighbours can only be decided in this key area when a much closer net-work of radiocarbon dates has been established.

Mesolithic Europe

In the case of territories such as the greater part of Europe, into which farming is known to have spread from outside, the Mesolithic peoples can be considered as transitional only in the latter sense. By the same token the span of Neothermal time during which Mesolithic societies prevailed was determined by the relative remoteness of different areas from the early centres of civilization, so that, to quote an extreme example, the Mesolithic period lasted much longer in say Denmark than it did in Palestine. Another fundamental difference is that, whereas in western Asia the Neothermal period began as one of stress, an era of aridity succeeding the plentiful rainfall of pluvial times, in northern Europe it was, on the contrary, one in which glacial conditions were relaxed and replaced by more genial ones. Thus, whereas in Asia worsening conditions promoted the development of a new way of life at the expense of the old, in Europe the emphasis was on adapting the old way of life to the spread of forest and on extending its geographical range to include regions formerly covered by ice-sheets or at least subject to periglacial

5-2

conditions. Between these extremes, over much of the West Mediterranean zone for example, the change in ecological conditions was much less marked and no outstanding cultural developments occurred.

Over a large part of Europe, including Iberia and Italy and much of France, Britain, central Europe and South Russia, the archaeological remains of Mesolithic cultures showed a marked falling away from those prevailing earlier in the same localities, suggesting a general impoverishment, due perhaps to some quite minor disturbance of the old equilibrium. A noticeable feature of the flint industries is an abundance of microliths shaped by a steep retouch from narrow flakes of small size and used in many cases to provide tips and barbs for wooden arrows; microliths had indeed played an important part in certain Advanced Palaeolithic industries, but the widespread dominance they now assumed was something new. Apart from this there was a marked reduction in forms, though scrapers continued to be a feature of most industries and burins continued, usually in greatly reduced numbers. In keeping with the decline of the burin went a general reduction in the importance of antler and bone as materials for implements and weapons and a scarcity of any form of art. The only exception to this was provided by the Azilian culture, named after the site of Mas d'Azil in the Ariège, which included numerous harpoon heads made from stag antler and barbed on one or both edges, and stone pebbles painted in red with conventional designs of ultimately anthropomorphic origin: and this culture, which was centred on the Dordogne, the northern slopes of the Pyrenees and the Cantabrian mountains, evidently evolved directly from the Late Magdalenian of the region. The precise sources of the cultures represented by minute geometric microliths and found over large parts of southern, western and central Europe are more difficult to trace, partly owing to their impoverishment and partly due to the effects of migration. The Grimaldian culture of Italy, indeed, seems to have developed without a break into an Epi-Grimaldian of Neothermal age, but no precise line of descent is evident for the Sauveterrian of France or the comparable industries of Britain or central Europe.

The Maglemosians

The hunter-fisher peoples who began to develop on the North European Plain in Pre-Boreal and reached their peak in Late Boreal times, stand in vivid contrast in that they exhibit something of the creative drive characteristic of the Advanced Palaeolithic peoples of southern and central Europe. The Maglemose people, named from the big bog (*magle mose*) at the Danish site of Mullerup where their remains were first recognized, have sometimes been classified as possessing a Forest culture but it is important to emphasize that they differed from those just described not so much in their environment—France and central Europe were forested as much as Denmark during Neothermal times—as in the use they made of it. The heart of the Maglemosian territory comprised the eastern part of Britain, the marshy region now covered by the North Sea, the North German plain and the lands bordering the western part of the Ancylus Lake, the form taken by the present Baltic Sea during Boreal times. From there they spread west as far as Ulster, east into the forest zone of Russia, and north to Middle Sweden and Norway as these territories were made accessible through the isostatic recovery of the earth's crust from the diminishing weight of retreating ice-sheets. The Maglemosians settled the banks of rivers and the margins of the lakes abounding in their territory, so that much of their refuse found its way into waterlogged deposits. This has led to the survival of an unusually large number of objects made from organic materials.

Like their contemporaries in central and southern Europe, the Maglemosians depended for their living on hunting and fishing supplemented on occasion by fowling and plant-gathering. The presence of quantities of antlers and bones at a number of their sites makes it possible to be sure that they killed large numbers of the elk, aurochs, red and roe deer and wild pig that sheltered in the virgin forest. Further, the discovery of microliths still mounted in resin on their pine-wood arrow-shafts proves beyond dispute that a main function of these was to barb and tip arrows. In addition to arrows of this type, blunt-ended ones of wood, intended for birds or small mammals with precious pelts, were found, together with bows made from single pieces of tapered wood and provided in the middle with carefully made hand-grips. As well as bows and arrows the Maglemosians used spears mounted with antler or bone heads barbed on one edge, either singly, or in pairs, for hunting and fishing. As might be expected from the nature of their habitat, they went in for fresh-water fishing on a considerable scale, using, in addition to fish-spears or leisters, lines with barbless bone fish-hooks resembling those from the Natufian culture of Palestine and nets made from twine twisted from fibres taken from the inner surface of line-bark and provided with sink-stones and floats of tree-bark. Numerous finds of wooden paddles, including one of late Pre-Boreal age from Star Carr, England, show that boats were in use and a well-made dug-out canoe from Pesse in Holland has been dated to c. 6250 B.C. by radio-carbon analysis.

One of the chief ways in which the Maglemosians differed from other Mesolithic groups lay in the positive attitude they adopted towards the forests that marked the climax of Post-Glacial vegetation in the temperate zone. Already before the end of Pre-Boreal times, during the period when birch forests were predominant, there is evidence that axes and adzes chipped from nodules of flint and sharpened and re-sharpened by blows struck transversely to the blade were used to fell trees and work timber. At first the blades were small and crudely made, but from the beginning they must have been mounted on handles in some form of holder or sleeve to absorb the impact. Larger and more regular ones were made during Boreal times and from this period we have a number of examples fixed in their original sleeves of antler or wood, into which wooden handles were inserted. By means of such tools the Maglemosians were able not only to initiate, though on a very restricted scale, the clearance of forest, which was not to be undertaken in earnest until the adoption of farming, but also to utilize wood on a more extensive scale, for example in making the dugout canoe already mentioned.

Another difference lay in their very extensive utilization of antler and bone. Whereas such peoples as the Epi-Grimaldians and the Sauveterrians contented themselves with awls, bodkins and various spatulate tools, the Maglemosians used these materials for making various forms of mattock-head, sleeves for axe- and adze-blades, barbed spearheads of various shapes and sizes, fish-hooks, netting-needles, leather-working tools, and objects of apparently ceremonial character.

Lastly, at the height of their development the Maglemosians practised art on a much more considerable scale. This took the form mainly of decorating objects of daily use, perforated and often smoothed antler beams or pendants or amulets. The techniques employed included line engraving, sometimes so fine as to escape casual scrutiny, and pits neatly drilled, presumably by fine flint awls, into the surface of the object decorated. The commonest motives were geometric patterns such as linear chevrons, criss-cross lines and various kinds of barbed line, all of which might on occasion be tied together to form an overall net-like design; in addition animal and anthropomorphic designs might be employed, the latter particularly on pendants or amulets. Occasionally, also, amber lumps might be carved into the forms of animals. The explanation for the flowering of this art at the peak of the Maglemosian culture and at the heart of its area of distribution may well be no more than that it represents a response to an environment peculiarly well-endowed for hunting and in which communities of hunters might be expected to have experienced some degree of cultural intensification.

Coastal settlement

During their final phase there is evidence that Mesolithic people in coastal areas were paying considerable attention to sea mammals, fish and shell-fish as sources of food, though there is doubt how far this represents a new departure and how far it is due simply to the submergence of the earlier Mesolithic coasts over most of Europe. Evidence that the resources of the sea were being vigorously exploited during the Atlantic phase of climate is available from the numerous middens of Denmark and South Sweden; from cave and midden sites occupied by Larnians and Obanians on either side of North Channel in north-east Ireland and south-west Scotland, from midden sites on islands off the present coasts of Morbihan and near the estuary of the Tagus in Portugal, occupied by makers of flint industries with trapeziform arrowheads; and from middens in cave-mouths abounding in the North Spanish province of Asturias but extending as far west as North Portugal.

Neolithic contacts

A significant aspect of the later stages in the history of some Mesolithic groups in Europe is the traces they show of influence from intrusive Neolithic economy. Thus, at a certain stage in the coastal settlement of Denmark, well exemplified at Ertebølle in North Jutland, we find a number of cultural traits that must have been Neolithic in origin, namely pottery, flat and radial flaking of flint axes, chisel-ended arrowheads made from sections of flint blades, and, most suggestive of all, agriculture and stock-raising alongside the older sources of food. Admittedly these have been explained in two ways, either as pointing to contact between indigenous hunter-fishers and intrusive farmers in Denmark or as evidence of the impact on the native Mesolithic culture of influences from Neolithic peasant cultures somewhere to the south. What is in any case reasonably sure is that the contacts set in motion a process of acculturation which serves to explain the distinctive character of Early Neolithic culture in the north. Again, in south-west Europe we find that peoples making flint blades and trapeziform arrowheads and living an otherwise Mesolithic way of life appear to have herded goats or sheep. Among such one may include midden-dwellers on the estuary of the Tagus or on the coast of Morbihan and the Tardenoisian cave-dwellers of Guyenne, who take their name from Fère-en-Tardenois in the Ile de France. Here also there are alternative explanations, but the fact remains that in both northern and southern Europe the later Mesolithic peoples bridged the gap between societies based exclusively on a wild economy and those who depended overwhelmingly on farming.

Expansion in northern Eurasia

Early Neothermal times also witnessed a certain enlargement in the area of human settlement, more particularly in northern territories as these were released from the grip of glacial or peri-glacial conditions. In the British Isles occupation was restricted during Late Glacial times to territories south of a line between Settle and Scarborough; and though much of Ireland provided lush grazing for giant Irish deer and reindeer, at this time the land was empty of men. Settlement seems to have expanded into the empty lands by two main thrusts: on the one hand makers of flint industries analogous to the French Sauveterrian, but with elements from native sources, moved up the Pennines to north-eastern England and eastern Scotland, sending a westward branch to the Isle of Man; and on the other off-shoots from the Magle-mosian centre, established in east Yorkshire as early as Late Pre-Boreal times, spread westwards across the sea to Ireland where they concentrated in the flint-rich province of Ulster. The Larnian–Obanian culture, which grew up on either side of the North Channel and ultimately spread up the west coast of Scotland, may well have received impulses of ultimately Azilian character from the Biscayan area to the south and quite certainly developed a regional character of its own, to which adaptation to coastal activities may well have contributed.

At the end of Late Glacial times the greater part of the Scandinavian peninsula was still buried under ice, the southern margin of which, marked by the Fenno-Scandian moraine, passed well south of Oslo and Stockholm; moreover, south of the ice-sheet a broad zone subject to isostatic depression was still submerged by the sea. As the ice-sheet shrank and the land was recovered, human settlement was able to expand, but it is worthy of note that the Mesolithic colonization was in fact restricted to territories outside the Fenno-Scandian moraine, and to the Atlantic coasts. The discovery of lithic industries at intervals around the Atlantic coasts of Scandinavia up to Finnmark and on to the Murmansk shore suggests a coastwise expansion of the coastal cultures identified in Denmark and West Sweden from early Atlantic times and in all probability established much earlier. The difficulty of overland movement up the fjord-indented coast of Norway and the discontinuity of settlement alike suggest that the northward spread of the Fosna-Komsa culture was effected by means of boats, the use of which enormously increased the possibilities of migration under primitive conditions.

Further east, in European Russia, a definite expansion in the area of settlement can also be noted. Thus, the Oka Valley into which Advanced Palaeolithic man had barely penetrated was occupied comparatively thickly by Mesolithic hunter-fishers. Further north there are signs that inroads were beginning to be made into the southern portion of the belt of pine forest that stretched from the East Baltic to the Urals. At Kunda and other sites in Esthonia abundant bone and antler gear for hunting and fishing, comparable but not identical with that of much the same age in the West Baltic area, is known from deposits of Boreal and younger age. Closely similar finds relating to an Eastern Maglemosian are known from north-west Russia and a further

800 miles or so east in the Schigir culture around Sverdlovsk, beyond a slight gap in the Ural mountains. Although, however, the Eastern Maglemosians had penetrated the coniferous forest over a front of more than a thousand miles, they did not do so very deeply, and much of the northern part of European Russia remained unoccupied. Further east in central Siberia no very marked change seems to have occurred in the external environment and in consequence no clear line can be drawn in cultural history until the appearance of pottery. The material from Verkholenskaia Gora, near Irkutsk, was associated with a modern fauna and dated from Neothermal times, but in all essentials it represents a continuance of the Advanced Palaeolithic of the region.

CHAPTER 4

THE INVENTION OF FARMING AND THE RISE OF MESOPOTAMIAN CIVILIZATION

Mixed farming as the basis of Old World civilization

The possibility of advancing towards civilization depended in the first instance on a new relationship between man and the animals and plants on which he depended for food. So long as he had to subsist on the game animals, birds and fish he could catch and trap, the insects and eggs he could collect and the foliage, roots, fruits and seeds he could gather, he was limited in the kind of social life he could develop; as a rule he could only live in small groups, which gave small scope for specialization and the sub-division of labour, and in the course of a year he would have to move over extensive tracts of country, shifting his habitation so that he could tap the natural resources of successive areas. It is hardly to be wondered at that among communities whose energies were almost entirely absorbed by the mere business of keeping alive, technology remained at a low ebb. It is true that peoples like the Kwakuitl and Nootka tribes of British Columbia, who were able to win a basic supply of food by catching and storing the salmon that came up their rivers at the spawning season, could maintain permanent settlements, build massive timber houses and support elaborate social institutions involving the ceremonial destruction of wealth. Yet the fact remains that no such peoples, other than the pioneers of farming, were able by their own efforts to emerge from the Stone Age. It was only through the control of breeding of animals and plants that early man was able to ensure himself a reliable and readily expandable source of food and thereby establish a secure basis for cultural advance. The invention of farming was indeed revolutionary in the sense that it alone made possible the rise of literate civilizations, though one does well to remember that the new economy was established so gradually and its effects upon other aspects of culture were at first so imperceptible as to be hardly discernible in the archaeo-logical record.

The historic civilizations of the Near East were centred on great rivers: the Euphrates and Tigris, the Nile and, somewhat later, the Indus; but archaeology, supported by radio-carbon dating, makes it clear that the antecedent stages, which witnessed the genesis of farming, metallurgy, urban settlement and a complex social hierarchy, were passed through elsewhere. The birth of farming and the origins of settled life in the Near East occurred somewhere in the zone extending from Palestine, Syria and Cilicia, and thence across the piedmont or foot-hill zone of Turkey and northern Iraq to Iran, the Caspian shore and Turkestan (Map 3). Whereas the alluvial lands had an arid climate and needed irriga-tion to render them fertile, the upland territories have a rainfall to-day exceeding 16 inches a year and even at the driest phase of Neothermal time must have been relatively more favourable to primitive farmers. Moreover, it was precisely in these latter territories that the prototypes of the relevant crops and livestock flourished in the wild state. At least it is the case that *Triticum dicoccoides* and *Hordeum spontaneum*, progenitors respectively of Emmer wheat and barley, the two cereals that dominated agri-culture in this zone, are both found wild in just these regions to-day; there is no evidence that either was available in Egypt before being introduced by man; and the only cereal growing wild in Europe, *Triticum aegilopoides*, known from Albania, Yugoslavia and northern Greece, is unlikely to have played a significant part, since Einkorn *T. monococcum*, to which it gave rise, seems never to have been cultivated as a separate crop and, having as a rule only one grain on a spikelet, was not much use for breeding

3. The heartland of Old World civilization, *c.* 8000–2500 B.C.

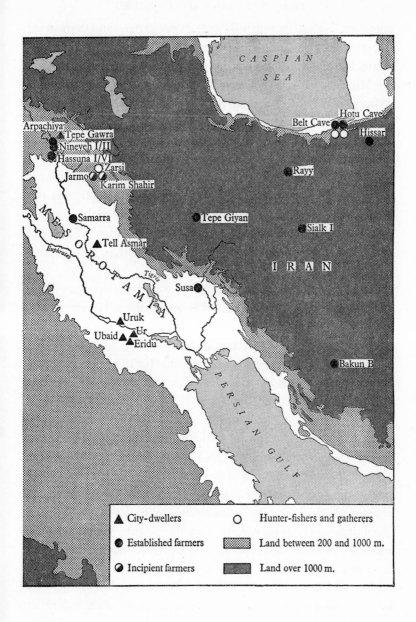

CASPIAN
SEA

Hotu Cave
Belt Cave
Hissar

Arpachiya
▲Tepe Gawra
Nineveh I/II
Hassuna I/VI
Zarsi
Jarmo
Karim Shahir

Rayy

Samarra

▲Tell Asmar

Tepe Giyan

Sialk I

Euphrates

Tigris

I R A N

Susa

Uruk

Ur

Ubaid ▲
Eridu

Bakun B

PERSIAN GULF

MESOPOTAMIA

▲ City-dwellers	○ Hunter-fishers and gatherers
● Established farmers	Land between 200 and 1000 m.
◉ Incipient farmers	Land over 1000 m.

purposes. Again, though wild prototypes of oxen and swine were rather widely distributed in the temperate zone during Neo-thermal times, wild sheep were much more narrowly confined, the Mouflon variety to a zone from Syria and southern Turkey to Iraq, the Urial to one from the Caspian across Iran to Afghanistan and northern Pakistan, and the Argali to the region from Turkestan to the Uzbek republic. Equally it was the piedmont and mountain zone that held metal ores and so offered conditions favourable to technological advance among societies whose economies long remained on a subsistence basis. It was not until social development was comparatively advanced that occupation of the alluvial territories, involving irrigation of the soil and wholesale importation of basic raw materials, first became feasible.

If the original focus of farming is to be located somewhere within the territory just defined, it is among the advanced hunter-fishers and food-gathers occupying the area at or near the beginning of Neothermal times that we have to seek the innovators, who in a sense were responsible for the whole future of civilization in the Old World. Insufficient is yet known about the Mesolithic peoples of western Asia to allow any firm conclusions to be drawn about those most likely to have been responsible. The possibility has to be allowed that in reality several different groups rose to the same challenge—the desiccation that marked the onset of Neothermal times in this area. In any case, even if some one group was in fact ahead of the others, conditions were such that people were more receptive than usual to new ways of easing the burden of subsistence, so that the picture would soon be blurred by diffusion. It would seem therefore that we must await a more exact definition of the Mesolithic groups occupying the region, and above all a network of radio-carbon dates sufficiently close to make it possible to trace the areas where the new form of economy first emerged.

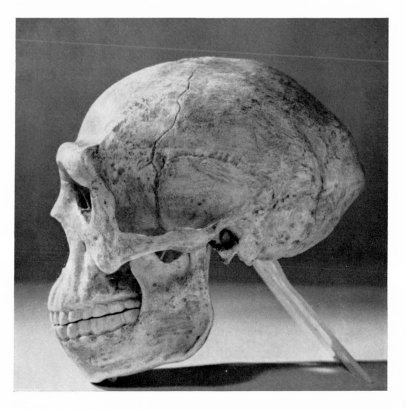

Reconstructed skull of Peking man (*Pithecanthropus pekinensis*)

(*facing p.* 80)

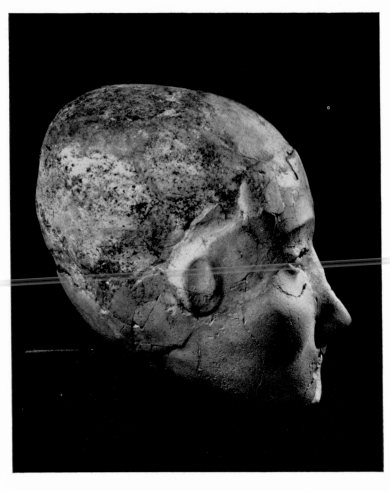

II   Skull of Proto-Neolithic man from Jericho with face
modelled in clay

The ' Proto-Neolithic' of Jericho and Jarmo

Meanwhile excavations in the Tell es-Sultan, the site of the ancient Jericho, in Jordan and at the mound of Jarmo in the Kurdish foothills of northern Iraq have thrown some welcome light on an early stage in the history of farming. The base of the tell at Jericho yielded traces of the Natufian hunter-fishers, whose remains, previously known from rock-shelters and open stations, mainly in Palestine (see p. 64), are the most complete for any Mesolithic group in western Asia. According to radio-carbon dates they were camping around the spring at Jericho about 7800 B.C. and to judge from the constricted space they occupied it would seem that they formed only a small group, probably a few primary families such as might have lived in the mouth of a large cave. Like their relatives at Mount Carmel they lived mainly by hunting gazelle, and supplemented their diet by harvesting grain by means of reaping knives inset with flint blades. Whether this grain was wild or in any sense domesticated has been much discussed, but it is worth pointing out that wild, self-grown cereals grow in the immediate neighbourhood at the present day and there is no evidence that the Natufians had any special arrangements for storing their grain or that they had developed any true querns or milling-stones, though they certainly used stone rubbers of the type employed in many parts of the world for preparing wild plant foods. Until specimens of the grain harvested by the Natufians have been examined by a competent botanist, one can hardly be sure about its precise status. What is certain is that the Natufians had hardly gained enough control over cereals to affect in any noticeable way their mode of life.

By contrast the forty-five feet or so of archaeological deposits overlying the Natufian layer, though they still yielded no real pottery, gave clear indications of greatly enlarged social groups and of more permanent settlement, and it seems reasonable to expect that when the plant remains have been reported upon they will show that definite progress had been made in the domestication of cereals; already comparison of the horn cores of the numerous goats from the site with those of wild ones has given some evidence for domestication. Two distinct stages have been distinguished in the Proto-Neolithic deposits. The earlier one, which yielded a flint industry in the Natufian tradition, though lacking certain types and supplemented by ground stone axes, was characterized by well-constructed round huts with sunken floors and beehive walls made from long oval bricks with flat bases and curved or hog-backed upper surfaces. In the course of this earlier or 'hog's-back' stage of the Proto-Neolithic, which to judge from the flints was an outgrowth from the Natufian, the settlement, which by now extended over the whole area of the tell, was defended by a ditch cut in the solid rock to a depth of 3 metres and a width across the top of 9 metres, backed by a massive stone wall with great round towers set at intervals and incorporating inner stairways for manning the defences.

The fact that such primitive people found it necessary to erect defences on such a scale suggests the presence of rivals at an analogous stage of development and it seems likely that these are represented in the upper Proto-Neolithic layer that began to form around 6000 B.C. This need not of course imply that the transition to a more settled form of life based on incipient farming, added to the hunting of plentiful game, was made by more than one Mesolithic stock in the region. More likely it reflects the possibility that the attainment of a more settled way of life favoured the development from the same basic Natufian stock of locally differentiated communities, and it is noteworthy that the lithic industry in the upper Jericho level, with its pressure-flaked tanged arrowheads and heavy, serrated reaping-knife blades compares closely with that of the Tahounian, previously recognized in the Judaean cave of El-khiam overlying successive stages of the younger Natufian. A feature of the upper Proto-Neolithic of

82

Jericho is the appearance of a specialized type of quern, wedge-shaped with a grinding hollow running out at the broader end, another sign that the use of grain for food was already long-established. The houses at this level consisted of rectangular rooms grouped round courtyards in which the cooking was done: the walls were built of sun-dried bricks on a stone foundation course and the floors were characteristically made of clay coated by burnished lime-plaster and covered by rush mats. Indications of what may have been family shrines were found in the houses, but the most telling evidence for spiritual development it so be found in the treatment of the dead. Already in the lower level the custom of severing the heads from the trunks and burying them in separate nests seems to have been established, a practice paralleled in a Mesolithic context in South Germany at Ofnet and Kaufertsberg near Nordlingen. A notable feature of the rite as practised by the plaster-floor people at Jericho was the way in which the skulls were filled with clay, the eyes inlaid with shell and the faces finely modelled in clay, the expressions of which are so personal as to suggest veritable portraits (Pl. II). Burial had been accorded to the dead since early in Late Pleistocene times and among Advanced Palaeolithic peoples it had become customary to inter them clothed and with their ornaments in place; but though burial had become formalized as a means of separating the dead from the living and though some differentiation in the objects placed with the dead might be made according to sex, there is no indication that individuals were memorialized as such in those early times. The modelled faces from Jericho on the other hand point the way to the funerary masks and portraits of later and more sophisticated cultures from Pharaonic Egypt to Stuart England. More vividly than anything else, unless it be the scale of the settlement and its defences, they emphasize the significance of the change initiated by hunter-fishers and carried forward during the seventh millennium B.C. by men who added to a plentiful supply of gazelle meat the increment of domesticated cereals and herds of goats, citizens of no mean community who were yet ignorant of pottery, for long regarded as a symbol of settled life.

Primitive farming communities also lived in the Kurdish foot-hills of northern Iraq, where descendants of the Advanced Palaeolithic Zarzi culture are known to have occupied, as at the open site of Karim Shahir, territory well supplied by species capable of being domesticated. Excavations at the mound of Jarmo on a promontory hill-top have yielded abundant evidence for a primitive Neolithic community that made no use of pottery until the last third of its existence. The houses, like those of the upper Proto-Neolithic of Jarmo, had rectangular rooms with mud walls built on stone footings and reed mats on the floors. The lithic industry combined blades and microliths of Mesolithic aspect with blades of reaping-knives and polished stone axes. Pestles, mortars and milling-stones bear further witness to the importance of plant-food, and what have been described as 'floor-basins' of clay baked in place may have been the bases of silos. The grains of emmer, spelt and two-rowed barley suggest that these cereals were still at a comparatively early stage of their emergence from wild prototypes. Among the meat bones wild animals accounted for only 5 per cent and the villagers evidently kept herds of sheep or goats, cattle and swine. If we were to follow the radio-carbon dates obtained from the original samples, the site would be no earlier than the first half of the fifth millennium B.C. and would therefore rank in relation to sites like Hassuna as a poor outlier rather than as an ancestor. Even so the site would remain of the highest interest, not merely as confirming that a simple kind of mixed farming might be carried on by people who had not yet acquired the art of potting, but as illustrating the process whereby the new way of life spread in a relatively primitive form at a time when in the main centres it was passing through a more advanced stage of development, a process which we shall find exemplified ever more vividly when in a later chapter we consider a secondary area of diffusion like Europe.

The 'Neolithic' of Syro-Cilicia

A new stage in the advance towards civilization in south-west Asia was reached when settled communities, depending on a mixed farming economy and still limited by a technology based substantially on lithic tools, took to potting, probably some time towards the end of the sixth millennium B.C. Three main foci may be noted, one centred on Cilicia and western Syria with contacts as far south as Jericho, another on northern Iraq and eastern Syria and a third on the Iranian plateau. In each case the villagers lived in rectangular-roomed houses that formed the nucleus of settlement mounds or tells. The pottery of the Syro-Cilician zone, best exemplified from the lowermost layers (XXV–XXXIII) of the Yümük Tepe at Mersin, Ugarit (Ras Shamra), and Byblos, comprises simple pots, often hole-mouthed, of dark burnished ware decorated by horizontal rows of impressions by a shell-edge that was sometimes rocked back and forth. Associated with this was a rich lithic industry, including blades of reaping-knives, polished axes and tanged lanceheads, often with pressure-flaking broadly analogous to those of the Tahounian industry of Palestine. To judge from the impressions of a textile garment under a crouched burial at Mersin (XXVI), weaving was practised as well as potting and flint- and stone-working.

The 'Neolithic' of Iraq: Hassuna and Halaf

Traces of broadly similar culture were found in the basal layer (Ia) of the great stratified mound of Tell Hassuna near Mosul in northern Iraq. To judge from the stratification and the absence of structural features, the earliest phase was marked by hardly more than camps and the emphasis evidently lay on stock-keeping, even if, as suggested by the use of straw for tempering the coarse pottery, cereals were also cultivated. The rich lithic industry including tanged projectile heads with pressure-flaking and the burnished pottery both point to the Syro-Cilician region as a source of the earliest culture represented at Hassuna and in this connection it should be noted that burnished ware occurs in the intervening Khabur drainage area at Tell Shaghir Bazar and at Tell Halaf; only the carinated storage vessels made from the coarse straw-tempered ware suggest local development. A further indication that at this time the whole area from the East Mediterranean to the Tigris formed in effect a unitary zone is that during the immediately ensuing period the same multi-chevron design was found painted on pottery from Mersin (XX–XXIV) as on that from Hassuna (Ib, c; II) or Nineveh (I). Moreover, pottery with incised herring-bone and chevron designs, associated with this at Nineveh I, is known from as far west as Mersin, Byblos and Jericho.

The first real indication that Assyria was beginning to form a distinct focus of early culture came with the last phase of this stage in northern Iraq, when the vigorous and distinctive pottery named after the original finding-place at Tell Halaf was developed. Halafian pottery is outstanding on account of the variety of its forms and above all of its painted decoration and because of the excellence of its firing; but it was still hand-made, and there is no reason to think it was necessarily or even probably made by whole-time potters. In addition to dishes and flasks the forms included bowls with sharp-shouldered bodies and flaring necks and bowls and flasks on hollow stands. The decoration comprised geometric patterns like triangles, chevrons, lozenges, chequers, stars, Maltese crosses, quatrefoils and rosettes; stipples, including egg and dot; and stylized representations of men and animals, including designs based on the bull's head. It was applied to a buff or cream slip by glaze paint. At the climax of the industry the decoration was polychrome; red, orange, yellow and black paints being used, sometimes high-lighted by white spots. The pottery was apparently fired to temperatures up to 1200° C. in great domed kilns with rectangular annexes, like those preserved at Carchemish with walls and ceilings of clay on stone footings. Some archaeologists, misled by the formal analogy in plan with *tholoi* (the circular underground tombs of Greece approached by sloping passages), have interpreted these structures as funerary or in some way religious, but there is no evidence that they were used for any other purpose than that revealed rather clearly at Carchemish. The Halafians appear to have depended on lithic tools and quarried obsidian as far afield as Lake Van. Metal tools have come from a number of Halafian sites, but these were either, as at Tell Halaf, from levels contemporary with the early Ubaid stage in southern Iraq or, as at Samarra, were in all probability intrusive from much younger deposits. Before the period of Ubaid influence copper was only used for such things as beads and then most probably from native metal. The Halafians were skilled at working hard stone, which they made into button seals, beads, amulets and small vessels, and they imported shells from the Persian Gulf to the Khabur area. Suggestions that they used wheeled transport should be discounted, being based on an incomplete and enigmatic vase painting. On the other hand there are indications that cult activities were well developed. Clay figurines of women, sometimes shown with exaggerated breasts and rump and at Arpachiya associated with doves, suggest fertility cults, as do models in clay, bone and stone of the common farmyard animals, notably including bulls, and representations of bulls' heads on pots and stone amulets. There are also signs in double-axe amulets and signs painted on pots that a thunder-god was recognized. At its greatest extent Halafian pottery extended westwards over the Syro-Cilician region to the West Mediterranean at Mersin (XVII–XIX) and Ras Shamra (III), northward to Lake Van and southward as far as the region of Baghdad and even further on the east of the Tigris; on the other hand it did not penetrate the alluvial lands of southern Iraq, which, as we shall see, were first settled by the Ubaid people from the east.

Iran: Bakun, Sialk and Hissar

The Iranian plateau, together with Baluchistan and Afghanistan, shared with the piedmont zone of Syria and northern Iraq an

endowment that favoured the early emergence of societies based
on mixed farming and capable of fixed settlement, societies that
soon learned to exploit the copper ores of the region and to
practise metallurgy. Although Iran formed part of the primary
zone in which prototypes of cultivated cereals and domesticated
sheep flourished in the wild state, very little is yet known of
peasant communities contemporary even with the early levels at
Hassuna. Crude, hand-made plain pottery found with a rich
lithic industry and numerous bone tools in the basal layer at the
tell of Bakun B near Persepolis suggest that the mountainous area
of south-west Persia was occupied before the development of the
painted wares chiefly characteristic of the region. Further north,
on the eastern slope of the mountains forming the western rim
of the Iranian desert, the lowest level (Ia) of the northern tell at
Sialk near Kashan has yielded well-documented material comparable in age with the Hassuna culture. The earliest settlement at
the base of the tell was evidently little more than a camp, but very
soon mud huts began to be built and the mound to grow. The
presence of lustred reaping-knife blades and saddle-querns and
of the bones of domestic cattle and sheep alongside those of some
game animals shows that the Sialk I people practised a form of
mixed farming and in the upper levels of this stage they had
already begun to hammer copper into small objects like pins and
awls. The most interesting feature of the pottery is that it includes
several distinct hand-made wares—plain undecorated, pale with
black paint, red oxidized (at first plain but later decorated with
black paint) and rare sherds of black—an indication that the
Sialk pottery is the product of a considerable history. Even so it is
significant that the Sialk I culture preserves some traits of Mesolithic ancestry, notably microliths and slotted bone reaping-knife
handles with animal head terminations, that recall in a general way
those of the Natufian. Another hint of the antiquity of Neolithic
culture in the region is the occurrence of soft pottery at the Belt
Cave on the south-east Caspian shore in a deposit formed

according to radio-carbon dating during the sixth millennium B.C. Yet until more systematic work on Pre-Sialk phases has been done it will hardly be possible to be sure at what stage Iran began to contribute to the history of cultures based on farming.

In common with the piedmont zone of northern Iraq and Syria, Iran was too arid to develop civilizations comparable in antiquity with those of the great riverine zones and indeed it was not until the first millennium B.C. that it effectively crossed the threshold of literacy. On the other hand this great upland territory formed so to speak a reservoir from which human floods broke out from time to time to interrupt, but on occasion to stimulate, the development of civilization in the riverine lands. Two main provinces of painted pottery have been distinguished for this region, one characterized by predominantly reddish, the other by predominantly buff wares. The former and more northerly group is found on sites like Sialk, Ravy and Hissar on the western and northern rim of the Iranian desert and at Anau in the former Turkestan: apart from the pottery, it is distinguished by a general absence of the clay figurines found in the southern group and by the practice of burying the dead among the houses instead of in separate cemeteries. The latter, on the other hand, is centered on the highlands of south-western and southern Iran, from Elam to Fars and eastward to Seistan and probably Makran in south Baluchistan, representative sites including Tepe Giyan, Susa I and Bakun A and B.

The 'Chalcolithic' of Iraq: Ubaid, Eridu, Ur and Tepe Gawra

It was from the buff-ware province that the first colonizers of the alluvial lands of southern Iraq came to lay the basis of the first historic civilization of Mesopotamia, that of the Sumerians. The Ubaid people, who take their name from a low tell not very far from the ancient site of Ur, arrived with a fully developed mixed farming economy and almost certainly with a knowledge of metallurgy acquired during their earlier history in the highlands.

They entered a territory lacking in minerals, building stone or even timber (other than palm stems), a land moreover which combined an arid climate with an absence of annual inundations and which therefore required artificial irrigation to provide a plentiful and assured supply of food. Yet it was a land of opportunity: given a certain level of technology and above all a degree of social integration permitting the growth of the political authority needed for public works, it was capable of producing food sufficient to support societies of increasing levels of complexity; and the great rivers both allowed access to distant raw materials and provided a means of exerting control ultimately over the whole of Mesopotamia. To anyone capable of occupying them the alluvial lands of southern Iraq presented a challenge, one that evoked in response nothing less than the development of a new form of city life and within less than a thousand years the emergence of a specific Sumerian civilization, embracing the whole Tigris–Euphrates basin.

The Ubaid people settled to begin with in the southern part of Iraq at a time when the northern parts of the country were occupied by the Halafians in the closing stage of the fifth millennium B.C.; but within a very few centuries they had imposed their culture over the whole of Mesopotamia and influenced much of Syria. The name site of Al Ubaid was a humble village set on a low mound or island of river silt close to the course of the Euphrates. The huts were built of the most abundant raw materials of the area; some had a flat roof, the walls formed of reed mats suspended between palm-stems and plastered with mud, and others a rounded one formed by bending bundles of reed over from one side to another, creating a structure like a Nissen hut. The peasants lived by farming: cereal crops were harvested by reaping-knives or sickles set with flint teeth, like those used on the highlands and in the Syro-Cilician region, or alternatively by sickles made of baked clay; and, though no bones have survived, the use of dung as plaster and the manufacture of animal figurines confirm that domestic livestock were kept. There is some evidence also for hunting and fishing in the marshes and rivers. To judge from a clay model with upturned ends, it would appear that they were already using boats made from bundles of reeds like the modern *bellum* to navigate the rivers. Potting was still mainly done by hand during the early stage of the culture, but already the foot-rings added to certain vessels before firing were being shaped on a slow-moving wheel or tournette turned by the potter's hand. The finer wares, of a light buff colour which turned when over-fired to a greenish hue, were decorated by painting with a smooth ferruginous paint having a matt surface, generally blackish but sometime reddish in colour. The patterns were made up pre-dominantly of relatively simple geometrical designs, such as zig-zag lines, triangles, lozenges and cross-hatching, but very oc-casionally animal motives, like those used more freely in the highlands, were employed. Although forming a distinctive ware on its own, the Ubaid pottery clearly relates to the buff-ware province of Iran and it is significant that figurines of women and animals were also a marked feature of the Mesopotamian culture.

The picture of village life given by the exploration of Al Ubaid has been corrected by later work on a number of town sites. Excavation of Tell Abu Shahrain (the ancient Eridu) and Ur in the south and of Tepe Gawra (XII–XIX) in the north has shown that the Ubaid people also lived in towns and erected their buildings from sun-dried bricks. Another sign of their relative advance over predecessors in Mesopotamia was that they practised metallurgy. In the south few copper objects have been recovered from Ubaid deposits, but at Tepe Gawra and Arpachiya and further afield at Tell Halaf a number of cast copper axes and other tools have been found; even at Al Ubaid the peasants made baked clay copies of copper tools, notably shaft-hole axes with expanded blades. The most striking monuments of the Ubaid people, not only on account of their physical size but even more because of what they imply in social organization, are their temples. At Abu

Shahrain no less than thirteen, the two bottom ones known only from a few walls, were found in the Ubaid levels underlying structures dating from the third Dynasty of Ur. The earliest temple of which a plan could be recovered (level XVI) was a small, nearly square room with a door near one corner, two short screens suggesting a division of the inner space, an altar in a niche in the rear wall and an offering-place showing signs of burning in the middle; by level VIII, on the other hand, the tripartite plan with a central cella flanked on either side by rows of small rooms had been evolved. This latter type occurred again in the two lowermost Ubaid layers (XVIII–XIX) at Tepe Gawra and was to recur throughout the succeeding Warka and Protoliterate stages of southern Iraq. The construction and above all the frequent reconstruction of temples, which might be of very substantial size, go to show that the Ubaid people had already so to speak created the characteristic form of early civilization in Mesopotamia, the sacred city whose economic, social and re-ligious life was centered on the temple and its priests.

Warka

On the Ubaid foundation Sumerian civilization developed comparatively rapidly in the south, where its progress can most conveniently be followed in the sequence of deposits found in the precinct of the Eanna Temple at Warka (= Sumerian Uruk, Semitic Erech). Here the Warka stage proper is represented by the bottom six layers (XIV–IX), the succeeding six (VIII–III) being assigned to the Protoliterate stage. The Warka stage is marked by the spread of a new kind of pottery which first co-existed with evolved forms of Ubaid ware and then replaced it. Culturally this pottery is interesting because it belongs to a ware at home in Anatolia and suggests an enrichment of Mesopotamia by impulses from the north. Economically its main significance is that it was turned on a free-spinning wheel, generally a sign that its manufacture had ceased to be a domestic craft and was in the

hands of whole-time potters. No architectural remains of outstanding interest were found in the levels of this phase at the
Eanna site, but in another part a succession of temples was
erected at this time to the god Anu. The earliest of these, represented only by a ramp, may have been earlier than Eanna XIV,
but those whose plans have been recovered were probably
contemporary with Eanna XI–VIII. The culminating structure
of the Warka phase was the White Temple, built on the traditional
threefold plan and having on the central axis of the cella a
rectangular pedestal with a low semicircular step bearing traces of
burning, presumably in connection with offerings or incense.
The White Temple measured 22·3 × 17·5 m. and it was set on a
great platform 70 m. long, 66 m. broad and 13 m. high, built of
rectangular mud bricks. The size of the temples erected during
the Warka phase and above all, perhaps, the frequency with which
they were rebuilt go to emphasize their importance in the social
structure of the day. Another feature to appear at this time,
destined to be of even greater importance in Sumerian society,
was the cylinder seal, which first occurred between two underlying building phases most probably of Eanna X–IX age.

Protoliterate Sumer

The Protoliterate phase at Warka was marked by a renewed
activity in the construction of temples. On the Anu site a true
ziggurat or stepped platform was erected for the first time in
Eanna VIII; on the Eanna site a tripartite temple was raised on
a limestone footing during period V and above it in period IV
a building with great free-standing columns; and on another part
of the site a temple was built directly on the level soil, the surface
being decorated by vast numbers of small cones of variously
coloured stones pressed into gypsum plaster, that gave the effect
of a vast mosaic covering not only the building itself but also
the wall round the court. The phase further witnessed a number
of innovations, including the use of vessels of copper and silver,

monumental sculpture and pictographic writing. The uppermost Protoliterate level at Warka (Eanna III) yielded an almost life-size human head of marble and a number of large sculptures of animal heads. Again, from a hole beside an altar at Tell Asmar we have a series of human figures (Pl. III) carved from yellow limestone with the eyes inlaid by shell, figures which are thought to represent in most instances individual devotees of the god whose temple they originally helped to furnish. It is significant, in view of the central role of the temple and its priests in Protoliterate society, that the earliest traces of writing and numeration belonged to the temple accounts. Pictographic signs first appeared in Eanna IV and by Eanna VIIb they had become notably more conventionalized. The numerical system associated with these primitive scripts combined features of the decimal and sexagesimal systems and emphasizes the way in which economic activities were controlled from the centre by the temple community. That means of transport over land as well as on rivers had been developed at this time is shown by the occurrence among the pictographic signs of representations of wheeled vehicles and of boats with upturned ends.

The Early Dynastic period

The Early Dynastic phase of Sumerian civilization, which began between 3200 and 2800 B.C., was marked from a material point of view by an overall increase in wealth rather than by any notable innovations in the sphere of technology. Many of its basic traits were already present in the Ubaid culture and, as we have seen, the use of the wheel for potting and for transport, monumental sculpture, cylinder seals and pictographic writing were all added during the ensuing Protoliterate phases. Among the most potent signs of increased wealth should be mentioned the greater abundance and elaboration of metal tools, weapons, ornaments and vessels, among which forms were evolved that spread in time to Syria, Anatolia, the Aegean, the Caucasus, central Europe and vast tracts of Russia. By the end of Early Dynastic times the Sumerian smiths were riveting and soldering, as well as casting, and were making bronze with a content of from 6 to 10 per cent of tin. Quantities of gold and silver were used for ornaments and vessels, as well as a wide range of more or less hard stones. Representations on painted pottery, models and remains from tombs give us more detailed information about the wheeled transport available at this time: chariots and waggons were evidently mounted on solid wheels, made from three pieces of wood held together by cross-pieces and bound by tyres held in place by copper nails, and drawn by Asiatic asses (onagers) or oxen harnessed by collars and yokes. From this time also engravings on cylinder seals indicate that animal traction was being applied to light wooden ploughs for cultivating the soil.

The rise in material well-being was accompanied by major changes in social structure, the most notable of which was the emergence of kings or officials of comparable status, at first as temporary war leaders, but in due course as established rulers of the city states. The immediate cause of this was undoubtedly the rise of warfare as an institution and this itself was linked with the increase in wealth already noted: thus, the growing affluence of the cities only served to increase their attraction to marauding pastoralists of the highland and the desert; the citizens needed to secure raw materials in increasing variety and volume from more or less remote territories inhabited by poorer and more barbarous peoples; and, even more to the point, rivalry between the cities grew as the opportunities for enrichment increased and this occurred at a time when armament was becoming more effective and the inhabitants found themselves able to support warriors. Whatever the factors responsible there can be no doubt that war had by this time become a well-organized institution: on the so-called 'Royal Standard' of Ur we see depicted not only the royal chariot with prisoners under guard, but three distinct grades of combat troops, namely ass-drawn chariots riding men down, a phalanx of heavy troops helmeted and cloaked, and light skirmishers in contact with the enemy. Eloquent insight into the status achieved by the Sumerian rulers is given by the Royal Tombs at Ur, which show that a whole procession of grooms, guards, courtiers and women, together with the oxen drawing the funeral car, were slaughtered to accompany the royal personage to the next world.

Mesopotamia down to Alexander

The political history of Mesopotamia during the two thousand years or so that elapsed before it passed under Persian dominion was in many respects depressing. Ever since its emergence in the fifth millennium the city state had been the basic political unit of the Sumerians and at least eleven of these, Eridu, Ur, Erech, Larsa, Kish and Nippur among them, supported independent dynasties. The struggle for predominance among these was seldom relieved by statesmanship or by the appearance of higher forms of political integration and on the rare occasions when these were achieved the promise was dissipated by the intrusion of desert or mountain-dwellers inferior in civilization and bent only on appropriating the wealth of the richer alluvial lands. Predominance won by piecemeal defeat of rivals was generally limited to the active life of the victor. It was not until Sargon founded his city of Akkad in c. 2340 B.C. that we find ourselves in the presence of a political innovator of genius, able not merely to conquer, but to secure his conquests by basing his regime on something more permanent than force. Sargon may well have owed his ability to weld into an imperial state the lands sharing in Sumerian civilization and extending from the Mediterranean to the Persian Gulf to the spread from the north of Semitic ideas and language with their greater emphasis on kinship and tribal loyalties. A uniform dynasty and calendar, indeed, secured his realms to his immediate successors, but around 2180 B.C. the Sargonid Empire was overthrown by

III   Sumerian statue of Early Dynastic times from
Tell Asmar, Mesopotamia

(*facing p.* 96)

IV   Relief carving of King Nar-mer on stone palette from
Hierakonpolis, Upper Egypt

hillmen from the east. Despite this set-back, Ur, under its Third Dynasty, was destined to enjoy its most splendid days, only to be overwhelmed around 2025 B.C. by Amorites from the west and Elamites from the east.

The victories of Hammurabi (c. 1800–1760 B.C.), by expelling the Elamites and establishing the First Dynasty of Babylon, ushered in a new cycle. Like Sargon before him, Hammurabi appreciated the need to establish an imperial organization: governors were appointed to rule over city states, a body of laws was promulgated and a state religion based on the cult of Marduk was established. This time it was Hittites from the north and Kassites from the east who overwhelmed the empire, the former sacking Babylon (c. 1595 B.C.) and the latter establishing a dynasty that lasted down to 1171 B.C. In the twelfth century B.C. the Assyrians emerged as a powerful military state and, though the Babylonians were able to maintain their trade with the Phoenicians and others bordering the Mediterranean, they lived, more particularly after the great period of Assyrian expansion during the ninth century, under the shadow of their ruthless neighbours to the north. This was only brought to an end by yet another irruption from the eastern highlands. By an irony of history it was the destruction of Elamite power by the Assyrians (640 B.C.) that made possible the rise of the Persians, who under Cyrus II of the Achaemenid dynasty first overthrew the Medes (c. 550 B.C.) and then descended on Babylon (c. 539 B.C.). The Assyrian dominions were overrun and before long the Achaemenid empire was extended east to the Oxus and the Indus and west to include Egypt. Soon almost the whole of the western focus of Old World civilization was engulfed in the Persian empire. Only the Athenian hoplites who on the plain of Marathon (490 B.C.) turned back the hosts of Darius, the Greek sailors who destroyed Xerxes' fleet at Salamis (480 B.C.) and the Lacedaemonians who defeated his army at Plataea (479 B.C.) preserved the growing point of European civilization. Within a hundred and fifty years or so the

Greeks under Alexander the Great had conquered the whole of the ancient world from Asia Minor and Egypt to Iran and the Punjab (334–323 B.C.). Alexander's conquest marked far more than the end of the Persian empire: it symbolized the eclipse of the ancient civilizations of western Asia and the Nile Valley and the advent of a European power on the stage of world history.

CHAPTER 5

ANCIENT EGYPT AND THE LATER PREHISTORY OF AFRICA

It is no longer seriously disputed that the arts of farming on which the Old World civilization were based were first learned in those parts of western Asia where alone the wild prototypes of the more important cereals flourished in the wild state. From this it follows that the spread of farming from this focal territory must have involved the introduction of domesticated species into new and unfamiliar environments. The first area to which cereal farming and stock-raising were diffused was probably Egypt and it will in any case be convenient to describe this next, because the Nile Valley gave birth to the earliest distinctive literate civilization outside western Asia.

EGYPT

Diffusion of farming

How and when farming first spread to Egypt and incidentally to Africa is still uncertain. The most obvious route is the overland one from Palestine to Lower Egypt, and traces of cultures of Neolithic aspect have been found there, notably at Merimde-Benisalame near the head of the Delta and on old shore-lines of the former Fayum lake (Map 3). On the other hand the fact that the main focus of the Predynastic cultures, in which the form of ancient Egyptian civilization had already begun to take shape, lay in Upper Egypt between Asyūt and Luxor suggests that influences from Asia may have reached Upper Egypt by way of the Wady-el-Hammamat and the Red Sea. The direction from which these impulses first arrived has an obvious bearing on the relations between the 'Neolithic' cultures of Lower and the Pre-dynastic ones of Upper Egypt: if the southern route was used, or at least used first, the existence of certain parallelisms between the two groups would argue that the former were poor, retarded relations of the latter; whereas, if the seminal influences moved upstream, quite opposite conclusions might be drawn. Present indications are that, though some of the 'Neolithic' communities of Lower Egypt in fact persisted during the early Predynastic period of Upper Egypt, the Fayum peasants have a clear priority, going back well into the latter part of the fifth millennium B.C., whereas the earliest radio-carbon dates for early Predynastic sites go back no further than the fourth millennium. Whether farming was established earlier in the lower Nile Valley we may never know, since in the course of six thousand years or so the river could well have eroded traces of any earlier settlements that may have existed.

Fayum, Merimde and El Omari

The earliest Neolithic communities yet known from Africa belong to the period of heavy rainfall following the arid period that formed the background to the invention of farming in western Asia. When the Fayum basin was first settled by farmers the level of the lake stood 180 feet higher than it does today and forest trees and swamps existed in what is now an arid environment. At the height of Altithermal times, indeed, the Fayum was no isolated oasis, but formed part of a zone of relatively favourable environment extending over large tracts of the Sahara. Traces of hunter-fisher peoples have been found there, with remains of crocodiles, hippopotami and fish, indicating conditions wetter than those of to-day. The widespread occurrence of barbed bone harpoon-heads suggests that a broadly similar way of life prevailed at the height of Altithermal times as far west as the Fayum depression and the Nile Valley down to the neighbourhood of Khartoum. Indeed the Fayumis can best be regarded as hunter-fishers who had adopted a Neolithic way of life originally

developed in western Asia, and it is worthy of note that they used
bone harpoon-heads and winged arrowheads of flint paralleled
in the French Sudan.

The Fayumi people kept sheep or goats, cattle and swine, and
cultivated emmer and flax. The equipment used in harvesting,
storing and grinding the grain, like the cereals themselves, were
those developed long previously in western Asia. The silos lined
with coiled basketry, in addition to carbonized cereals, yielded
fine baskets, used in all probability for sowing, and wooden
reaping-knives with flint blades set in slots, like the much older
bone ones of the Natufians. Although fire-holes were noted in
the mounds of midden material, no definite traces of dwellings
were observed, from which it has been inferred that tents or
similar structures were used. Numerous axe and adze-blades made
from polished flint or stone suggest that timber was nevertheless
utilized on a considerable scale and it may prove that more
substantial dwellings were in fact made. Traces of linen show that
weaving was practised. Pots were made by hand in simple shapes,
mainly undecorated flat-based bowls without handles, spouts or
other features. Apart from shells, some of which were brought
from the Red Sea and the Mediterranean, and beads of amazonite
or microcline felspar of uncertain, but certainly exotic origin, the
Fayumis made do with local materials and their economy was of
simple subsistence type.

Traces of communities practising the same economy and whose
way of life and material equipment closely resembled that of the
Fayumis, are also known from Merimde and from El Omari near
Helwan. The exact age of the Merimdian is still unknown, but a
radio-carbon date for El Omari (*c.* 3300 ± 230 B.C.) suggests that
poor peasant cultures of this type could survive for some time
alongside more advanced communities. An apparent difference is
that the Merimdians buried their dead, as a rule contracted on
their right side and without grave-goods, among their dwellings
rather than away from the settlement. They occupied light shelters

of oval or horseshoe plan. They sometimes used large pots as silos as well as baskets, and supplemented the produce of farming by hunting and fishing; like the Tasians of Upper Egypt they made barbless fish-hooks resembling in general those used long earlier by the Natufians of Palestine.

Badarian of Upper Egypt

Other communities of relatively simple farmers, depending on flint and stone for their basic technology, established themselves in Upper Egypt, notably in the region near Badari, where they seem to have laid the basis of the Early Predynastic culture. Traces of the temporary settlement of such early farmers were found at Hammāmīya stratified below Early and Late Predynastic levels, but the bulk of our information comes from burials. The Badarian peasants cultivated emmer and barley which they harvested with reaping-knives set with bifacially flaked sickle-teeth and stored in clay silos; and they kept cattle and sheep or goats, though not apparently swine. In addition they hunted, using arrows tipped with heads of leaf- or hollow-based and winged form. As craftsmen they also wove, made baskets and turned out pottery by hand. This latter comprised bowls and open dishes, commonly black inside and near the rim, the lower part of the body being red or brown through oxidization; the finer ware was finished with a burnished rippled surface and patterns were sometimes made on the inner face of open vessels by means of burnished lines. Flint, stone and bone were freely used, but copper appeared only in the form of beads that had been hammered into shape, presumably from native metal. The dead were interred in a contracted attitude in oval trench graves clothed in linen with skin outer garments, as a rule with the head at the west end, facing south and so lying on their right side. The men were clean-shaven, but wore their hair long; and the women plaited theirs and wore ivory combs carved with animal heads. Finds of stone palettes, occasionally with red pigment or with malachite, suggest the use of cosmetics. Perforated shells were used for head-dresses, girdles and necklaces; and anklets, bracelets, rings and ear- or nose-plugs were also worn. A feature of Badarian practice of special significance for the future was their careful burial of domestic animals wrapped in textiles.

Among the graves with Badarian grave goods were others with distinctive, though evidently closely related, furniture, which is commonly attributed to a separate culture named after the site of Der Tasa. Although no radio-carbon or absolute dates are available for the Tasian it is generally held on not very impressive evidence to have preceded the Badarian. The absence of copper beads, on which some stress had been laid, could well be due to chance; and in any case the presence or absence of small trinkets of native copper has no real economic or technological significance. The distinctive beaker pots, slender, with round base and flaring rim, are decorated by incised patterns that suggest basketry prototypes.

Early Predynastic

The Early Predynastic or Amratian culture has been found at Nakada sandwiched between the Badarian, from which it apparently developed, and the overlying Later Predynastic. Radiocarbon dates suggest that it was flourishing about a third of the way through the fourth millennium (3627 ± 300; 3794 ± 300 B.C.). Whereas the villagers of Merimde and Badari camped on spurs overlooking the Nile and the Fayumis settled the margins of the Fayum lake, the Predynastic peoples seem to have been the first to exploit the possibilities of the naturally irrigated valley. The size of the Nakada settlement, an aggregation of mud and reed huts at least 100 yards across in either direction, and the number of the graves in the cemetery both suggest enlarged social units. Schematic representations of a variety of animals painted or scratched on pottery may have been intended as symbols of totems and it is significant that similar ones recur as emblems of nomes or territorial divisions during the historic period. It may well be therefore that the Amratian villages were occupied by totemic clans. Their technology was still basically lithic, copper continuing to be used only in its native form and for such small objects as pins with rolled heads. On the other hand, flint was no longer obtained merely in the form of surface nodules; it was now mined and the roughing out and manufacture of tools was carried out on the site of the quarries. Bifacially flaked arrowheads continued to be made in numbers, including leaf and triangular as well as hollow-based forms. The finest pieces were fish-tail lanceheads and long dagger blades, which had been ground into shape before being subjected to a final process of superbly controlled pressure flaking. This process, the object of which was no doubt to impart a surface finish, was also applied to polished flint axes and adzes. In general Amratian pottery was coarser than Badarian, probably because the Predynastic people were beginning to develop elegant stone vessels, cylindrical ones from alabaster and footed ones from basalt. Black-topped ware continued to be made, but a new departure was White Cross-lined ware in which patterns recalling basketry, together with others depicting animals, men and boats, were applied in dull white paint to a polished red surface. To judge from the clay figurines found in the graves, men appear to have gone unclothed apart from penis sheaths and sandals, though they wore plumes in their hair, and both sexes went in for a variety of ornaments, most of them elaborations of ones used by the Badarians, such as ivory combs carved with animal figures, glazed beads and a variety of bracelets. Stone palettes show that making up was still popular and indeed their more elaborate character—they might be shaped to animal profiles—suggests an even greater accent on cosmetics. In addition to personal ornaments the dead were accompanied by food and figurines, which might be carved from ivory, as well as being modelled more roughly in clay, in graves that were still simple holes in the ground.

Late Predynastic

The Late Predynastic culture, represented by Nakada II, extended further north into the northern part of Middle or the southern part of Lower Egypt and indeed takes its name from Gerza near the entrance to the Fayum depression. In the extreme south, however, it never displaced the Amratian in Nubia, nor at the opposite extreme did it penetrate northern Lower Egypt with the Delta which was occupied by a quite different culture, represented by the settlement of Maadi near Cairo and by the cemetery of Heliopolis on the margin of the Delta. The Gerzean culture probably arose in Middle Egypt on an Amratian basis enriched by the permeation of cultural elements of Asiatic origin. Thus, whereas Black-topped pottery continued to be made for a while, White Cross-lined ware gave place to Decorated ware, painted in Asiatic fashion with dark red paint on a pale buff ground, to represent the natural markings of the stone vessels on which the forms were based. Stone vessels themselves continued to be made and the use of hard porphyry marks a further advance in an exacting craft.

A highly significant innovation was the introduction of metallurgy, which had appeared in western Asia a thousand years or so previously: in addition to the small objects which the Badarians and their immediate successors had made from native copper, the Gerzeans were now able to cast flat axes, ribbed daggers and flat knives. Swallow-tailed blades and curved knives continued to be thinned by polishing and finished off by controlled pressure-flaking, which on the latter might take the form of oblique, parallel fluting of extreme regularity. On the other hand new features to appear at this time, almost certainly from Asia, included the widespread use of blades struck from carefully prepared prismatic cores, and the introduction of chisel-ended or transverse arrowheads and pear-shaped stone mace-heads. In place of glazed stone, faience began to be manufactured, a complex substance consisting of an artificial core of finely powdered quartz grains cemented by fusion and coated with a glass glaze. Important raw materials were obtained from a distance: copper came from the eastern desert or from Sinai, but lead and silver were imported from Asia, and lapis lazuli from an ultimate source in northern Afghanistan, presumably by way of Mesopotamia. In this latter connection it is significant that a local copy of a Mesopotamian cylinder seal of Protoliterate type was found in one of the Gerzean graves at Nakada. Boats made of bundles of reeds, but of substantial size and provided with cabins, served for the transport of materials like mined flint or stone vessels on the Nile. These native boats were propelled by oars, but foreign-looking ones with upturned prow and stern painted on Gerzean pots were fitted with a sail. For overland portages asses were used, and it should be noted that wheeled vehicles, though long known in Mesopotamia, were not introduced in Egypt until the New Kingdom, which began *c.* 1570 B.C.

Gerzean society was firmly based on farming, and hunting had markedly declined as an economic activity. The villagers lived in more substantial houses, rectangular in plan and fitted with a wood-framed doorway in the side. Graves were no longer orientated regularly and it is noteworthy that they began to show a greater range of wealth in terms of burial offerings, some being provided with ledges, others with compartments separated off by wattle partitions, to contain extra offerings; the most one can say is that during Gerzean times there were signs of a growth in wealth accompanied by a more integrated social structure.

Unification

The ancient Egyptians attributed the unification of their country to a single individual, Menes, whom they supposed to have welded the twenty-two nomes of Upper and the twenty nomes of Lower Egypt into a single realm and to have initiated in his own person the First Dynasty of pharaohs. In reality the process must almost certainly have been a gradual one, lasting for at least two or three generations. The unification is unlikely, for one thing, to have been accomplished without a good deal of fighting, and we have evidence for this on a number of well-known archaeological objects. For instance scenes of royal conquest are carved in low relief on either face of a great stone palette some two feet in length from the old royal capital of Hierakonpolis in Upper Egypt: one (Pl. IV) depicts king Nar-mer, the crown of Upper Egypt on his head, despatching an enemy with a stone-headed mace and surrounded with captives and enemy dead; and the other shows the same ruler, this time with the crown of Lower Egypt, confronting four chiefs of nomes and surmounting a heap of decapitated enemies. It is interesting to note that two animals are depicted on this latter face with their necks intertwined, a convention also found on a dagger handle from Gebel et Tarif, but only at home in Mesopotamia. Another knife handle, this time of ivory from Gebel el Arak, has been carved to show on one face combats between men and boats with standards and upturned ends and on the other a man dompting two lions. This last is especially interesting because the man is wearing a hat and skirt of Sumerian type and because the whole scene recalls the Sumerian epic of Gilgamesh.

The occurrence of elements of Mesopotamian origin among the representations on these key objects raises the question how far the unification of Egypt was brought about by foreign influence or even by alien intruders. There can be no doubt of the existence precisely at the period of transition from the Predynastic to the Protodynastic or Archaic period of Egyptian history of innovations that stemmed from Mesopotamian sources of Protoliterate (Jamdat Nasr) age. In addition to the cylinder seals and the art motives already mentioned, one could cite brick architecture, which after a long history in Mesopotamia appeared suddenly in Egypt during the First Dynasty in the construction of tombs and which exhibited a series of detailed agreements, such as the size of bricks, the use of three rows of stretchers alternating with one of headers and the decorative use of buttresses and recesses. Another innovation to appear about the same time was writing, with ideograms, phonetic signs and determinatives, even though at first mainly as an element in monumental art rather than for the practical purposes for which it had been devised in Mesopotamia.

Dynastic Egypt

Yet it has to be emphasized that, important though Asiatic impulses undoubtedly were at this decisive juncture, the civilization that emerged in the Dynastic period was essentially Egyptian, the culmination of a thousand years or so of prehistory in the Nile Valley, distinct from and in some respects in marked contrast to that of Mesopotamia. The continuity of Egyptian civilization from its prehistoric beginnings down to the Hellenistic Age and even to the spread of Islam owes much to geography. Whereas the inhabitants of Sumer had to contend with rich and warlike mountain dwellers both in the east and north, as well as with occasional incursions from the western desert, the ancient Egyptians were comparatively insulated in the Nile Valley. They were not so remote as to be cut off from the stimulus of Asiatic civilization, deriving from that quarter first the arts of agriculture and then metallurgy and the techniques of incipient civilization, but they were far enough off to escape invasion, save at periods of exceptional weakness; and even when this did occur their civilization was too deeply rooted to be much affected by temporary political domination. Meanwhile the economic wealth conferred by the Nile floods and the cultural advantages derived from proximity to Asia ensured that the Egyptians were at all times so superior that they had nothing to fear from their immediate neighbours in the Libyan and Eastern Deserts and in tropical Nubia.

The main political danger was rivalry between Upper and Lower Egypt arising from the narrowness and great length of the alluvial zone of the Nile. It was because of this that the conquerors from the south found it worth while to set up an important centre at Memphis to match their old capital at Heirakonpolis and that down to the end of the New Kingdom the Pharaohs wore the two crowns. The river Nile provided a physical means for uniting the country, but it was the supremacy of the Pharaoh that guaranteed that unity. As a divine ruler he symbolized the whole community and it was his unchallenged sovereignty that engendered confidence and stability. The whole administration was carried on by authority delegated from the Pharaoh, whether through governors of nomes or through officials of the central government, one of whose main concerns was to channel a sizable proportion of the social surplus into the hands of the ruler. The importance of leading officials even during the Archaic phase of the Dynastic period is witnessed by the scale and richness of their tombs recently explored at Sakkara. On the other hand the supremacy of the Pharaoh is well displayed on one of the great ceremonial stone maces from Heirakonpolis, showing Nar-mer raised up nine steps, on his throne, confronted by captives and attended by a priest, a sandal-bearer and fan-bearers. Another shows the 'Scorpion' ruler presiding at the opening of a canal, a symbolic act emphasizing how the people of Egypt depended for their very sustenance on the mediation of the Pharaoh. From the beginning crops must have benefited from the natural irrigation brought about by the Nile flood, but for any great extension of the fertile zone it was necessary to cut channels and lift the Nile water into them by some such device as the *schaduf*. The increase in population that seems from all appearances to have marked the Predynastic period, suggests that some such works must have been initiated before the end of the prehistoric period. On the other hand the institution of a highly centralized government, while in itself expensive to maintain, made it possible to undertake public works on a scale not hitherto possible.

In addition to centralizing sovereignty and administration, the Pharaohs were careful to promote an official religion. This was centred on the solar cult whose priests evolved a cosmogony, accounting for the genesis of nine main deities, at their head-quarters in Heliopolis (the ancient Egyptian On), a little north of Memphis. Of the progeny of Ra-Atum, the sun-god, the most influential was Osiris, lord of the regions of the dead, whose cult was a direct counterpart. Preoccupation with death, or rather with the continuance of life after physical death, played an immensely important part in the life of ancient Egypt. The basic belief was that the spirit could survive only if the body was adequately preserved and provided with what was needed for its well-being in the after life. As the Egyptians grew richer and their social structure became more elaborate the tombs of the more important members of the community took on a monumental form and were furnished richly to accord with the position in life of the dead. By the First Dynasty substantial structures of sun-baked bricks, known as Mastabas, began to be erected over the graves of promi-nent people, and by the Third Dynasty stone was employed for royal tombs. The first or Stepped Pyramid, erected by Zoser at this time, was built over a Mastaba, already twice enlarged, the burial being made amid a maze of passages and rooms at the foot of a deep shaft beneath. The Old Kingdom was symbolized above all by the regular pyramids, which began to be made in the Fourth Dynasty and reached an early climax in the Great Pyramid built for Cheops and his queen. The dimensions of this structure—approximately 756 feet square at the base, which covered over 13 acres, and rising, when complete, to a height of 481 feet—are impressive in themselves, but the great cause for wonder is the sheer labour involved in the preparation and transport of the stone. Approximately 2,300,000 blocks, weighing on the average some 2½ tons, were used and the mere transport of these by man-power would have involved the labour of perhaps 100,000 levies for a three months' spell in each of twenty years, the time it took to complete the work, according to the story recorded by Hero-dotus; and in addition to this a permanent force of masons and labourers would have been needed on the site, perhaps as many as 4000 in all. When it is recalled that upwards of twenty pyramids, none so large, but all substantial, were erected during the Old Kingdom alone, the overwhelming force of the idea behind them, the conservation of the bodies of the Pharaoh and his consort and their provision for life after physical death, and the almost incredible concentration of the forces of an essentially poor society on the needs of one man will be even more apparent.

By contrast, no trace of the houses or even of the palaces of these divine rulers survives. For the purposes of transient life even the greatest were content to live in flimsy structures, while lavishing their power and substance on the construction and provisioning of their own tombs. In this respect the difference between Egypt and Sumer is marked, even when we remember the riches of the Royal Tombs of Ur. Although in abstract terms civilization had developed by way of the same broad stages of development, the actual expression or form of the two civilizations was markedly distinct. Nourished by the Nile and sheltered by protective deserts and their own superior technology, the ancient Egyptians were able to maintain their way of life with remarkably little change over something like three thousand years of recorded history. The breakdown of central authority that marked the end of the Old Kingdom would in an Asiatic state almost certainly have led to alien domination, but in Egypt it was the local nomarchs who profited and when the royal power was re-established with the Middle Kingdom (c. 2132–1777 B.C.) the construction of pyramids was begun again as though no interruption had been. During the second intermediate period, it is true, Egypt fell under the yoke of foreign rulers, the Hyksos or Shepherd kings, but it is significant that their eviction (1573/0 B.C.) inaugurated, in the New Kingdom, the greatest phase in the history of the land, during which Egyptian armies warred against the leading powers of western Asia and campaigned as far east as the Euphrates. Even during the period of decline that followed the close of the Twentieth Dynasty (*c.* 1090 B.C.) and witnessed conquests by Assyrians, Persians and Greeks the fundamentals of Egyptian civilization survived: indeed, under the earlier Ptolemies, whose rule began with the death of Alexander in 323 B.C., the Egyptian state experienced something of an imperial revival; and independence was only ended with its conversion into a province of the Roman Empire on the death of Cleopatra in 30 B.C.

THE LATER PREHISTORY OF AFRICA

Ancient Egypt owed its history to the twin facts of being near enough to share in the basic advances made in the creative zone of south-west Asia, while at the same time being remote and self-sufficient enough to mature and conserve its own distinctive civilization over what in terms of other and later traditions must be accounted an immensely long period. For the rest of Africa the consequences were less happy. The ancient Egyptians, secure in their homeland, made no conscious effort to extend their civilization or even their sphere of influence over other peoples: they defended their frontiers and during the New Kingdom extended these far into south-west Asia; but in their African homeland they contented themselves with holding their neighbours at arm's length. In effect therefore Ancient Egypt served as a buffer rather than as a connecting link between the progressive territories of western Asia and a continent that had already during Late Pleistocene times slipped far behind in the race of progress.

This is not to say that the ancient Egyptians refrained from all contact with other African peoples: apart from anything else they were constrained from time to time to campaign in Nubia, send trading expeditions to the land of Punt or employ Libyan mercenaries, each of which might in one way or another result in a limited degree of cultural exchange. Whatever the precise mechanism, certain elements of higher culture managed, however fitfully and belatedly, to spread over more or less extensive tracts of Africa, even if outside a limited zone of the Nile Valley Africa remained in the Stone Age until the diffusion of iron-working. Such feeble impulses as can be discerned from societies depending to a significant degree on farming spread on the one hand westward to North Africa and on the other southward by way of the Sudan to East, central and West Africa.

The Neolithic of Capsian tradition in North Africa

Neolithic impulses passed westward along the northern fringes of the Sahara to enrich the lives of the Capsian hunter-fishers of the Maghreb. Examination of caves and open-air middens has shown that, though they continued to rely to a large extent on hunting and on the collection of molluscs, these people had begun to keep domestic animals as an additional source of food. They continued to make lunate and trapeziform microliths for arming their arrows, but in addition they used chisel-ended arrowheads. Other acquisitions from the east included polished stone axes and coil-built pottery, mainly in the form of round- or conical-based bowls with perforated lugs and impressed decoration. Blades of reaping-knives or sickles, on the other hand, were notably absent and there is no evidence that agriculture was practised. Confirmation that they lived by hunting and pastoral activities is provided by the rock-engravings, which in addition to elephants, rhinoceroses, buffaloes, giraffe and a number of carnivores, depict domesticated sheep. In style and content and technique—they were either pecked or deeply incised and polished—these early naturalistic engravings of the Maghreb compare closely with those of Upper Egypt with which they are linked geographically across Libya. Similar engravings, together with paintings, are widely distributed over the Sahara. The tradition of engraving and painting rocks certainly endured into the New Kingdom, because horse-drawn chariots occur as far west as the western Sahara; indeed, representations of domesticated camels shows that it must have been continued into the Christian era. The art of potting seems to have spread by the fourth millennium B.C. to communities of hunter-fishers in the Khartoum area, whose barbed bone spear and harpoon-heads recall those of the Fayum and to less degree those of the French Sudan. They also made lunate armatures for arrows of a type stemming ultimately from Epi-Levalloisian sources (p. 46). The first signs of domestication in the form of small straight-horned goats appeared at the site of Shaheinab (3493 ± 380 B.C.) on the left bank of the Nile some thirty miles north of Omdurman, together with pottery and hollow-ground adzes like those from the Fayum, in a context best described as Sub-Neolithic: lunate microliths, bone harpoon heads and barbless hooks testify to the importance of catching activities; and it is important to stress both the absence of any trace of agriculture and the fact that only 2 per cent of the animal bones were those of domesticated species.

Pastoralism in East Africa

It was presumably from the upper reaches of the Nile that the practice of breeding and maintaining herds of sheep or goats as an adjunct to wild sources of food spread south to Kenya. Here it occurred already at Hyrax Hill, the first of a series of cultures marked in the archaeological record by stone bowls and pestles used presumably for crushing wild plant foods, by coil-built pottery decorated in a variety of styles including some suggesting basketry prototypes, and by lithic industries with lunate microliths like those widespread in the Late Stone Age of Africa. The precise age in terms of years of the sequence formed by the Hyrax Hill, Gumban A, Gumban B and Njoro River cultures cannot yet be told, but it is suggestive that a faience bead of a kind that spread most widely during the period 1500–1300 B.C. has been found with a burial at Nakuru assigned to Gumban B. There is no certain evidence that pastoral activities spread further south until much later, but isolated 'neolithic' traits, like polished stone axes and pottery, were adopted by Nachikufu and Wilton groups in the Rhodesias and even as far south as the Union of South Africa without disturbing their hunter-fisher mode of subsistence. No doubt it is to this southward drift of culture that we may attribute the earlier styles of naturalistic rock art characteristic of much of East and South Africa.

Polished stone-axe cultures of the equatorial forests

Although polished stone axes have been found sporadically in Kenya and occur with implements of Wilton type in the Rhodesias and even in South Africa, it is only in the northern part of the forest zone from French Guinea to the northern and eastern parts of the Congo that they are present in really large numbers. The fact that the densest concentration of these tools falls in the forest zone, where many have been encountered in modern clearings, as well as on tracks and in a variety of diggings, argues that they were discarded in the process of temporary clearance of the ground for raising crops, in the manner practised in the same region down to modern times. What crops were grown is still unknown, but modern analogy might suggest yams, more than one species of which is native to the region. Cultivation today is simply effected by removing the eyes from tubers and planting them in plots temporarily cleared from the forest to admit light: as the yield declines after a year or two the plots are abandoned and new ones cleared; this process, practised in the past, would naturally have led to a wide distribution of discarded axeheads. The excavation of rock-shelters in French Guinea and Ghana has shown that the people who first adopted polished stone axes also made pottery with impressed decoration and possessed a lithic industry of Late Stone Age type with lunate microliths, backed blades and some chisel-ended arrowheads. The upper levels at the Bosumpra cave at Abetifi, Ghana, testify that in due course these same people adopted iron-working and made more advanced pottery decorated with grooves. Recent discoveries in alluvial tin-workings at Nok and other localities in Nigeria have brought to light a series of remarkable terracottas of Negroid type (Pl. V), which appear to belong precisely to the time when iron tools were beginning to supplement ones of polished stone.

The diffusion of iron-working

The first community in Africa to make general use of iron tools seems to have been at Carthage, founded near the site of modern Tunis by Phoenicians from Tyre at a date set traditionally at 814/13 B.C. From Carthage the new technology spread to the borders of Cyrenaica by the end of the sixth century B.C. The ancient Egyptians made no general move to adopt iron until subjected to intensive Greek influence under the Saite or Twenty-sixth Dynasty around the middle of the sixth century B.C., but it was ultimately from Egypt that iron metallurgy spread far and wide over central and southern Africa. The immediate source of diffusion was probably Meroe, situated on an island at the confluence of the Nile and the Atbara, and which served as capital of the kingdom of Nubia or Ethiopia from the fifth century B.C. to the third century A.D. From this centre iron-working seems to have spread westward along the steppe corridor between the Sahara and the forest belt, where, as at Abetifi, it was adopted by the local Late Stone Age people, and southward by way of East and central Africa.

The southward spread of iron-working came with immigrants, many of whom were probably Bantu-speaking. Everywhere they brought with them a high standard of potting and also the practice of agriculture, generally associated with stock-raising. Various millets were cultivated, together with ground nuts and peas, all of them derived from wild species indigenous to Africa and each, together with maize introduced by the Portuguese, still cultivated by Africans to-day. Although compelled through ignorance or lack of manure to shift their cultivation at frequent intervals, the prehistoric farmers found it worthwhile to terrace valley slopes for their crops. Already before the end of the first millennium A.D. the Arabs, who controlled trade in the Indian Ocean until they were displaced in the sixteenth century by the Portuguese, had established trading-posts on the east coast of central Africa. From these they were able to draw precious substances like ivory, gold and presumably copper in exchange for such things as cloth and beads of Indian manufacture. One result of this trade and of the contacts which it involved was the adoption among the Bantu peoples of building in dry-stone technique. The commonest structures of which the ruins confront us today were clusters of round huts in irregular enclosures. One of the most impressive of these kraals at Zimbabwe, Southern Rhodesia, was built on such a scale as to attract the misleading designation of 'temple'. Other outstanding structures are best interpreted as forts, and many of these were doubtless erected against the Portuguese colonists.

European exploration and colonization

South of the Nile Valley and of the strip of territory north of the Sahara, which were successively absorbed into the Roman Empire and, in the mid-seventh century, overrun by the Moslem religion and the Arabic language, the greater part of the continent of Africa was brought within the range of civilization through maritime exploration from without. Between them the mountainous country of Abyssinia and the Sahara imposed formidable barriers to the expansion of civilization overland, even if we must not overlook the influence of camel-riding Moslems in the formation of the ancient kingdoms of the western Sudan. On the east it was Arab traders who controlled the Indian Ocean and through their trading stations on the coast created a market and so stimulated mining activities in the interior. On the west it was not until the middle of the fifteenth century that the Portuguese under the lead of Henry the Navigator emulated the voyage undertaken around 450 B.C. by Hanno the Carthaginian and reached the Senegal; the first European settlement was effected in Guinea in 1481; in 1488 Batholomew Diaz rounded the Cape of Good Hope and ten years later Vasco da Gama crossed the Indian Ocean to

Calcutta. Within the next few years the Portuguese wrested control of the Indian Ocean from the Arabs and established their influence on the east as well as on the west coast of Africa. When in due course the Dutch gained maritime supremacy they founded a station at the Cape and so inaugurated the European settlement of South Africa.

Down to the beginning of the nineteenth century Europeans occupied only comparatively small areas of what is now the Cape province. The prehistory of large parts of central and East Africa were first brought to an end during the latter part of the century, through the extension of exploration, missionary endeavour, trade, settlement and government administration. It is well to remember that at a time when North Americans and Europeans were already riding in railway trains and reading newspapers the Bushmen of South Africa were still practising a culture in many respects comparable with those existing during Neothermal times in the northern temperate zone. Even today the Bushmen of the Kalahari and the pygmies of the equatorial forests maintain a basically 'Mesolithic' mode of life, modified by barter with their agricultural neighbours. Of even greater relevance to our times is the circumstance that many of the Africans working in mines operated by Europeans return to families whose general way of life recalls that prevailing in Britain during the earlier part of the pre-Roman Iron Age.

CHAPTER 6

THE FOUNDATIONS OF EUROPEAN CIVILIZATION: 'NEOLITHIC' PEASANTS AND ARCTIC HUNTER-FISHERS

The status of European 'Neolithic' cultures

The beginnings of settled life in Europe and the possibility of a distinct European civilization depended in the first instance on the spread of farming from the focal territories in which cultivated forms were first elicited and on the adoption in due course of this new and alien way of life by indigenous hunter-fishers. The only part of Europe in which possible prototypes of cultivated cereals have been found in a wild state extends from Greece to Yugoslavia and even here it is only with wild forms of einkorn and millet that we have to do: over the continent as a whole, up to the northern margin of the temperate zone that formed the boundary of cereal cultivation during early times, all cultivated cereals had to be introduced into environments differing to some extent from those in which they were originally domesticated.

Even in those parts of Europe first colonized by farmers, settled life began much later than in Palestine, Cilicia, Syria and northern Mesopotamia; though to judge from radio-carbon dates no more recently than in the Nile Valley. Although the earliest peasant communities in Europe were 'Neolithic' in the sense that they were ignorant of metallurgy and that their technology was governed by the possibilities inherent in the utilization of flint and stone tools, they were contemporary with societies in western Asia conversant from the latter part of the fifth millennium B.C. with the casting of copper and from the middle of the fourth with that of bronze. Even more to the point, early in the third millennium the Minoan civilization had already begun to develop in Crete along independent lines, though under the influence of those of Asia Minor, Syria and Egypt; and active centres of culture were established in the Cycladic islands and on the mainland of Greece. Already during the latter half of the third millennium B.C. both central Europe and the Mediterranean were permeated by a knowledge of copper metallurgy, and even in western and northern Europe, where Neolithic communities were unable to afford metal tools, flint and stone axes might be influenced by metal prototypes. Another striking illustration of the status of these northern 'Neolithic' peoples is that they adopted the rite of collective burial from the technologically more advanced Aegean world and felt impelled, despite their comparative poverty, to share the funerary customs of peoples much richer than themselves and to erect megalithic chamber tombs.

The basic reason why parts of south-west Asia were so far in advance of Europe in adopting farming is the differing conditions to which the rather drastic transition from Late Pleistocene to Neothermal times gave rise in the two areas: whereas in the former the desiccation of hitherto rich hunting grounds presented a challenge to people now fitted biologically and culturally to respond by a fundamental change of outlook towards their environment, in the latter a gradual increase of temperature, while bringing ecological changes in its train, offered no comparable challenge to prehistoric man. Thus an environmental change which precipitated the so-called Neolithic Revolution in one, encouraged in the other the persistence under progressively more genial conditions of old ways of life stemming from the Old Stone Age and expressed in the Mesolithic cultures described in a previous chapter (see pp. 67f.).

The new farming economy, giving a hitherto unknown degree of control over the supply of food, was inherently expansive, but

it was not until the return of wetter conditions in the neighbourhood of the focal region during Altithermal times that the Neolithic
way of life was able to spread to North Africa, south-eastern
Europe and Inner Asia. As a field for colonization by farmers,
Europe fell into three major ecological zones. The first was a
Mediterranean zone which formed an extension, progressively
modified as one moves west, of that in which the basic discoveries
were made and into which in consequence they were able to
penetrate without the need for major changes. The second was
a temperate zone, differing more or less markedly in climate,
vegetation and soils and into which the new economy was only
able to penetrate selectively and sometimes with difficulty. The
third was a circumpolar zone into which only certain elements of
Neolithic culture were able to filter and over which the old hunting
and fishing economy continued to reign supreme.

Since men learned to farm in parts of western Asia long before
they began to make pottery vessels, the question arises to what
extent agriculture was introduced into Europe in advance of
pottery-making. The only certain evidence for this comes from
Thessaly, where traces of huts and fire-places were found at the
base of mounds at Argissa near Larissa and at Sesklo, stratified
below the earliest pottery-levels, but belonging to farmers who
grew cereals and pulse, kept sheep or goats and presumably made
do with baskets or other non-ceramic containers. These pre-
pottery farmers had a flint industry producing blades and trapeze-
shaped points, together with stone palettes and simple bodkins and
skin-working tools of bone. Similar blade and trapeze industries
from the Mediterranean area may indicate a wider extension of a
pre-pottery Neolithic and it is significant that remains of sheep
or goats have been found with industries of similar type in France
known as Tardenoisian: decisive evidence might well be obtained
by an exhaustive study of the organic refuse from a site like
Châteauneuf-les-Martigues, near Marseilles, where a blade and
trapeze industry underlay early Neolithic impressed pottery.

Another reason for thinking that agriculture may have been introduced to Europe by people ignorant of pottery is that few of the earliest pottery vessels from most of Europe can plausibly be traced to specific Asiatic sources.

The Balkans, central and eastern Europe

Nevertheless, the first farmers certainly verifiable over any extensive tract of Europe made hand-built pottery, comprising bowls and flasks with round bases, simple rims and handles in the form of lugs perforated so that the pots could be carried or

TABLE F. *Sequence of early peasant cultures in parts of Europe down to* c. 1200 B.C.

South Britain	Denmark	Danube	Greece	South-east Balkans	Ukraine
		VI			Black burnished
Bronze Age (Wessex)	Bronze Age	V	Late Helladic (Mycenaean)	Karanovo	
Secondary Neolithic	Late Neolithic	IV	Middle Helladic (Minyan)		
	Middle Neolithic	III			Tripolje
Primary Neolithic	Early Neolithic	II	Early Helladic	Gumelniţa	
			Late Neolithic (Dimini)		Izvoare
		I (Spiral-meander ware)		Boian	
			Middle Neolithic (Sesklo)		
			Early Neolithic (Impressed; Otzaki)	Starčevo	
			Proto-Neolithic		

suspended. The most important region settled during this early phase was the Balkan peninsula, which formed as it were a funnel, the narrow end open to western Asia and the broad one to the expanses of central and eastern Europe. The earliest pottery-using farmers to penetrate the Balkans were shifting agriculturists who cultivated temporary clearings in the forest and moved on after cropping the initial fertility of the virgin land. The Starčevo people, named after the site on the north bank of the Danube near Belgrade, seem to have spread north from the Aegean coast mainly by the Vardar–Morava route into what is now eastern Yugoslavia and on into the Middle Danube valley. Western Bulgaria may have been colonized partly by way of the Struma Valley, in part from the Morava Valley by way of the Nišava, and in part by following the Danube downstream. Further north they pressed into Hungary where they concentrated on the Tisa and Körös rivers. It may prove significant that the Starčevo people cultivated einkorn and millet, the wild prototypes of which are known from the south Balkans; and it is noteworthy that they had reaping-knives with flint insets and querns like those from western Asia; in addition they kept livestock and did some hunting. Some of their pottery vessels were more specialized in form, including bowls with ring feet and, more particularly in the Körös Valley, lop-sided flasks with perforated lugs, probably designed for slinging on the back. Impressed decoration was common, though cardium shells were not used for this purpose as they were in parts of the Mediterranean area, and other favoured varieties included roughening of the surface and plastic relief, including representations of animals and men; and footed bowls in fine ware might be decorated by painting. The widespread use of the Aegean mussel *Spondylus gaederopus* as a material for beads and bracelets shows that contact was maintained with the south. Clay seals, apparently barbaric versions of stone stamp seals of ultimately Asiatic origin, marble vessels, bone and clay idols and four-footed pottery stands that may have served some cult purpose are among enrichments which may well have been acquired from the more settled villagers whose settlement mounds had begun to accumulate in Greece and the south Balkans.

Immediately north of the Starčevo province, over a territory which extended from south of Lake Balaton to near the estuary of the Oder—a distance of nearly six hundred miles—and laterally from the Rhine and the Maas to the Vistula and the Upper Dniester—a span of a thousand miles—the earliest peasants made pottery decorated with spiral-meander patterns and exhibited a cultural uniformity so great as only to be explained if we suppose that the whole area was colonized comparatively rapidly. From the Middle Danube region, comprising much of central Hungary, Lower Austria and Bohemia, the pioneer farmers pushed along the great rivers, east to the Vistula and the Upper Dniester; north down the Vistula, Oder and Elbe; and west by way both of the Upper Danube and overland across Saxony and Hesse to the Rhineland and the Maas. The rapidity of their spread—according to radio-carbon dating they had reached South Germany and Dutch Limburg before the end of the fifth millennium B.C.—was due in part to their extensive system of agriculture, in part to the discontinuous distribution of the fertile and easily worked loess on which they settled, and in part to the lack of opposition. Emmer and barley were grown, as well as einkorn, peas, beans and flax, and the common farmyard animals were kept. Material equipment remained very simple during this first phase in the settlement of the Danubian zone. There is no evidence either for weaving or for metallurgy. The pottery was made from carefully prepared clay that required neither slip nor burnish, and took the form of the standard early Neolithic shapes, round-based bowls and flasks, the latter sometimes flattened on one face, having plain rims and no handles other than lugs. Plastic ornament, like that on Starčevo ware, was used, especially in the Middle Danube area, but the most characteristic form of ornament consisted of bands defined by two or three more or less parallel incised lines and conforming to spirals or meanders; in addition designs were sometimes painted on the surface after firing. Where flint was readily available it was flaked into the form of blades which might be inserted into slots to provide cutting-edges for reaping-knives, or worked into end-scrapers and trapeziform arrowheads. The commonest stone tool, a polished stone adze-blade of D-section with a slightly hollow-ground working edge, was probably used mainly for dressing the timbers needed for building. The peasants lived in large houses, generally of rectangular plan, but in parts of Germany and in Poland often wedge-shaped with one end markedly broader than the other. They were commonly of twenty or thirty and might be up to fifty metres in length and it is thought that they must have provided space for storage and possibly for sheltering livestock as well as for the peasant family. The Danubian I peasants seem to have lived in fair-sized villages, which at first they found no need to defend by more than a palisade; but the nature of their economy caused them to shift their cultivations at frequent intervals, though commonly re-building on the same site. Like the Starčevo people they continued to import *Spondylus* shells from the far distant Aegean and to deposit with the dead, interred in cemeteries of single graves, ornaments that more vividly than anything else recalled their southern origin.

Permanent settlement that gave rise to tells on the Asiatic model was confined to the Balkans. In Greece settlement mounds began to accumulate immediately over the encampments of pre-pottery peasants and it is significant that two layers, the lower of which yielded a primitive painted ware, had been formed at Otzaki before the appearance of cardial-impressed and Starčevo pottery. After the Starčevo culture had passed north, Thessaly was the scene of the flowering of a culture named after the site of Sesklo, a culture which, though having Syrian analogies, is distinctively Thessalian and may have developed there from an earlier Neolithic spread. The Sesklo potters made a fine burnished ware which they baked to reddish colour in kilns. Many of the finer pots, which included flat-bottomed dishes with flaring sides, footed bowls, and mugs with well-made handles, were painted by hand before firing with red paint on a white slip or alternatively with white on a red ground. The designs were geometrical in character: these included a variety of multiple linear chevrons; and in the 'block-painted' ware rectangles, lozenges and triangles, probably inspired by the ornament on birch-bark vessels. In addition to the use of the kiln for firing painted pots, mud-bricks, stone button seals and the use of the sling all point to Asia as an ultimate source; but shoe-last adzes, the use of *Spondylus* shell for bracelets and portable clay altars were among features widely spread in the Balkans. Late Neolithic layers containing a local ware named after the site of Dimini commonly overlie Sesklo ones in the Thessalian mounds. The distinctive pottery is more elementary in form, bases being flat and lugs replacing the handles, but designs painted on the surface now included spirals and meanders.

Outside Greece the kind of settlement that gave rise to tells did not begin until the basis of a farming economy had been laid by pioneers who moved their corn-plots and their livestock at frequent intervals and occupied no more than temporary villages. Thus the mound at Vinča near Belgrade, type site of a culture that extended over much of Yugoslavia and parts of western Roumania and Bulgaria, overlay traces of Starčevo people. Again, the Gumelniţa mound-culture of central and eastern Bulgaria replaced a pioneer peasant culture that took its name from the Boian lake near the head of the Dobrudža.

The Boian pioneers cultivated einkorn and millet and occupied rectangular houses with matting on the floor. For felling and working timber they used a variety of stone tools, including polished adze-blades of bevelled and shoe-last form. Their pottery, which included bowls with ringed-feet, biconical jars and large pear-shaped storage jars, was decorated by several different methods, but most commonly by incising or excising the surface to form in the first case either spiral or other curvilinear patterns and in the second rectilinear ones, each of which were emphasized by encrusting with red or white paint. The Boians were of more than local interest because they initiated the spread of peasant economy over much of Roumania and the Ukraine as far east as the river Dnieper. The first stage in their expansion, well exemplified at the site of Izvoare in Moldavia, penetrated the Alt valley on the west of the Carpathians and on the east extended as far as the Bug; it was only during the developed or classical phase of the culture, commonly named after Cucuteni on the Pruth or Tripolje near Kiev, that the full extent was attained. The excised technique continued to be fashionable during the Izvoare stage, but this was replaced by painting before firing, a technique already practised by the Starčevo peasants, or by U-sectioned grooves designed to hold encrustation. The spiral, a motive already exploited by the Starčevo and Danubian peasants and one that may well have been suggested originally by making coiled basketry, continued to play a leading part in decorating pottery. As regards the forms of pots, the simple rims, flat bases and absence of handles other than lugs are all persistent features. Other Balkan elements include polished stone adzes, a lithic industry based on blades, and clay stamps and female figurines made from baked clay. Like the Danubians, whom they dispossessed on the Upper Dniester, the Tripolje peasants shifted their settlements at frequent intervals as they took into cultivation fresh areas of the fertile black earth that directly overlay the loess. Likewise they lived in substantial rectangular houses, up to 30 metres in length, but they differed at least in the Ukraine in arranging these in circles or even in concentric rings, as at Kolomiishchina or Vladimirovka. It seems likely that this circular arrangement may have been designed for security against their warlike pastoral neighbours of the steppe who decorated their pots with cord imprints.

In the Middle Danube area there is evidence for the penetration, possibly as early as the beginning of the third millennium B.C., of renewed impulses from the south-east. The pottery ascribed to the Danubian II stage of settlement in this cortical area is more sophisticated in form than that of the Danubian I stage, having flat bases and including footed bowls. It was also much more diversified and one may distinguish even in Hungary between the monochrome ware of Lengyel and the encrusted ware, painted after firing, of the Theiss Valley. Apart from the painting of pottery, southern traits include female figurines and model houses of fired clay, clay stamps reminiscent of stone seals, cubical clay block vases recalling Early Minoan ones of stone, and spiral ornaments made of copper wire.

While these innovations were making themselves felt in the Middle Danube area and spreading thence over Czechoslovakia and into Germany, the heirs of the original colonists occupying the extensive outer tracts of the Danubian I territory were undergoing a certain degree of barbarization. In default of any more intensive occupation of the loess soil, such as might be implied by the growth of settlement mounds, the peasants were driven to spread on to poorer soils and develop hunting as an accessory source of food, both processes that brought them into contact with Mesolithic hunter-fishers. Among the leading features of this time was the disappearance of the spiral and meander from the decorative motives used by potters and the substitution of horizontal lines and chevrons—designs that reproduced the webbing in which round-based pots were commonly carried; and further the incised line was replaced or at least supplemented by impressions made by toothed stamps or combs, producing the so-called stroke-ornamented ware. Other more specialized wares included that named after the cemetery of Rössen near Merseberg in Saxo-Thuringia, which spread over much of the Middle and Upper Rhineland and beyond, and was decorated by broader furrowed lines apparently made by a jabbing motion and intended to secure white incrustation. Wild animal bones show that the Rössen people went in for hunting on a considerable scale and it is significant that the arrowheads belonging to the younger phases of the Danubian were of devolved Tardenoisian type, trapeziform and triangular and commonly with flat flaking. A final point to mention is that on the margin of their distribution in the west the Danubian peasants in their later phase began to come into contact with others of alien culture. No doubt it is this which explains why in its last period the great settlement at Köln-Lindenthal was defended and why in South Germany the Rössen people chose to occupy such a natural fortress as the Goldberg. What is certain is that Rössen pottery occurs on settlements of the earliest peasants of Switzerland, whose cultural affinities lie in the west.

The Mediterranean and western Europe

The earliest pottery from western Europe is that from the islands and shores of the Mediterranean, simple bowls and flasks with round bases and lugs, plain or decorated by impressions of cardium shells. Closely similar pottery has been recovered from western Asia, for example from the lowest levels in the tells at Mersin in Cilicia and Ras Shamrah (Ugarit) in Syria. The distribution of cardial impressed ware in the Mediterranean area strongly suggests that it was transmitted by sea: it is found on the islands of Leukas and Corfu; on the coast of Yugoslavia and the Adriatic coast of Italy, including the Tremiti islands; on Malta, Sicily, Elba and Sardinia; on the coast of Liguria; in the French provinces of Languedoc and Provence; and on the east and south-east coasts of Spain and the south coast of Portugal. The impressions, which were frequently made by toothed stamps and other objects as well as by cardium shells, were most commonly arranged as horizontal or vertical lines, zig-zags or hanging arcs. Most of the settlement material has come from caves or rock-shelters and represents what appear to have been temporary occupations. The lithic industries of these early farmers were based on the production of blades, from sections of which trapeze and transverse arrowheads were made; hunting evidently played some part in a mainly pastoral economy. Polished stone axes and adzes testify to the felling of trees and the working of wood. Among the simple objects made from bone the most noteworthy were spatulae used, in all probability, for eating cereal food. For personal ornamentation perforated animal teeth, shells and foot-bones of hare were used as beads, and bracelets were made from polished stone or shell.

Whether the predominantly plain, round-based wares associated with Neolithic farmers in France, parts of Iberia and beside the Swiss lakes stemmed from the same source as the impressed wares or whether they represent a distinct and to some extent parallel tradition remains uncertain. Although the pottery from the Camp de Chassey in the French department of Saône-et-Loire was frequently plain it was sometimes decorated by geometrical patterns incised before firing or scratched on afterwards, and the pots of the younger stage of the Swiss Cortaillod ware, named after the locality on Lake Neuchâtel, might be ornamented by patterns cut out of birch-bark and applied to the surface of the pot by means of resin. Plain western ware is found with flint blades, trapeziform arrowheads and polished stone axes and adzes on settlements like El Garcel in Almeria and with collective burials in southern Iberia. The Chassey culture spread extensively over France from the Mediterranean, by the valley of the Rhone and Saône to the Paris basin and west of the Massif Central to the Atlantic coast of Brittany; and it is significant that fired clay female figurines have been found as far north as Fort-Harrouard, Eure-et-Loire. The makers of the Cortaillod pottery, which has a counterpart to the south of the Alps in the Lagozza culture of North Italy, occupied rectangular wooden houses resembling those made by the Rössen and other Danubian II groups from whom they may well have derived them. The lakeside locations of their settlements favoured the survival of a much greater range of material equipment than is normally available from Neolithic sites and has shown that the Cortaillod people made an extensive use of wood and bark for containers and other things, as well as making baskets, nets and a great variety of linen textiles. Yet the Alpine countryside set limits to agriculture, and the proportion of wild animal bones shows that hunting contributed in a significant way to the supply of food; moreover, stag antler played a conspicuous role as a raw material for making a wide range of objects, such as mattock-heads, holders for adze- and axe-heads, harpoon-heads and personal ornaments.

The West Baltic area

Meanwhile a distinctive culture, characterized by beakers with flaring, funnel-shaped necks, was beginning to develop on the North European Plain beyond the frontiers of the Lengyel and Rössen groups of the Danubian II tradition. In spite of many differences of detail between its various sub-groups, the Northern culture was marked by features common to its whole extent from Mecklenburg to the Vistula and from central Prussia to Denmark and South Sweden. Its distinctive character rules out the possibility that its appearance can have been due solely to the expansion of any of the Neolithic cultures previously established in territories further south; and yet, at the same time, the appearance of basic Neolithic traits, notably stock-raising, cereal-growing and the making of pottery containers, can only be attributed to impulses from the south. On geographical grounds the most likely source is the Danubian province, and indeed pottery of Danubian II–III character has commonly been found in the same graves as Northern forms in Silesia and Poland. Quite plainly the northward spread of Neolithic civilization was accomplished by means of acculturation rather than of colonization. The North European Plain supported in the Maglemosian culture and its successors the most vigorous Mesolithic settlement in Europe. The hunter-fisher populations of the region were correspondingly selective in their borrowings: thus, the coast-dwelling Ertebölle people, while adopting the arts of domestication, continued to rely substantially on hunting, fishing and the gathering of shell-fish, and, in taking over the art of potting, applied to the manufacture of their larger, coarse vessels the technique of coiling used in basketry; similarly, the stone shoe-last adze failed to penetrate in face of flint forms evolved over millennia in a territory lavishly provided with the essential raw-material, though flint celts were now for the first time in this region finished by polishing. The vigour of the indigenous 'Mesolithic' heritage is shown in other ways, for example in the lavish use of amber, but the adoption of rectangular houses as far north as the Vrå culture of middle Sweden shows the force of the intrusive impulses. In burying their dead in single graves, the Funnel-neck Beaker people conformed to the general Danubian practice, but in constructing stone monuments they were making the most of their own habitat and giving expression to their own genius. Definition of individual graves by means of the glacial boulders so widely distributed on the North European Plain was practised by the Danubian groups north of the Sudeten mountains as well as by the Funnel-neck Beaker people, but the use of thin stone slabs or large blocks of megalithic proportions to form closed cists was peculiar to the northerners. Still more was this the case with the mounds erected over the graves and frequently themselves defined by boulders: in Denmark these mounds might be circular, but over the North European Plain in general they were built like the houses of the living on the elongated plan, which in the west was generally rectangular, but in the east, again corresponding with the local house-plan, was characteristically wedge-shaped.

The primary Neolithic culture of southern and more particularly of south-western Britain drew some elements from French sources, but it is becoming increasingly evident that much of its inspiration came from the North European Plain to the east, a conclusion which in view of the common Maglemosian heritage should hardly occasion surprise. The earthen long barrows, occasionally parallel-sided, but more often wedge-shaped in plan, have been notoriously difficult to parallel in France, but find analogues as far east as the Kujavian graves of Poland, even though, apart from the Medway group, their structural elements are of timber and turf rather than stone. The causewayed camps, for which again no adequate parallel has been adduced from France, have been wrongly compared with the fortified sites of Urmitz and Mayen in the Middle Rhineland; a more significant, if rather loose, analogy lies with enclosures formed by radial settings of houses noted at Kolomiishchina and other Tripolje sites in South Russia. Again, the flint-mines for which parallels admittedly exist in North France and the Low Countries, can be matched by the examples with vertical shafts and radiating galleries at Krzemionkach Opatowskich and other sites in Poland.

On its western margins the Northern culture came into contact with the Western province both in the Middle Rhenish and Alpine zones. From these contacts arose the Michelsburg and Pfyn cultures respectively, the former named after a hill-fort overlooking the Rhine plain a few miles north of Karlsruhe and the latter designated by the locality to which it is confined in the eastern part of Switzerland. The Michelsberg culture, typified by the tulip beaker and a series of ceramic forms, was centered on the Main, the Middle Rhine and the Neckar, whence it spread east into Bohemia, south into Alsace-Baden and north into the Koblenz area and Belgium.

Copper-working in central Europe

Meanwhile impulses emanating ultimately from the East Mediterranean had already begun to carry exotic burial rites, metallurgy and the use of metal tools over wide zones of Europe. Several central European groups of the Danubian III stage, notably the Bodrogkeresztur of north-east Hungary, the Jordansmühl of Bohemia and Silesia and the Baden of Austria and much of Czechoslovakia, fabricated copper artifacts, including perforated axe-adzes and a variety of ornaments. The sources of the copper ores used by these early smiths are still not fully known, but it is likely that the copper ores of the eastern Alps and of central Germany were already being worked, and certain that flat axes made from copper won in the latter region were being traded to the peasants of the Northern neolithic culture before this had emerged from its early phase. The replacement of the flint axe with pointed butt and lozenge section by one polished all over and having a thin butt and flattened sides, which took place towards the end of the Northern Early Neolithic, was almost certainly inspired by the flat copper axe that was too costly for general use. Before considering any further how the comparatively simple peasant societies of temperate Europe were affected by impulses from the East Mediterranean, it will be necessary to turn to the relatively advanced civilizations of Crete and the Greek mainland.

Minoan civilization

The island of Crete, legendary home of the Minotaur and hence of the Minoan culture, was originally colonized by immigrants from Asia Minor in a Neolithic stage of culture, but from an early period Egyptian influences made themselves felt in the central and southern regions. The Early Minoan culture grew up in eastern Crete under the impact of fresh immigration from Asia Minor, but it was on the Messara Plain in the area cross-fertilized by Egyptian contacts that the richer culture of Early Minoan II–III developed. During this time copper came into more prominent use for daggers and axes, and circular dry-stone structures up to 13 metres in diameter, having portals made from heavy stone lintels resting on monolithic jambs, were built as collective tombs to house successive generations of the dead. The Early Minoans stood at the same general level of culture as the Early Helladic people of the Greek mainland, who were likewise largely recruited from Asia Minor. On the other hand, like the Early Cycladic islanders, they were better placed to enrich themselves by maritime trade: indeed, their situation at the southern margin of the

Aegean world was even more favourable, since it encouraged contact with Egypt and the eastern coasts of the Mediterranean.

It was a combination of wealth gained by trade and of inspiration derived by contact with the civilized peoples to the south and east that made possible the decisive advance that led to the development in Crete of the first distinctively European civilization. The Middle Minoan period (c. 2000–1580 B.C.) was marked by many of the features associated with the rise of the earlier oriental civilizations: a finer sub-division of labour made possible advances in technology reflected in the manufacture of bronze and the adoption of the potter's wheel; population increased in density and concentrated in the larger units represented by towns with two-story buildings; authority was centralized in the hands of rulers who combined religious and political authority and whose palaces were also centres of economic importance; and centralized control was assisted by improved communications in the shape of wheeled transport and roads as well as by the development of writing, primarily for purposes of accountancy. The first approach to literacy took the form of hieroglyphs engraved on seals, but by Middle Minoan III times a true linear script—linear A—was being inscribed on unbaked clay tablets.

The zenith of Minoan civilization was reached during Late Minoan I–II times (c. 1580–1400 B.C.) between the rebuilding of the palace of Cnossos after its second wrecking by earthquake and its final destruction, presumably at the hands of the mainland power centred at Mycenae, that took over the hegemony of the Aegean world during Late Minoan III times. Although they owed much to Asiatic and Egyptian influences, the Minoans were unique in far more than the style of their decorative art, for they created the first European civilization and the first one anywhere to depend for its well-being on maritime contacts. Their art, as expressed most freely on the palace frescoes and on some of their finest pottery, betrays a pleasure in the representation of natural forms, maritime as well as terrestrial, for which no parallel exists in the ancient oriental world; and by comparison with the bearers of earlier civilizations the Minoans were freer from either priestly or militaristic oppression.

Early Helladic

The Early Helladic people of the Greek mainland, like their contemporaries in Asia Minor or in Macedonia, Bulgaria and southern Roumania, occupied permanent villages or townships and these were set as a rule on the mounds of their Neolithic predecessors. Yet innovations in pottery and architecture and the rise of metallurgy itself speak, if not of ethnic movement, at least of trade or other contacts with various parts of Asia Minor, some of which may have passed through intermediate islands. The rite of collective burial in rock-cut tombs or built ossuaries on the other hand reminds us that Greece was a Mediterranean land. Another reminder is the facility with which the Early Helladic people entered upon maritime trade that extended directly or indirectly to Egypt.

Aegean trade

The vigorous civilizations that arose in the East Mediterranean early in the third millennium were the first in the ancient world to rest primarily on the basis of maritime trade. The Neolithic colonization of the larger Aegean islands and of Crete presupposes traffic over the sea, and the flowering on these islands of cultures based on metallurgy and on the utilization of raw materials from a distance indicates a close and well-maintained network of sea-borne commerce. An excellent example is given by the Cycladic islands, many of which, left to themselves, would have been too barren or too small to sustain more than a handful of poor peasants on a subsistence basis. The islanders owed the possibility of developing the kind of urban life displayed by the ruins of Phylakopi on Melos to their activity as traders: indications of this are indeed provided by the distribution of raw materials narrowly localized in nature, like the copper of Paros and Siphnos, the emery of Naxos and the obsidian of Melos, or by evidence for the export of manufactured objects like marble idols and vases to Greece, Thermi, Troy, Crete and Egypt. Equally, there can be no doubt that trade relations extended as far afield as the West Mediterranean. Thus idols of local marble from Sardinia reflect Cycladic influence; one might also cite beaked pottery, flagons of Melian type, not to mention a tanged dagger of Cypriote form from the Rhône delta. Again, though it is known that Crete entered on a phase of intensified trade activity in the East Mediterranean during Middle Minoan II times, there are signs, for instance in the pottery or the bossed bone plaques, representing female forms, from the Tarxien culture of Malta and from Castelluccio in Sicily, and in the copper daggers of the Remedello culture of North Italy, that impulses may have begun to reach the Middle Mediterranean before the end of the Early Minoan period. The Aegean peoples had long been practised mariners: their boats, probably up to 20 to 30 metres long, were provided with oars and projecting keels to reduce the impact on landing; and, though incapable of tacking or sailing close to the wind, they could presumably have run fairly rapidly before it. It seems likely therefore that the coasts of Tuscany, the south of France or Iberia could each have been reached quite quickly from the East Mediterranean.

The main drive behind early exploration in the Mediterranean may well have been, as was the case with the Vikings, the comparative poverty of the homeland, but prospecting for metals may also have been a particular attraction so far as the far west is concerned. Yet, while there is no evidence that the mariners were impelled by missionary zeal, they certainly carried their religious convictions with them, and these were sufficiently strong to impress themselves in due course on many of the native peoples with whom they came into contact. Many of the elements of Aegean religion, notably the mother goddess, the sacred bull, the horns of consecration and the double-axe, stemmed directly from western Asia, but the practice of collective burial, whether in natural caves or in artificial tombs hollowed out of the rock or constructed in dry-stone masonry, seems to have been a peculiarly Mediterranean development. Collective use of natural caves for places of burial, in itself a practice of very remote antiquity, was undertaken in Crete in Early Minoan I times; by Early Minoan II the islanders were building circular dry-walled tombs above ground; and in the South Cyclades collective tombs were being provided with corbelled or cupola roofs. Again, on the southern part of the Greek mainland Early Helladic folk were burying their dead in family vaults that might be cut from the rock or built in dry-walling.

Diffusion of chamber tombs

It is hardly possible to doubt that it was from the Aegean area that the rite of collective burial, associated with belief in a mother goddess, spread widely over the Middle and West Mediterranean or that this was associated with the voyages of exploration and prospecting at which we have already hinted. The earliest collective tombs in Malta, Sicily, the Balearic islands, the south of France and southern Iberia were as a rule cut in the rock, as though they were artificial caves, but in the latter case they might be rendered in dry-walled structures at ground-level to form corbelled graves approached by passages. These rock-cut and dry-walled collective tombs emanating from the East Mediterranean were reproduced in Sicily, Sardinia and the Balearic islands by diverse structures of cyclopean masonry, and in Malta, the south of France and Iberia by megalithic chambers walled and roofed by upright and transversely laid stones. When the idea of collective burial spread widely over western and north-western Europe it was embodied mainly in tombs of megalithic construction, though the chalk-cut grottoes of the Marne and the corbelled vaults of certain Breton, Irish and Orcadian chambers remind us in out-lying regions of ultimate Mediterranean sources, as do the representations of goddesses on the grottoes and gallery-graves of the Paris basin or the more schematic ones on passage-graves in

Brittany, Anglesey or Ireland. The diffusion of the idea of building megalithic chamber tombs, like that of Neolithic economy itself, was accomplished partly by primary intrusions of adventurers from without and partly through adoption by aboriginal populations with a more or less devolved culture.

The route followed by the pioneers is marked by megalithic chamber tombs approached by passages and covered by round mounds (Map 4): from Atlantic Iberia they sailed across the Bay of Biscay to the southern shore of Brittany, up the western seaways to Ireland, Anglesey, the Hebrides, northern Scotland and the Orkneys, and ultimately either down from the north or by way of the English Channel to the West Baltic area. Although noticeably concentrated in the western part of their distribution on areas rich in copper, it was only in southern Iberia that the passage-graves yielded metal objects: elsewhere it was only in the forms of lithic artifacts, like the greenstone axes of Breton tombs, that their chalcolithic background finds any reflection in their contents. The vast majority of megalithic chamber tombs were secondary to the pioneer spread: they were erected by Neolithic peasants and pastoralists, who themselves were often comparatively recent converts from a Mesolithic hunter-fisher way of life. Although they adopted the rite of collective burial, they departed more or less widely from the architectural prototypes. Over large parts of western Europe they built tombs that were clearly degenerate passage-graves, often no more than small chambers with or without some kind of portal.

An alternative to the passage-grave that was widely adopted was the gallery-grave, a long chamber, generally under a long mound, which, though it might be sub-divided, had no separate entrance passages. Among the many variants of this type one might mention the gallery-graves of the Severn–Cotswold area of Britain having pairs of opposite side-chambers or transepts, prototypes of which probably came from the Biscayan area of France, and the segmented ones with concave forecourts, which with their elaborations are found in Ulster and south-west Scotland, both associated with variants of the Western Neolithic pottery. Another important group is that of the Paris basin, comprising long subterranean chambers lined and roofed with

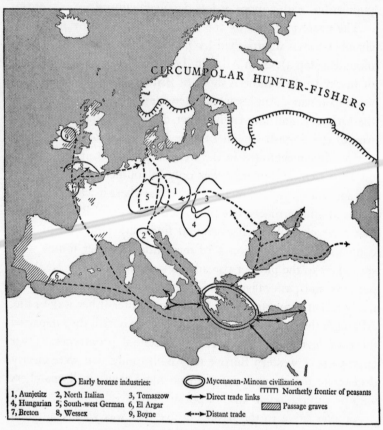

4. Europe in the mid-second millennium B.C.

megalithic slabs, often with porthole entrances. Representations of what may be funerary goddesses were occasionally carved on slabs at the entrance to the tomb and this was more frequently the case in the tombs of the upper Marne Valley that were cut entirely from the chalk rock. The people of the Seine–Oise–

Marne area, though they continued to depend to a significant degree on hunting and made crude pottery, nevertheless used daggers of honey-coloured chert from the quarries at Grand-Pressigny in Touraine that were evidently designed as substitutes for copper.

Small tombs of megalithic construction (*dysse*) were already being built in Denmark during the final phase of the local Early Neolithic, but these were only variants of cist graves intended for single burials. The idea of collective burial reached the West Baltic area from outside in two main waves. Passage-graves came in at the beginning of the northern Middle Neolithic, evidently by one or other of the western sea-routes; and gallery-graves or long cists appeared in the final stage of the northern Stone Age, the period of the flint daggers that ran parallel in time with the Early Bronze Age both in central Europe and in the Hiberno-British province. Although a few of the northern passage-graves stand fairly close to the prototype in plan, none show signs of corbelling or traces of rock-engravings, and the great majority diverge more or less markedly: some have oval plans, but often the chamber was long and rectangular leading with the passage to a T-plan. The grave-goods were in the main indigenous; the pottery comprised a succession of styles identified from settlements and originating in different parts of the North German plain; the thick-butted flint axe was evolved locally from the thin-butted one with squared sides, itself inspired by copper prototypes; and the commonest ornaments were beads and pendants of West Baltic amber.

'Secondary Neolithic' groups

The diffusion of collective burial and of megalithic tomb-construction in the west and the rise of copper-working in central Europe and North Italy, at a time equivalent to Danubian III in central and Early Neolithic C in northern Europe, are only symbols of the influence exerted from the Aegean towards the close of its Early 'Bronze' Age on the still predominantly Neolithic peasantries of barbarian Europe. By contrast, in the more marginal territories of the temperate zone the process of acculturation, by which surviving Mesolithic groups were led to adopt elements of Neolithic culture, was still actively proceeding. Some such process must have been involved in the genesis of secondary Neolithic groups like the Tripolje, Funnel-neck Beaker and Western, in territories immediately adjacent to zones of primary Neolithic spread. Examples of what might be termed tertiary Neolithic groups include the Alpine Horgen and the Seine-Oise-Marne of the Paris basin, both of which continued to lay emphasis on hunting and the use of stag antler and made pottery of debased character. In the same category may be placed the Clacton-Rinyo, Ebbsfleet and Peterborough groups of eastern Britain, though from an insular standpoint these have been dubbed 'secondary'. Although in the case of the last two there is no evidence that originally they practised farming, none of these groups seem to have found difficulty in commingling with Western pastoralists and cereal-growers: moreover it is worth noting that it was these most recently acculturated groups which contributed the tradition of ritual structures comprising ditches of horseshoe plan and settings of ritual pits that formed the initial stage in the evolution of Stonehenge, in many respects the most outstanding monument of barbarian society in Europe.

Battle-axe and beaker peoples

The close of the Stone Age was marked over large parts of temperate Europe by the rapid movement of ethnic groups, which through their impact on the static peasantries and through their blazing of new routes helped to prepare the way for the spread of metallurgy. East of the Rhine pastoral groups, armed with stone battle-axes, spread widely, burying their dead everywhere in single-graves. They issued from the lands between the Vistula, the Baltic and the Dnieper, from which the Funnel-neck Beaker folk had emerged in a previous period, but the custom of barrow burial, which not all of them adopted, came in all probability from the steppe region further east. There were spreads in several directions and each of the main regional groups that emerged was distinguished by differences of style both in battle-axes and pottery. To the north they spread across the Baltic to Sweden and Finland and through the East Baltic lands to the Gulf of Riga; and in the forests of the Oka–Volga watershed east of Moscow there grew up the distinctive Fatyanovo group. To the south others moved into central Europe and some few penetrated as far as Greece at the close of Early Helladic times. Another main drive was to the west: some turned north into Jutland, where they contrasted notably with the megalith-builders, who practised mixed farming on the richer soils of the drift; and others proliferated in Saxo-Thuringia and spread into the Rhineland on a broad front from the Alps to the Low Countries. In the Rhenish area they came into contact with powerfully built, broad-headed bowmen, having distinctive archer's wristguards, barbed and tanged arrowheads of flint, copper daggers, V-perforated buttons and bell-shaped beaker pottery, the latter decorated in horizontal zones by means of toothed stamps. These Bell-Beaker folk seem to have spread immediately from Iberia, following the megalithic sea-routes, but also finding their way into central Europe and in small numbers into Denmark, as well as into the Rhine Valley and thence, as well probably as from the south, to the British Isles. In thus linking Bohemia, a major source of tin, with both the Mediterranean and Denmark, the Beaker prospectors pioneered routes essential to the development of metallurgical industries in central and ultimately in northern Europe; and there is evidence that another group, this time coming ultimately from the Rhine-land, first opened up the copper deposits of Ireland and so initiated the Hiberno-British industry.

Arctic hunter-fishers

The development of bronze metallurgy in Europe will be reserved for the next chapter. Meanwhile it needs to be emphasized that the spread of Neolithic farming economy in Europe was limited by ecological factors and that, beyond the northern margin of the deciduous forest, hunting, fishing, fowling and gathering provided the only or at least the principal means of subsistence. The circumpolar zone, with its great tracts of coniferous and birch forest and areas of open tundra and extending from the Atlantic coast of Norway to the Urals and far beyond, supported a type of Arctic culture which, though overlapping in South Scandinavia and the Baltic coasts with cultures based primarily on farming, rested fundamentally on a 'Mesolithic' type of economy. The emphasis laid on different aspects of the food-quest naturally varied: on the Atlantic and Arctic coasts of Norway deep-sea fishing with hook and line was particularly important; whereas the hunting of elk played a leading role in the interior of Sweden, Finland and northern Russia; and seal-hunting was a main activity on the coasts of the southern territories, in which alone mixed farming was combined with catching activities. Certain cultural elements of Neolithic origin were appropriated by the Circumpolar people, notably the making of pottery, which they built up by coils to conoid forms and decorated by sinking pits in the thickness of the walls, as well as by impressing combs or toothed stamps, commonly arranged in zig-zags over the whole surface of the vessel. Although they turned out projectile heads, knives and, in north-west Russia, some notable profiles of animals, from flint or alternative materials by means of bifacial pressure-flaking, the sub-Neolithic Arctic people were notable above all for the extent to which they utilized slate. Both the forms, and the techniques of sawing and polishing used to shape them, suggest familiarity with the working of bone. The antlers and skeletal material from game animals provided material indeed for harpoon-heads perforated near the base for securing to a line, barbed spearheads, arrowheads, handles slotted for flint insets and fish-hooks; nearly all of these were of Mesolithic ancestry, though the hooks were now commonly barbed and sometimes made in two pieces bound together at the base. Polished adzes, frequently hollow-ground and evidently inspired by tools made from split tubular bones, were another widespread feature and presumably indicate the importance of wood-working.

The Arctic people were aided in their quest for food by various means of transport. On the sea and inland waters they almost certainly used skin boats which, to judge from the north Norwegian rock-engravings, were of *umiak* type and propelled by paddles: vessels covered by seal-skin which would have been tolerably resistant to floating ice. For traversing the snow, which in Scandinavia lay for nearly half the year over most of the zone, heavy dog-drawn sledges, built up on struts set in grooves and braced to runners up to 12 feet long, were used as well as two kinds of ski, one for compact snow, having straps passing through a raised foot-rest, and the other for slushy snow with foot-thongs threaded through side flanges. Boats and devices for moving rapidly over land during the long winter made it possible to carry on trade over surprisingly long distances; thus axes and adzes of Danish flint were traded up the west Baltic coast and across Sweden to the north-west coast and adjacent islands of Norway; others roughed out of a kind of slate at Olonets in Karelia found their way over much of Finland and the East Baltic states; and amber pendants and figurines from East Prussia found their way across Scandinavia to the west coast of Norway. The existence of this trade helps to emphasize the broad homogeneity of culture over very extensive regions, a homogeneity only partly explained by an underlying ecological and economic unity.

In Finland, Norway and Sweden settlement tended to concentrate on the coast so that advantage could be taken of the resources of the sea and the shore as well as of the interior. In Russia on the other hand and in the interior of Scandinavia the shores of lakes and rivers were main foci of settlement. The hunter-fisher way of life commonly involves migration and this applies particularly to the circumpolar regions where seasonal differences are so pronounced. Thus, where they were available, as on the west and north-west coasts of Norway and on the island of Karlsö off Gotland, caves might be used during the summer for particular catches of seals or fish. As a rule, no doubt, tents or other light structures were used at this time of the year. On the other hand, during the winter, dwellers on the exposed coasts of north-west and northern Norway built rectangular semi-subterranean houses having thick walls of earth and rubble faced with dry-stone work, the roofs supported on two rows of vertical posts. Although it is difficult to be sure how many houses were occupied at once, it seems that under favourable conditions the Arctic hunter-fishers were able to live in sizeable groups. This is confirmed by the existence of cemeteries like those of Olen on Lake Onega in Russian Karelia and Västerbjers on Gotland. The first of these, though partly destroyed, yielded more than 150 graves. The dead were normally buried in an extended position wearing skin garments fringed with perforated animal teeth and accompanied by personal ornaments, weapons and tools.

The wealth of grave-goods suggests that the Arctic people practised their economy, the only one feasible at the time over most of their territory, at least as successfully as their contemporaries practising farming further south. In addition to repetitive patterns applied to pottery, which they shared with the peasant communities of Neolithic Europe, they created an impressive body of art—rock-engravings, plastic models in fired clay, carvings in amber, bone, slate, greenstone and wood, profiles chipped from flint and outlines impressed by toothed stamps on pottery—devoted primarily to representations of the animals on which they depended, above all elk, bear, reindeer, seals, small toothed whales, fish and water birds, but also including human-beings and boats. In the case of the rock-engravings several distinct local styles may be recognized, but the general style of the carvings is remarkably uniform as far east as the bog of Gorbunovo in the Mid-Urals.

CHAPTER 7

THE FOUNDATIONS OF EUROPEAN CIVILIZATION: FROM MYCENAE TO THE AGE OF EXPANSION

Mycenaean origins

About the same time as the Battle-axe people were swarming in central and eastern Europe, the Middle Helladic phase of Greek prehistory was ushered in by warriors who apparently spoke the Greek language and so belonged linguistically to the Indo-European family. Their wheel-made, grey 'Minyan' pottery, which included among its forms high-handled cups based on silver prototypes, belongs to a ware found widely over Asia Minor and as far afield as north-east Iran and Turkmenia, a fact consistent with a homeland on the steppes of South Russia for speakers of the pristine and undivided Indo-European language. Whether the warrior incursion reached Greece by way of Asia Minor or, as others think, from Macedonia, the event gave a decisive flavour to the Late Helladic or Mycenaean civilization that flowered in Greece during the sixteenth century B.C. Though clearly subject to strong Minoan influences, Mycenaean civilization is no longer believed to have been introduced fully formed by conquerors from Crete. The mainlanders adopted many elements of the island civilization, but the Mycenaeans and their culture were deeply rooted in mainland Greece. This is illustrated by the fact that the site of Mycenae was occupied already from Early Helladic times and that the royal shaft graves, which yielded many of the finest objects from the beginning of the Mycenaean civilization, formed part of a cemetery of Middle Helladic origin. Again, though sharing the centralized palace organization of the Minoans, the Mycenaeans incorporated the megaron or great rectangular hall with porch and inner chamber, a plan absent from Crete, but which existed in Troy II and in Late Neolithic Thessaly. Even more to the point, the records maintained by Mycenaean scribes in connection with the palace economy introduced from Crete are now known to have been written in the Greek language, though the script (linear B) was palpably derived from one (linear A) used by the Minoans as early as the seventeenth century B.C. for a language yet to be identified; by common consent this was not Greek and the suggestion has been made that the change in script was in fact due to the need to adjust to a different tongue.

The mainland was a larger and naturally richer unit, which only needed the stimulus of the 'Minyan' incursion to realize its potentialities. No doubt it was this economic pull that drew Cretan artificers as well as Minoan manufacturers to Greece and led in due course to the introduction of the palace economy. The most vivid picture of the wealth attained in Mycenaean Greece already by the middle of the sixteenth century B.C. is to be gained from the goods placed with the dead in the shaft graves. Vessels of gold and silver, mirrors with carved ivory handles, lavishly decorated personal ornaments and weapons and the use of exotic substances give evidence not merely of wealth, but of wealth concentrated in the hands of chieftains whose warlike attributes and status are symbolized by light war-chariots, drawn by horses and running on spoked wheels, vehicles of a type that had first spread with the Hyksos to Palestine and Egypt and with the Hittites to Anatolia. When it came to blows with the Cretans, it was the mainlanders who won and the burning of the Cnossian palace c. 1400 B.C. marked the beginning of Mycenaean dominance in the East Mediterranean. It was during the following centuries that Mycenaean trade reached its peak and it was to this period that the cyclopean walls and the palaces of Mycenae and Tiryns belong, as well as many of the tholos tombs, whose great circular underground chambers approached by sloping passages are roofed with domes that might be up to 45 feet high.

Bronze metallurgy in central Europe

Until the intensified working of the East Alpine copper mines had begun to cheapen metal and so to influence technology on a broad front during the last century or two of the second millennium, the spread of tin-bronze metallurgy had only a limited effect on the peasant and pastoral societies of prehistoric Europe. The broad pattern of Neolithic cultures, as this was modified by the spread of the Beaker and Battle-axe peoples, persisted; flint, stone, bone and wood continued to be the most important materials; and few important appliances came into use at this time, unless we except the wooden ox-drawn ard or scratch-plough and the farm waggon with solid one- or three-piece wheels, of a type that was probably transmitted from South Russia through the territory of the Funnel-neck Beaker people of the north European plain. While metal was still expensive, its use was mainly confined, apart from the all-important axe, to weapons and personal ornaments. The metal-smiths themselves were either itinerant, peddling their own wares, as in the west, or, as in central Europe, working at a few centres for middlemen who apparently organized the sale of their products. The conjunction of copper and tin needed for the rise of a bronze industry admittedly implied trade that might extend over long distances, but neither this nor the basic activity of mining was in itself new, since it had been developed, even among hunter-fisher peoples, for the stone axe and adze blades needed for felling and shaping wood. On the other hand the metal trade opened up greater possibilities for the concentration of wealth and there seems little doubt also that it marked a further intensification of the prospecting activities of more advanced peoples centred on the East Mediterranean, the early stages of which have already been traced. This is confirmed by the fact that the early smiths of central Europe practised techniques invented earlier in the Near East. Among these was the use of valve moulds consisting of two pieces pegged together, which allowed the casting of objects having raised features like mid-ribs and flanges on either face, and of the *cire-perdue* process whereby wax models were encased in clay and after firing replaced by molten metal, a method which made it possible to produce a wide range of complex forms with greater ease and economy. Many of the leading metal types manufactured during the Early Bronze Age of central Europe (Danubian IV, *c.* 1800–1450 B.C.) among the Perjámos, Tószeg A, Aunjetitz and Straubing groups of the Maros, Upper Theiss and Middle Danube, Bohemia and Bavaria respectively, such as for example racket-shaped and knot-headed pins of bronze, gold wire earrings and copper torcs or neck-rings with coiled ends that served as metal ingots, were likewise of Near Eastern origin.

Mycenaean trade with barbarian societies

Although bronze metallurgy was thus established in limited parts of central Europe before the rise of Mycenaean civilization, it was the Mycenaean market (Map 4) that more than any other factor was responsible first for its spread to other centres and then for its intensification. Although copper was worked in Crete and certain Cycladic islands on a small scale and in Cyprus on a larger one, the requirements of the Minoans and later of the Mycenaeans grew with every advance in their technology. The adoption of standard bronze in Middle Minoan times accentuated the need for prospecting and trade, because the East Mediterranean area was notably deficient in tin. It was the need for metals that in the first instance attracted Mycenaean attention to central Europe and it was doubtless there that their emissaries came into contact with the Jutish amber that was already during the final phase of the Northern Neolithic being traded south. Their interest in the fossil resin with its magical 'electric' properties seems to have been aroused at first sight because Danish amber, distinguishable from that found in the Mediterranean, was already being buried in the shaft-graves of Mycenae; as it turned out it was their sustained appetite for this substance, as well as their hunger for metals, that determined in large measure the course of trade in Bronze Age Europe down to the breakdown of Mycenaean power in the twelfth century. The original route by which amber travelled south from the west Jutland coast was up the Elbe to the junction with the Saale, thence by way of both rivers across the territory of the Aunjetitz culture to the Brenner pass and so by way of the Po Valley to the head of the Adriatic and down by sea to Greece. When in the second phase of the central European Bronze Age a distinctive bronze industry, associated with tumulus burial, arose among descendants of Corded-ware folk occupying the highlands of south-west Germany, a western loop was added, making first for the Middle Rhineland, passing up the Neckar, thence across to the Danube and so downstream to join the old one. The amber route formed a veritable hub around which the Early Bronze Age industry of much of Europe revolved. East of the Saale and extending as far as the Warthe another distinct centre marked by rich tumulus burials grew up, which like that in south-west Germany, was carried by descendants of the Late Neolithic Corded-ware people. Another distinctive industry developed in North Italy adjacent to the southern end of the overland route, and at its northern end the Danes, still in the final stage of their Stone Age, were importing bronze manufactures both from central and also from western Europe.

The only manufactured objects of East Mediterranean origin found in barbarian Europe and sufficiently numerous to define commercial routes are beads of faience, an artificial substance consisting of a core of fused quartz grains and a covering of glass glaze. Almost certainly the trade in these beads to the west and north-west was in the hands of Mycenaeans or their emissaries. The large numbers present in the Aunjetitz territory and in that of the adjacent Tomoszów culture of the Upper Vistula and a single find from north Jutland confirm the importance of the central European trade, but equally the distribution of the beads points to an alternative route by way of the Mediterranean and the western sea-ways. Faience beads from the cremation cemetery of Hal Tarxien, Malta, and from sites with Late Helladic III A pottery on Sicily and the Lipari islands mark the passage of traders towards the western Mediterranean. On the other hand the scarcity of finds on the coast of eastern Spain and their relative abundance in the south of France from Languedoc to Provence makes it plain that the main routes to the west no longer encircled Iberia. The El Argar culture that followed and carried forward the Almerian in the east of Spain was relatively provincial in character, and its metal-smiths had to make do with an insufficient supply of tin. Trade now flowed north of the Pyrenees, down the Garonne to Morbihan, itself a source of tin, and on across the open sea to Great Britain and Ireland, attracted no doubt by the tin of Cornwall and possibly of Wexford, by the copper of Waterford, Cork and Kerry and by the copper and gold of Wicklow.

Although two main routes can be distinguished, these were themselves interconnected; for instance the chieftains' tumulus burials in Brittany probably indicate a movement from the Saale-Warthe province, and the Hiberno-British region was linked by two-way movements both with this and with the West Baltic area. Indeed, it was the position of Wessex at the cross-roads of the two routes that made it possible for the ruling class to gain riches from Irish gold, Cornish (and possibly Irish) tin and Baltic amber. Clues to the ultimate destination of at least some of the tin are given not merely by the presence of segmented faience beads in a fair proportion of the Wessex tumulus burials, but also from the many indications that Wessex goldsmiths had learned from the more sophisticated practitioners of Mycenaean Greece.

Wessex and Stonehenge

In the wealth of their tumulus burials the Wessex chieftains have many analogues on the Continent, but in the lintelled circle and horseshoe setting of trilithons erected from sarsen blocks at Stonehenge they can show a monument unique in barbarian Europe and one which they have autographed by means of engravings pecked on certain of the uprights. Much attention has rightly been paid to the representation of a metal dagger of a kind found in the shaft-graves at Mycenae, but it is at least as significant that more than sixty representations occur of an ordinary Wessex type of cast flanged axe. Further, while it is true that the sarsen settings stand apart in sophistication both as to form and finish, it should be remembered that they relate to a comparatively late stage in the history of the monument. Stonehenge began, as we have noted, as a circle of ritual pits surrounded by a penannular bank and ditch, and was originally constructed during the Secondary Neolithic phase. The first stone erections on the site were made from bluestones quarried on the Prescelly Mountains, and dragged and floated all the way to Salisbury Plain by the Beaker people. In view of the role of these people in opening up the copper resources of Ireland and initiating a native Hiberno-British metallurgical industry, it is worth noting that according to an old tradition incorporated in the chronicle of Geoffrey of Monmouth (c. A.D. 1136) the bluestones were derived from Ireland. It is also a fact that under the right conditions it is possible to descry Wicklow from the crest of the Prescelly mountains.

Recession in the East Mediterranean

Enough has been said to make it evident that the Mycenaeans or their agents played a decisive part, both in fostering the development of native bronze industries in central and north-western Europe and in creating conditions that favoured the enrichment of chieftains whose wealth was conspicuously displayed by individual tumulus burial. It is possible also, though in the existing state of knowledge this is only a hypothesis, that Mycenaean skill and technical knowledge and the pull of the Mycenaean market were between them responsible for intensifying the winning of copper in central Europe, which made possible the far-reaching industrial changes of the Late Bronze Age in temperate Europe. It has been suggested that it was expansion from central Europe that precipitated the fall of Mycenaean civilization and helped to set in motion movements of peoples which troubled the whole of the East Mediterranean world during the first half of the twelfth century B.C. Of the existence of disturbances at this time there can be no doubt. We know from the records of Ramses III (1198–1166 B.C.) that the Hittite confederacy, previously threatened during the closing decades of the thirteenth, was broken up by an eastward thrust of population during the first part of the twelfth century, at a time when Philistines were settling on the coast of Palestine and Egypt herself was threatened by islanders from the north. Again, according to later sources, Troy VII A was destroyed some time around the end of the twelfth or the beginning of the eleventh century (between 1209 and 1183 B.C.); and Thucydides tells us that the Dorians entered the Peloponnese some eighty years later. Archaeology confirms that many of the leading Mycenaean cities were destroyed by people whose immediate source was Mount Pindus, but who probably originated in Macedonia. Yet many of the detailed analogies between central European, Greek and Anatolian material used to support the idea of movements from the Middle Danube area might equally suggest movement in an opposite or even from a third direction and no definite answer can be expected until the chronology has been more exactly worked out.

Urnfield cultures in central Europe

A notable feature of this time in central Europe was the adoption by the descendants of the Aunjetitz people of the practice of burying their dead in urnfields, a practice that presumably spread from Hungary and which, significantly, occurred at Troy VI as early as the fourteenth century B.C. Likewise the warts and fluting on the cinerary urns themselves have Hungarian affinities and fluted pottery had a very long history in Anatolia, as well as being used by the destroyers of Troy VII A and of Late Mycenaean villages on the Vardar. The Urnfield cultures of central Europe are symbols of the independent potentialities of European peasants at a time when civilization in the East Mediterranean was undergoing a temporary eclipse. They are immensely significant as laying the basis on which, under Greek, Etruscan and Scythic influence, the prehistoric Iron Age civilization of Europe depended. The earliest Urnfield group was that established in Hungary and exemplified by the C-level of the mound at Tószeg. Another grew up in the old Aunjetitz territory of the Lausitz between the Elbe and the Oder and north of the Sudeten mountains and later spread east to the Vistula and south to Lower Austria. A third, of special importance to the genesis of the Hallstatt Iron Age civilization of temperate Europe, was located in the North Alpine area, where two distinct cultures flourished, namely the Knoviz of Bavaria and south-west Bohemia and the Hötting of Austria.

Copper-mining in the Tyrol

It was the Hötting people who were mainly responsible, under the initial stimulus of the Mycenaean market, for opening up the copper-mines of the Tyrol. The best explored mines are those of the Mühlbach–Bischofshofen area near Salzburg, which tapped deep veins of copper pyrites. The miners had bronze-headed picks, but their main weapons were fire and water. Veins would first be attacked where they outcropped, but as soon as the miners had worked themselves into the hillside they were able to bring the fire to bear on the ceiling as well as on the rock immediately ahead. Very soon it would be necessary to build a wooden staging to carry the rock-waste and support the fires, and under this a passage would be left for the air currents needed to keep the fires burning and the atmosphere clear. By the time the workings had reached a practicable limit they might be as much as 160 metres in length and 30 metres in height at the entrance. Such a mine at the peak would probably have called for a labour force of some 180 men, a third of whom would have been employed on felling the wood needed for fuel and staging purposes. The total quantity of crude copper produced by the Mühlbach–Bischofshofen mines during the Late Bronze Age has been estimated at around 20,000 metric tons.

Mining operations on such a scale greatly increased the supply of copper and it must be remembered that the collapse of the Mycenaean market soon left the whole of this to the peasant societies of prehistoric Europe. Some of the metal was undoubtedly exported, to be incorporated for example in the products of the Nordic bronze-smiths in their splendid hey-day; but the bulk was used by the Urnfield people themselves, either directly or for fabricating wares for export. Among the techniques first practiced by Urnfield people in temperate Europe was the art of hammering vessels, an art long previously practised in in the East Mediterranean world. Socketed axes, the idea of which may have originated in central Eurasia, were among the numerous forms that required core-casting. The cheapness of metal made it practicable to turn out an increased range of tools and these included such things as chisels, gouges and saws, which in turn made possible notable advances in wood-working. The scale and number of the urnfields, the highly organized character of the extractive industries and the advanced standards of bronze-smithing suggest a denser population and a more productive basis of subsistence than that which sufficed for the earlier peasant communities of much of Europe. Although there is evidence that the ox-drawn ard or light scratch-plough may have started to be taken into use during an earlier stage of the Bronze Age, it would seem that the Urnfield people consolidated a system of settled mixed farming that was to prevail over extensive parts of Europe down to the Roman period.

Expansion of the Urnfield cultures

It is hardly surprising therefore that after a period of consolidation in the North Alpine area, during which they elaborated their way of life and accumulated wealth from copper- and salt-mines, the Urnfield people should have entered on a phase of further expansion at the expense of their less developed neighbours, an expansion which took the form of a series of thrusts over a period of centuries and continued into the time during which iron had come into use for tools and weapons. The expansive power of the Urnfielders, based in the first instance on an enlarging population, was enhanced by the mobility made possible by a fuller use of horse-drawn vehicles and given a sharp cutting edge by the slashing swords first introduced to central Europe from Asia Minor during the disturbed period that ushered in the break-up of the Hittite empire and the decline of Mycenaean power. The expansion of the Urnfield people, by displacing the populations that existed in the territories into which they first penetrated, brought about movements of population far more widespread than those involved directly in their own migrations. Moreover, through their control of vital commodities like copper and salt and as a result of their pre-eminence as metal-smiths, they exercised an important influence through the medium of trade, and it is often difficult from the imperfect evidence of archaeology to determine the precise historical significance of particular Urnfield influences.

The Urnfield expansion is significant both on account of the movements of population and of trade that it set in motion and because it laid the economic foundations of the last major phase in European prehistory, a phase in which iron tools were destined to play a role of increasing importance. South of the Alps Urnfield influence penetrated to the Po Valley and Latium, and round about 1000 B.C. a distinctive culture marked by cremation cemeteries and known as Villanovan began to develop between the Po and the Tiber on the basis of the old Apennine civilization. The Villanovans placed the ashes of their dead either in biconical urns, decorated in the Apennine style and covered either by a small cup or by a crested bronze helment, or in urns shaped like store-houses with entrances high up in the walls and of a type probably derived from the Middle Elbe. They grew prosperous by intensi-fying the exploitation of Tuscan metal resources initiated long previously, probably under Minoan influence; developed a rich bronze industry, of which many of the leading forms, including swords with antennae-like projections at the base of the hilt, razors, helmets, girdles, safety-pins or fibulae and cult objects, were of Danubian derivation; and in due course adopted iron-working. North of the Alps on the other hand Celtic-speaking people seem actually to have penetrated as ethnic groups as far west as Catalonia and ultimately as far north as southern Britain, incidentally setting in motion a number of groups with traditions formed in the Middle Bronze Age. The earliest incursion seems to have passed through the Belfort gap into south Alsace and north Franche-Comté. Late movements during the first quarter of the first millennium B.C. reached as far south as the Saône, pressed forward in a westerly direction towards the Atlantic coast, and during the latter half of the eighth century B.C. crossed the south of France to complete the movement into Catalonia. Meanwhile a distinctive bronze industry grew up in the Atlantic zone of Iberia, based on Cantabrian copper and Galician tin, the original stimulus for which was probably given by refugees from the Loire region displaced by the westward thrust of Urnfielders. By the seventh century B.C. the region had apparently entered into active trade relations with Brittany and the British Isles, a commerce that greatly enriched the later bronze industries of the islanders.

Southern England was strongly influenced from across the Channel by the economic growth and ethnic expansion of the Urnfield people. Doubtless it was through trade that such conti-nental types as socketed axes and slashing swords first came into

the country, and it must be significant that it was during the
opening centuries of the first millennium that the distribution of
the products of metallurgical industry was reorganized on continental lines and the travelling tinker replaced by the more elaborate organization implied by large hoards of finished wares or of
scrap. Ethnic movement, on the other hand, seems to be implied
by the adoption of globular urns recalling prototypes in northern
France, and above all by the introduction of the new system of
agriculture based on the cultivation of short, broad fields by
means of ards or light scratch-ploughs, a system destined to
provide the principal base of the agricultural economy of much of
lowland England throughout the prehistoric Iron Age and the
Romano-English period.

Protogeometric Greece

As we have seen, the catastrophes which temporarily eclipsed
Aegaean leadership redounded to the economic advantage of
central Europe, and set in motion changes which transformed the
way of life prevailing over extensive tracts of the then barbarian
world. Even in Greece itself the disaster failed to impair the basis
on which civilized life was recreated during later centuries. The
destruction of Mycenae and of other urban centres is a fact
attested by archaeology, whoever the attackers, traditionally
referred to as Dorians, may have been in particular cases. Urban
sophistication gave place to rustic simplicity; economic life re-
verted very largely to the activities immediately concerned with
subsistence; trade languished; and crafts like masonry-building,
gem-cutting and writing fell into desuetude. Yet even at a
material level the decline was not unrelieved; Protogeometric
pottery may have been ruder in some respects than Mycenaean,
but it was by no means without merit; and the importation of iron
ornaments and weapons marked the onset of a new era in European technology. Moreover, the break was by no means equally
marked in all the Greek lands. If Mycenaean civilization was

destroyed in the Peloponnese, substantial continuity was maintained in Attica, Boeotia and Ionia, and it can hardly be a co-
incidence that it was in these latter regions that, to quote Miss
Lorimer, 'all Greek poetry, both archaic and classical, all the
great forms which the literature of Europe was destined to imitate
and elaborate through the centuries, have their ultimate origin'.
No doubt it was this continuity also that helps to explain why it is
that Greek mythology, with the gods dwelling on Olympus in
subjection to Zeus, is Mycenaean in conception and the Greek
temple a descendant of the Middle Helladic megaron. Again, it is
a striking fact that the oriental influences that brought Classical
civilization to birth were transmitted through territories like
Rhodes and Cyprus, where Mycenaean civilization had been
subject to the least disturbance.

Genesis and diffusion of iron-working

As so frequently happens, the decline of one phase of culture
marked the genesis of its successor. Thus the fall of the Hittite
empire at the beginning of the twelfth century was the immediate
cause for the spread of iron technology. Although much more
widely spread in nature than copper and still more than tin,
telluric iron did not come into general use until much later than
bronze, even though insignificant quantities were occasionally
produced accidentally in early times in the course of such activities as firing pottery in closed kilns. Traditionally the earliest
skilled iron-workers practised their craft in the lands bordering
the southern shore of the Black Sea, and it is significant that the
first historical references occur in the archives of the Hittite kings
at Boghaz-Keui. There are grounds for thinking that the Hittites,
conscious of the advantages conferred by iron weapons in war,
guarded the secret of their production and restricted exports to
daggers, personal ornaments and the like, designed as presents for
rulers of foreign states. What is certain is that it was not until the
downfall of the Hittites that iron-working spread for example to

V   Terracotta Negroid head from Nok, Nigeria

(*facing p.* 160)

VI   Plastic vase of kneeling boy, Agora, Athens

Palestine, where it soon came to be applied to general economic activities such as farming in the shape of hoe-blades, plough-shares and sickles. It must have been from Anatolia or Syria, probably by way of Cyprus, that the Greeks of the Protogeo-metric period obtained their sword- and dagger-blades and in due course the knowledge needed for establishing their own iron-working industry.

The alphabet

It was in the same historical context and from the same quarter that the Greeks derived the alphabet. The fall of the Hittites, the decline of Egypt, following the death of Ramses III (1166 B.C.), and the collapse of Mycenaean power combined to play into the hands of the Phoenicians, a Semitic trading people of the coasts of Lebanon and Syria, who even managed to enjoy political independence from the twelfth to the ninth centuries. During an early phase of this period and most probably by c. 1100 B.C. the Phoenicians had evolved, probably to assist them in the conduct of their commerce, the first alphabetic script, the actual symbols of which were adapted from Egyptian hieroglyphs. Considering that the alphabet had to be adapted to the needs of a non-Semitic language, the agreement between the symbols on the earliest Greek inscriptions and those of the Phoenician alphabet is so close as to leave no doubt of their source, in addition to which the names and order of letters and the direction of writing from right to left in many inscriptions are all features of early Greek practice and only readily explained on the hypothesis that the alphabet was originally devised for inscribing a Semitic tongue. The prob-ability is that the Phoenician script was first adopted around the mid-ninth century B.C. by Greek traders based on the Asiatic coast of the Aegean and operating through the Phoenician trading station on Cyprus. Although devised and spread in the cause of commerce, the alphabet was doubtless a main factor in reducing the Homeric poems, hitherto passed on by word of mouth, to their final form, probably towards the end of the eighth century, just as it was destined in its variously modified versions to transmit down to our own day the literature of western man.

Greek colonies

Ever since Neolithic times the coasts and islands of the Aegean had been the subject of exploration by mariners eager for trade or new areas for colonization; at the height of their power the Mycenaeans had posts as far west as South Italy, Sicily and the Lipari Islands and trade connections over broad tracts of Europe from Iberia and southern Britain in the west to the Ukraine and even Transcaucasia in the east. It is a sign of their renascent energy that the Greeks of the Geometric period not merely caught up with, but in due course eclipsed their predecessors. This is particularly true of the Euxine, into which Mycenaean trade had penetrated only feebly and settlement not at all. Already during the eighth century Ionian Greeks had begun to explore the northern shore of Asia Minor and in due course trading stations were established at Trebizond and Sinope, the first for loading iron, copper and gold from Transcaucasia and the latter perhaps for transhipment into larger craft. Doubtless it was the adventures of these pioneers which nourished the myth of the Argonauts in search of the Golden Fleece that we find incorporated in the *Odyssey*. During the following century exploration was extended to the western and northern shores and here no doubt the leading attractions were the fish that abounded in the great rivers of South Russia, the Bosporus and the Sea of Azov and which were traded dried or preserved in jars; the salt that could so conveniently be prepared in the great estuaries; and the honey and wax, known to have abounded in medieval Russia and of which the importance was already implied by Herodotus. In addition to its importance as a source of food and metals, the Euxine also offered scope for settlement, and numerous colonies sprang up at favourable points on the coasts. Among the most prosperous were those which paid tribute to and lived in profitable harmony with the Scyths, such as Olbia at the mouth of the Bug and close to that of the Dnieper, Pantikapaion on the west shore of the Bosporus and Tanais at the head of the Sea of Azov.

In the Mediterranean the Greeks met formidable rivals in the Phoenicians and Etruscans. To begin with they had to content themselves with establishing colonies in South Italy, from Calabria to as far north as Naples on the west coast, and in Sicily. They were effectually prevented from venturing further over the open sea by the Phoenicians, who had founded Carthage and other colonies on the Tunisian coast and established depots on the coasts of Sicily and Sardinia as early as the eighth century B.C. Assyrian pressure on the trading cities of the Lebanese and Syrian coasts first made it possible for the Greeks to spread to Egypt and Cyrene and ultimately to the western Mediterranean, where they founded Massilia (Marseilles) around 600 B.C. and Emporion (Ampurias) on the modern Catalan coast, approximately 550 B.C. From Massilia Greek traders reached out to remoter parts of Europe for tin and other materials. By the middle of the sixth century they had ventured through the Straits of Gibraltar to Tartessos, the modern Cadiz, probably to collect Asturian tin. But once again Greek enterprise was affected by events far away at the east end of the Mediterranean. The destruction of the Ionian cities by the Persians weakened the Greeks and made the Carthaginians powerful enough to close the Straits of Gibraltar. One effect of this was to deflect the Greek quest for tin to the deposits of Morbihan and Cornwall. These were reached by way of the Carcassonne gap, the Garonne river and the Biscayan sea-route with a port of call at Corbillo by the mouth of the Loire.

Athenian repulse of Persia

The overwhelming of the Ionian cities also constituted a mortal threat to the Helladic homeland where the arts of Classical civilization were already beginning to develop (Pl. VI). Before long Athenian support for Ionian rebels incurred the active enmity of Darius, who set his armies in motion to stamp out the distant source of disaffection. Conversely, it was the defeat of the Persian army at Marathon in 490 B.C. and the destruction of the fleet ten years later at Salamis that, in dispelling the Persian menace, ushered in the greatest age of Classical Greece. That this proved to be brief was due to a fatal flaw in political life: the existence of so many sovereign city states in a land as small as Greece was bound to lead to destructive rivalry and conflict. In the event the state which emerged as victor from the Peloponnesian war (431–404 B.C.) was the most disciplined, but also the most philistine. With the predominance of Sparta the most creative, though not necessarily the most influential, phase of Classical art and thought was over. Before long the emergence of a strong Macedonian kingdom under Philip II (359–336 B.C.) put an end to the Greek city state as a political entity of importance. Yet in other respects Philip's achievements were immensely significant, since they made possible the conquests of Alexander the Great and so ultimately brought within the sphere of Hellenic influence the ancient civilizations of western Asia and Egypt and prepared the way for the expansion of the Roman Empire in the east.

The Etruscans

Both on the Italian mainland and in the North Tyrrhenian sea the Greek colonists encountered the Etruscans: a people of non-Indo-European tongue, whose literature has yet to be deciphered and whose origins have long excited interest. The idea that the Etruscans arrived in Italy with a ready-made culture from the Lydian homeland in western Asia Minor attributed to them by Herodotus has few supporters today. The culture which appeared in full view around 700 B.C. between the Arno and the Tiber was in essence no more than an enrichment of that of the Villanovans, explicable in terms of economic growth and the impact of exotic influences; Phoenician, Cypriote and Greek. The Etruscans drew their wealth from the deposits of copper, iron and tin in the mountains and from their own skill as metal-workers. From their early homeland they gained control over most of western Italy north of the Greek zone, though, except in the north, they nowhere crossed the Apennines or disturbed the Italic bearers of the old Apennine culture: Elba was seized early on account of its iron deposits and Corsica fell into their possession as a result of a sea-victory in league with the Carthaginians over the Greeks around 540 B.C. In the course of the sixth century Etruscan civilization spread widely over the old Villanovan territories in the Po Valley and southward as far as the Campanian plain, where the northern Greek colonies on the Gulf of Naples were enveloped.

Whereas the Villanovans were essentially villagers, the Etruscans preferred, like the Greeks, to live in stone-built towns with public buildings: it was after all Etruscans who first enclosed the Seven Hills of Rome with a wall and converted a cluster of Villanovan villages into a city with forum and temple. The most impressive signs of their wealth are furnished by their tombs, great stone chambers domed or vaulted and heaped over with earthen mounds: the scenes painted on the inner walls, no less than the sculptured urns, the bronze figures, mirrors and vessels, the ivories, the imported Greek vases and the exquisite gold smithery testify to a society that was not only affluent, but sophisticated and highly stratified. Politically the Etruscans were organized in self-governing cities, each with its dependent territory, a system which, as with the Greeks, was favourable to a high level of culture, but which was unable long to survive the pressure of larger and more coherent units. The overrunning of their territories in the Po basin by Celtic-speaking warriors between 450 and 350 B.C. began the process of disintegration which the Romans did so much to accelerate. By the middle of the third century B.C., indeed, Etruria had submitted to Rome, even if culturally the absorption was not complete until just before the beginning of the Christian era. Although the Roman republic ostensibly owed its birth to the expulsion of the Tarquinian dynasty and its growth was largely at the expense of the Etruscan state, Roman civilization was deeply indebted to the Etruscans: apart from their capital city and its forum, the Romans owed them many of their leading characteristics, such as their prowess with drains, their system of land survey by centuriation, their preoccupation with divination by the *haruspices* and, in the fasces, their very emblem of authority.

The Scyths

By the middle of the sixth century B.C. the Phoenicians, Carthaginians, Greeks and Etruscans had thus between them settled the coasts, islands and peninsulas of the Mediterranean Sea and had already begun to penetrate by means of trade and exploration the extensive territories to the north that still remained prehistoric. Before tracing the impact of these influences on the heirs of the Urnfield and earlier prehistoric inhabitants of western and middle Europe, it will be convenient to consider the nomad peoples of the Eurasian steppes, who contributed important influences of their own to the cultural life of the Celtic and Teutonic peoples. Everywhere the natural grasslands of the steppe were defined on the north by the forest zone. At their western extremity the steppes came down to the shores of the Euxine, and east of the Volga they graded on the south into deserts. In this way the steppes formed a natural corridor linking the northern margins of China with the Altai, the southern Urals, Caucasia and the southern Ukraine, along which nomad horse-riders could move rapidly. Moreover, the fact that the nomads depended for their bare existence on the natural pastures of the steppe meant that pressure at any one point was liable to involve progressive displacements of population over vast territories.

To gain a living from the steppe called for a highly specialized knowledge of animal husbandry and a notable degree of cultural adaptation, notably in riding, clothing and habitations, so it is hardly surprising that well-defined nomad groups did not make their appearance until well into the first millennium B.C. One of the first indications dates from the end of the ninth century, when fore-runners of the Huns began to harass peasant cultivators in the frontier lands of North China, and it may well have been the driving of these raiders to the west by the Chou emperor Suan that set in motion the widespread displacement of nomad groups which brought the Scyths to South Russia, probably around 700 B.C. Although mainly concentrated in the South Ukraine and the Kuban, the Scyths penetrated in some numbers into Hungary, where they formed immediate neighbours of the central European Celts, with whom they appear to have intermixed in Hungary and Transylvania. The Scyths were pre-eminently nomads: by the fifth century, it is true, some groups in contact with settled peoples had adopted agriculture and even occupied townships on the Dnieper and in the Crimea; but the overwhelming proportion were at home on the open steppe. There they subsisted to a large extent on mare's milk and cheese, helped out by game and fish. Ever on the move from one pasture to another, the men rode on ponies, on whose harness they lavished the best materials and the most skilled craftsmanship, and the women and children reclined in waggons under the shelter of felt roofs. It is likely that when stationary they lived in felt tents, which, to judge from the frozen tombs of the Altai, where such things survived in a wonderful state of preservation, had wool-pile rugs and brightly worked wall-hangings. Leather, wool, felt and fur provided materials for clothing, which in the case of men included soft boots, trousers for riding, jackets pulled in tight round the waist to allow maximum freedom in the use of the bow while in the saddle, and conical hats. They wore plenty of jewellery, and bronze mirrors of Greek manufacture or copied from Greek models were common possessions.

A notable feature of Scythic culture was the decorative art manifested in metal belt-plaques, harness-fittings, scabbards, dagger-hilts, drinking-vessels and jewellery and also in wood-carving, leather- and felt-work and even tattoo marks. Although much of the metal-work was executed by alien craftsmen and though the art derived elements from south-west Asia and Ionia, Scythic art was essentially barbaric in style and feeling. It was animated above all by a lively feeling for animals—stags, goats, lions and birds of prey prominent among them—such as one might expect to animate men who spent much of their life in the open and for whom hunting was a main interest. Yet there is a strong tendency towards stylization: the artist sometimes combined several aspects of a single animal into one representation, or he might use parts of one creature, such as the head and beak of a bird of prey, to enrich a representation of another quite different one; nor did he hesitate on occasion to contort and manipulate the beasts to conform to some decorative pattern. Among the tricks which the Scyths could have derived either from China or from south-west Asia, and which they probably transmitted in turn to Celtic art, was the rendering of projecting muscles on shoulders, haunches and other joints by means of curls.

As might be expected of a people to whom war, the chase and the management of animals were all-important, Scythic society was strongly masculine and authoritarian. This is strongly brought out in the burials, which seem to have provided a main focus of religious sentiment and which incidentally have yielded by far the greater part of our information about the Scyths. The dead were buried under barrows in chambers roofed over with timber and provided with grave-goods. In the case of the leaders the tombs were sometimes of vast size and the grave-goods of outstanding wealth. The barrows of the royal Scyths in the Alexandropol region of South Russia, for example, might range up to from 30 to 70 feet in height and from 400 to 1200 feet in circumference and the chamber might exceed 40 feet in depth below the old ground surface. The archaeological evidence strongly bears out the account left by Herodotus, who records that the body of the dead leader, having been embalmed, was laid on a waggon and for a period of forty days was drawn in procession round his territory. The great man would be accompanied to the grave, not merely by material possessions, such as clothing, jewellery, weapons, food, drink, drinking-vessels and containers, but also by his favourite horses, his wife and his chief servants, recalling the practices of the Han emperors of China or from much earlier times those of the Sumerian rulers, witnessed by the contents of the royal graves at Ur.

Hallstatt Iron Age

The spread of iron-working north of the Alps gave rise to a new group of cultures which takes its name from the cemetery of Hallstatt near Salzburg. Although most of the bearers of Hallstatt culture must have been direct descendants of the Urnfield people, the ruling class probably stemmed in part from the old Tumulus culture, and in part from immigrants from the east. The most notable find relating to the earlier phase of the Iron Age Hallstatt culture, defined by the characteristic long swords of bronze or iron with scabbards having metal terminals, or chapes, of winged type, are the burials of the chieftains. Instead of being cremated and deposited in flat urnfields, they were now inhumed under timber chambers covered by substantial burial mounds. Some of the richest burials in the cortical area of Austria, Bavaria and Bohemia have yielded remains of four-wheeled waggons that remind one vividly of the funeral carts described by Herodotus in connection with the burial of Scythic leaders. Although they had adopted iron-working for some purposes, the Hallstatt peoples made great use of bronze: for instance, they used a variety of vessels, helmets, shields and greaves of sheet bronze in the North Italian style, as well as a variety of smaller objects and ornaments; and on occasion they even made their characteristic swords in this metal. Whether these were really designed for fighting from horseback, as many have held, is far from certain. There is no doubt that the Hallstatt warriors rode horses, but there is no proof that they used them for true cavalry fighting; it could well be that they treated them, as the La Tène and other early charioteers did their vehicles, as means of transporting warriors to the most advantageous point for ground combat. In any case their ability to ride, which they doubtless owed to impulses from the east, enabled them to spread fairly rapidly over the old Urnfield territories in the west, down the Rhine to the Low Countries, into the Alpine area and across France to northern and central Iberia. In an opposite direction elements of Hallstatt culture appeared in several distinct Urnfield groups, among them the Lausitz culture, regarded by Polish prehistorians as the basis of the Slav people; the East Alpine, occupying much of the Middle Danube basin; and the Bosnian, extending over much of Yugoslavia south of the Sava and the Danube. The wealth of personal armament and above all the widespread prevalence of military defences in the form both of hill-forts and marsh-fortresses like Biskupin in Poland leave one in no doubt that the period was one of warlike activity, but how far the diffusion of Hallstatt types was due to mere fashion, how far to raids by warriors and how far to anything like folk-movements are problems which need to be considered on their merits in particular cases.

During the final phase of Hallstatt culture, defined by short swords and beginning around 500 B.C., the centre of gravity seems to have moved west, and it was then that Greek influence, stemming from the colony at Massilia and passing up the Rhône and across to the Upper Rhine and Danube, began to play directly, at least on the upper classes of Celtic society. The most numerous imports from the Greek world were concerned with wine-drinking, which seems to have been taken up by Celtic chieftains almost as a symbol of status: amphorae, still retaining traces of the pitch commonly added to wine in the Mediterranean down to the present day, pottery wine-cups, bronze mixing-bowls and flagons of Rhodian type combine to give a convincing picture of a trade symbolizing an influence that was to do far more than transform the drinking habits of the Celtic aristocracy. Another striking instance of Greek influence at this time is given by the brick bastions of the Heuneburg hill-fort near the headwaters of the Danube.

La Tène

During the last quarter of the fifth century a new art style, taking its name from the famous votive find of La Tène at the eastern end of Lake Neuchâtel in western Switzerland, came into being in the territory between the Upper Danube and the Marne. Many elements of La Tène art are most easily explained by the breakdown of Classical Greek motifs like the tendril and the palmette (an ornament with narrow divisions somewhat resembling a palm-leaf), in the hands of craftsmen schooled in the geometric Hallstatt style. Some of the earliest vehicles of Greek art to reach the area in question were bronze wine-flagons with beaked spouts, manufactured in the Etruscan workshops of the Po Valley, but carrying Greek patterns on the handle-attachments, which crossed the Alpine passes in the course of trade; it was not until the conquest of the Po Valley by Celtic-speaking people and the inauguration of Cisalpine Gaul around the middle of the fourth century that contacts with Italo-Greek art proceeded on a broader front. The fantastic treatment of animals or parts of them was on the other hand almost certainly derived from the Scyths, who as we have seen were immediate neighbours of the Hallstatt peoples in east central Europe. Celtic society was oraganized on an aristocratic basis and the finest products of La Tène art flashed in bronze or gold on the helmets, shields, spears, scabbards, harness-mounts, lynch-pins and terret-rings (driving rein rings) of warriors, their horses and their chariots as well as on the head, limbs and clothing of their women; but some of the basic motifs were reflected in the work of humble potters and wood-carvers. From its original focal area La Tène art spread east into the Danube Valley, where was probably made the silver vessel found in the bog of Gundestrup (Pl. VII) in Denmark, south into Cisalpine Gaul and west and north over France, the Low Countries and the British Isles. Over the whole of this territory it continued to flourish until replaced by Roman provincial culture within the advancing frontiers of the Empire; and on the far north-west perimeter of Europe, in Ireland and the highland zone of Britain, it continued to survive until much later historical times.

During the prehistoric La Tène period the Celtic peoples of Gaul and Britain borrowed much from their more civilized contemporaries in the south. Thus, the revival of chariots was almost certainly due to contacts with the Etruscans. Again, during middle La Tène times the rotary lathe, used mainly for working wood and shale, reached south-west Germany from North Italy, where it had been introduced by the Etruscans, and from there spread widely over temperate Europe. The rotary quern, invented in the Graeco-Roman world for large-scale milling by means of donkeys and slaves, was introduced to barbarian Europe in the portable form used by legionary troops. The native coinage developed in Gaul stemmed from two main sources: the gold coinage was modelled on Macedonian staters; and the silver one on coins of Massilia and the western Greek colonies. The appearance of native coinage in Gaul, and in due course in southern Britain, marked an important advance in political consciousness and organization and it is significant that the late La Tène period also witnessed the development in Gaul and South Germany of the considerable fortified townships or *oppida* described and in some cases stormed by Caesar.

Expansion of the Roman Empire

Meanwhile the tiny and rather rustic Roman republic, born in 509 B.C. of the eviction of the Tarquins, was making ready to extend the boundaries of the civilized world. By the time the Gauls irrupted into Italy around 400 B.C. the Romans had began to dominate their Latin neighbours, but it was not until the victory of Sentinum in 295 B.C. that they finally emerged as the dominant power in middle Italy. In the second stage of their expansion they consolidated their hold on Italy as a whole: they began by bringing under control the Greek colonies of Magna Graecia, went on to evict the Carthaginians from Sicily in the course of the First Punic War (264–241 B.C.) and within the next twenty years had subdued the Po Valley. The third stage, during which they gained control of the Mediterranean, was initiated by the Second Punic War (218–201 B.C.), which not only brought them Spain, but also, as a result of the battle of Zama, Carthage itself and with it full control of the straits of Sicily; further than that, through the Carthaginian alliance with Macedon, Rome became involved in campaigns in the East Mediterranean which led indirectly to the conquest of Pergamum and so to Roman intervention in the affairs of Asia. The annexation of Syria and Crete in 62 B.C., and of Egypt in 30 B.C., virtually completed the encirclement of the Mediterranean, which became in effect a Roman lake. Meanwhile the fourth and final phase of expansion, during which the Romans incorporated within the Empire most of the remaining territories of the Celtic La Tène peoples, had already been initiated with the conquest of the rest of Gaul by Caesar between 59 and 51 B.C. The subjugation of Britain, much of the southern part of which had since Caesar's incursion been subject to strong influences from Roman Gaul, was begun by Claudius between A.D. 43 and 47 and completed even beyond the Firth of Forth by Agricola (A.D. 78–84), appointed for the task by Vespasian. By the death of Trajan in A.D. 117 the Empire had reached the Rhine–Danube line, which it was destined to hold until the collapse of imperial authority in the west; and beyond this it had extended to the Low Countries, the enclave between the Middle Rhine and the Upper Danube, and the province of Dacia.

The Germanic Iron Age and the migration period

Meanwhile, beyond the most extended limits of the Empire the forces that were ultimately to disrupt it were gathering strength.

The heirs of the Nordic Bronze Age had acquired a knowledge of iron-working from the south by around 400 B.C.: during the ensuing four centuries they drew their main inspiration from the Celtic La Tène peoples with whom they came into contact on their southern borders; but during the opening centuries of the Christian era they came predominantly under Roman influence. By means of trade, to quote just one instance, bronze accessories of wine-drinking, manufactured in Italy, Gaul or the Rhineland, were taken into use by prosperous farmers as far north as the Trondelag; but even more important than trade in many respects was the return of individuals from service in the Empire. Thus the free Germans were growing in wealth and knowledge at a time when the inhabitants of the Roman provinces were being thwarted by bureaucratic interference and fiscal exactions; moreover the provincials' power of war-like resistance was progressively lowered by the very peace secured within the frontiers by an army in which the barbarian element was ever on the increase. Beyond the frontiers the small possibility of internal growth allowed by subsistence farming and the barrier to northward colonization set by the adverse climate of Sub-atlantic times led inevitably to southern thrusts of population. The first of these indentified in history was the drive of the Teutones and Cimbri from northern Jutland, that began in 120 B.C. and was only checked by the destruction of the Teutones on the field of battle near Aix-en-Provence in 102 B.C. More widespread movements occurred during the second century A.D., when for example the Goths crossed the Baltic from their homeland in South Sweden and drove north of the Carpathians down to the region of Olbia on the north-east shore of the Black Sea. Such movements as these increased the flow of new ideas back to the old homelands. It was from the Goths in their new territories that many exports from the Roman world, and art conventions from the steppes, reached the north. Another feature to spread north was the runic script, first adapted from the Latin in all probability by the Marcomanni of Bohemia, a script that was to reach Britain with the Anglo-Saxon invaders and to survive in Scandinavia in full flower down to the Christian Middle Ages.

Although it has been argued that westward thrusts of Huns from the steppes, by engaging the eastern Germans delayed their assault on Italy, in the long run it was the complex system of folk-movements which they set in motion that brought down the Empire in the west. The death of Theodosius I in A.D. 395 and the division of the Empire, the Latin west falling to Honorius and the Greek east to Arcadius, was the signal for wholesale invasions. The full brunt of these was borne by the western half of the empire. Although the formal end, symbolized by the deposition of Romulus Augustulus, was delayed until 476, the invasion of Italy and the sack of Rome by Alaric and his Visigoths in 410 was really decisive in that, bereft of an effective head, the provincial limbs proved unable to withstand the multiple and often lightning thrusts of the barbarians (Pl. VIII). No account of these can be offered here, but it is important to recognize a primary distinction between those of the eastern and western Germans. Whereas relatively small bands of the former, Visigoths, Ostrogoths, Burgundians, Lombards and Vandals, penetrated great distances and left little ethnic trace behind—the last-mentioned for example passed through Gaul and Spain and across North Africa to fall upon Rome from the Carthaginian shore—the latter, spreading only over neighbouring territories, laid the foundations of Anglo-Saxon Britain and Frankish Gaul.

The spread of Christianity

The prehistoric peoples beyond the old imperial frontiers were first brought within the sphere of civilization by Christian missionaries. Although subject at times to severe persecution, Christianity spread widely throughout the Empire during the Antonine period (138–92) and between 313 and 325 it achieved a settled status through its recognition by Constantine and the clarification of its doctrines at the council of Nicaea. When the western Empire collapsed, much of its ecclesiastical organization survived even though in the areas most overrun by barbarians there was some relapse into paganism. Thus the continuity of civilized life in south-east Britain was so disrupted by the Anglo-Saxon invaders that Christianity had to be reintroduced from Rome when more settled conditions set in by the end of the sixth century. In the long run the Anglo-Saxons brought about an enlargement of the Christian world by displacing Christians from the most populous parts of the Roman province and driving them to the remoter parts of Britain and even across the sea to Ireland. As a result thriving centres of Celtic Christianity grew up in northern Britain and in the far west, separated from the remainder of Christendom by a welter of Germanic barbarians, and it was only during a lengthy period after St Augustine's mission (597), in the aftermath of which the Synod of Whitby (663-4) was an outstanding episode, that the two were reunited. Even so the Celtic church continued as in a sense a separate force, making for example a distinctive contribution to the conversion of Bavaria and West Germany.

The bringing in of northern and eastern Germany had to wait on political progress. The defeat of the Huns at Troyes (451) and the conversion of the Frankish ruler Clovis to Christianity encouraged the emergence of a well-founded state under the Merovingian dynasty (486-751). Great advances were made under Charlemagne, who extended the Frankish frontiers to the Elbe and the Pyrenees and was crowned in the year 800 as emperor of the Romans at the hands of Pope Leo III. Yet the ninth century was to witness the temporary return of conditions reminiscent of those prevailing some four hundred years earlier, with Vikings taking the place of Germans and Magyars that of Huns: the former issued from Scandinavia to ravage the coasts of the Baltic, the North Sea, the Western Isles, the Irish Sea, the English Channel, the Bay of Biscay and even the West Mediterranean; and the latter, of remotely east Ural origin, were pushed by the advancing Petcheneg hordes from their immediate homeland in the Ukraine across the

VII   Representation of the Celtic god Cernunnus on a panel of the
bowl from Gundestrup, Denmark

(*facing p.* 176)

VIII   Bronze mould showing Teutonic personages of the Migration
Period, Torslunda, Sweden

Carpathians into the Middle Danube basin, where their forays terrorized more settled peoples.

It was not until the middle of the tenth century, after half a millennium of unrest, that the German kings Henry the Fowler and Otto were able to establish more or less settled conditions in central Europe, the latter beating the Hungarians decisively at Lech and reviving the Holy Roman Empire at his crowning in 962. The extension of Christianity and indeed of literate civilization itself to the remaining parts of Europe was the work of missionary endeavour from Rome and Byzantium, the twin capitals of the Roman Empire. Henry and Otto had carried the frontier up to the Oder and the closing years of the first millennium were marked by a series of dramatic advances, among them St Adalbert's mission to Prussia (997), the adhesion of Hungary (1000), the conversion of Olaf Tryggvason, king of Norway (995–1000) and a former Viking, and the establishment of Christianity in Sweden, whence in the twelfth century missionaries crossed to Finland. Meanwhile Byzantine missions had already before the end of the ninth century gone among the Bulgars, Croats and Serbs. In 988 Vladimir the prince of Kiev introduced Christianity to his dominions, which extended north to Novgorod over territory crossed by the old trade routes linking the Swedish Vikings with Byzantium. Pressure of nomads from the eastern steppes led to Novgorod taking the lead from Kiev during the later twelfth century, but during the fourteenth and fifteenth centuries Moscow rose to prominence, and when at length the ancient capital of the East Roman Empire fell to the Turks it was to the metropolitan of Moscow that the headship of Orthodox Christianity passed and it was the principality of Moscow that formed the core of the future Russian Empire. It was the expansion of Muscovite power and Orthodox Christianity that brought the remaining areas of prehistoric Europe within range of literate tradition. By the death of Ivan III in 1505 the frontiers had reached the Arctic territories and the Urals and the prehistory of Europe was to all intents and purposes concluded.

A counterpart to the northward expansion of Christianity, which followed the achievement of more stable conditions towards the end of the first millennium, is to be seen in the staying and reversal of Islamic expansion in the south. Within twelve years of Mohammed's death in 632 his followers had overrun much of the Byzantine Empire, including Cyrenaica, Palestine, Syria and Iraq, and in addition Persia and Armenia; and by 700 they had added to their conquests the rest of North Africa, Afghanistan, West Turkestan and north-west India. At the peak of their power in the mid-tenth century the Moslems had come near to engulfing the entire Mediterranean, having occupied most of Spain, as well as Provence, Sicily and South Italy, and threatened Asia Minor and Byzantium itself. From this point of view the stability that made possible the Crusades came to Christian Europe only just in time: in the event not only was all Spain regained by the middle of the thirteenth century, but the fall of Byzantium was delayed sufficiently long for it to be in some respects an advantage to western Christendom.

The age of exploration

By the middle of the thirteenth century Christendom was no longer on the defensive in the west and was indeed ready to reach out into other continents. Already by 1260 Venetian and soon after Genoese merchants had begun to establish trade relations with China from bases in the Crimea using the same route as that followed a thousand years previously for conveying silk to the Roman world; and during the earlier half of the fourteenth century envoys were reaching China by sea from the Persian Gulf. The conditions on which this eastern trade was based ceased to exist when the Mongol was replaced by the Chinese Ming dynasty (1368/70) and xenophobic influences regained the upper hand. The Europeans had to turn elsewhere for the spices and other eastern produce to which they had become accustomed. A new age of geographical discovery and as it turned out a new era in the history of mankind was inaugurated, in which the lead passed from the Mediterranean to the nations of the Atlantic sea-board. The Portuguese began by edging round the west coast of Africa and by 1498 had succeeded in reaching India by way of the Cape of Good Hope (see p. 117). Meanwhile, six years before Vasco da Gama's culminating exploit, Christopher Columbus, a Genoese holding the commission of Ferdinand and Isabella of Spain, made landfall on one of the Bahama islands and before returning planted a small colony of Spaniards on Haiti. Christendom had thus in the course of two or three centuries initiated a process that within the ensuing three or four was destined to bring the whole world within the purview of literate civilization.

CHAPTER 8

INDIA AND THE FAR EAST

INDIA

India, like the greater part of Africa, lay outside the realm of the Advanced Palaeolithic peoples whose successors initiated early in the Neothermal period the processes that led in due course to the emergence of civilized life in the Old World. At a time when tells, marking permanent settlements by peoples subsisting on the products of cereal farming and stock-raising, had for centuries been incorporating the ruins of successive houses and temples over a great tract from Palestine, Cilicia and Syria to northern Mesopotamia and the Iranian plateau, the greater part of the Indian subcontinent remained the refuge of low-grade hunter-fishers, whose microlithic flint-work stemmed from Lower Palaeolithic sources (see p. 49).

Early farmers in Baluchistan and Sind

The earliest traces of communities based on farming in India are confined to Baluchistan and to a contiguous area of Sind on the right bank of the lower reaches of the river Indus (Map 5). At the present day Baluchistan is so arid that most of the inhabitants are perforce nomadic, but the numerous tells indicating permanent settlement, together with the stone-built dams (*gabarbands*), suggest that rainfall must have been higher during the third millennium than it is to-day. Although a few of the mounds have yielded assemblages lacking in pottery or with only hand-made wares, as in the first and second phases respectively of the site of Kile Gul Muhammed, near Quetta, the great majority relate to communities using copper tools and turning pottery on the wheel.

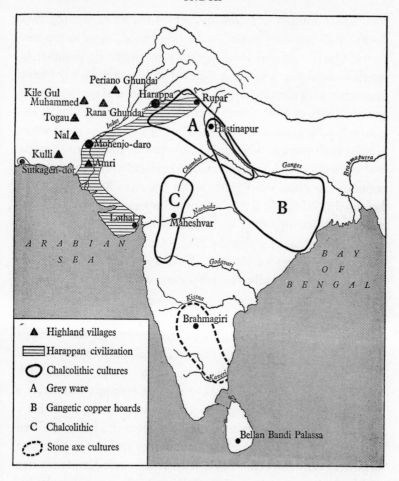

5. The Indian sub-continent in late prehistoric times (*c.* 2500–500 B.C.).

Several distinct varieties of wheel-turned pottery have been detected in different parts of the territory, differing in the colour of the ware and the character of the designs painted on its surface, local differences analogous to those observed over the same territory in the designs of rugs made at the present day. Wares of reddish hue are found in the Zhob valley in the north and again in central Baluchistan, where the Togau pottery exhibits designs based on naturalistic animals and humans and on friezes of stylized ibex heads. Buff-coloured wares, on the other hand, occur in the area round Quetta, painted predominantly in geometric designs; in south Baluchistan, where the Nal and Kulli wares each combine geometric with naturalistic and stylized animal designs; and in the outlying area of Sind, where Amri ware was painted almost exclusively with geometric designs. The chronology of these wares relative both to one another and to the urban civilization of Harappa and Mohenjo-daro is still uncertain. Yet already it seems clear that some of the Zhob and Quetta wares began to be manufactured before that of Amri, a fact of some importance when it is remembered that this ware underlay remains of the Indus Valley civilization at several sites in Sind. On the other hand many of the hill-villages of the Nal, Kulli and Quetta groups were without doubt broadly contemporary with the great riverine civilization.

Too little is yet known about antecedent stages in the human settlement of the Indus Valley for the origins of the Harappa civilization to be anything but obscure. Yet already it is known that painted wares of ultimately Iranian origin—Amri ware in Sind, and Rana Ghundai (Zhob Valley) ware at Harappa—underlay a number of the settlements, and it can hardly be doubted that a formative part was played by colonists from the hills, endowed with a technology that included metallurgy and the manufacture of pottery on the wheel. What is more problematical, and too often overlooked, is the contribution made by the aboriginal population, most probably represented by the proto-Australoid stock which, together with Mediterranean and Alpine elements, made up the population buried in cemeteries of the Indus Valley people. Direct contacts with the older civilization of Sumer, for which concrete evidence exists mainly in the form of small objects of value, such as engraved seal-stones and etched beads, may well have provided stimuli, but one has only to compare the Indus Valley and Sumerian civilizations to see that they are distinct and largely independent entities. Both responded to the challenge and opportunity of great river plains on each flank of a vast highland region peopled with settled metal-using farmers who delighted to decorate their wheel-turned wares in paint.

Indus Valley civilization

Thanks to the trade contacts just mentioned, it is possible to say that, by around 2500 B.C., the Indus Valley civilization had assumed the form it was destined to maintain with comparatively little change over the best part of a millennium. Geographically it covered a larger area than either the Egyptian or Sumerian civilizations: the great metropolitan centres, Harappa on the river Ravi and Mohenjo-daro lower down on the main river, were themselves over 350 miles apart as the crow flies; but smaller townships and trading centres covered a much more extensive area from the foot of the Simla hills to the neighbourhood of Karachi, nearly 700 miles apart, and again over a distance of some 950 miles extending from Sutkagen-dor near the coast of the Arabian Sea to Lothal and Rangpur in Gujarat.

Culturally speaking the Indus Valley people (Pl. IX) stood at a level comparable with that of the Early Dynastic peoples of Egypt and Sumer. They inhabited cities with monumental architecture and exercised political authority over extensive territories. Economically they could show a relatively advanced degree of subdivision of labour: urban populations were maintained on food grown in surrounding rural areas; many distinct crafts were practised, including metallurgy, potting on the wheel, faience-manufacture and gem-cutting; and trade connections were maintained by means of ships with lands as far afield as Sumer. On the intellectual level they had achieved partial literacy, even if their script, essentially pictographic in character and mainly engraved on seals, though also stamped or scratched on pottery and inscribed on small copper tablets, is confined to texts of hardly more than twenty characters that have yet to be deciphered.

On the other hand the general configuration of the Indus civilization was quite distinct. The leading characteristics betrayed by the excavated remains include a high degree of civic discipline and organization, uniformity over an extensive area and stability over long periods of time. The rectangular grid of the street plan, differing so notably from the cramped irregularity prevalent in ancient Mesopotamia, the elaborate system of sewers and rubbish shoots, the carefully maintained wells, the great communal granaries and the standardized systems of weights and measures all reflect an ordered and settled society. What was the basis of this discipline maintained over so long a period of time? There is no indication that military authority was at all prominent: weapons were relatively inconspicuous and defences were apparently confined to the citadels, a reflection no doubt of the comparative isolation of the Indus people from neighbours at a comparable level of technology. Nor has any obvious sign of royal authority been found, whether in the form of palaces, outstanding tombs or regalia. A likely alternative is that the sanctions behind this ordered way of life were religious and that the Indus Valley civilization, like that of modern Tibet, was essentially theocratic. The existence of a definite institutionalized form of authority seems to be indicated by the great citadels at each of the capital cities, which stand to a present height of some 40 feet and measure between 200–300 by 450–500 yards in length and breadth. The buildings on the citadel at Harappa were too much robbed to interpret, but those at Mohenjo-daro, though incompletely explored, are of outstanding interest: in addition to a massive granary and loading platform, the citadel was crowned by a great bath or tank surrounded by a veranda and cell-like rooms suitable for changing, the whole suggestive of ceremonial cleansings, such as are featured by modern Hinduism; and close by was an extensive range of buildings that may have housed a high priest or even a college of priests or monks. As to the religious life of the people, there is evidence, in the form of numerous terra-cotta figurines, of a domestic cult of the mother goddess, a widespread feature of the ancient world. Of special interest are features which, like the bathing tank already mentioned, suggest a pre-Aryan beginning for modern Hindu practices: these include stones suggestive of phallus- or *linga*-worship and a variety of deities engraved on seals, including ones combining animal and human characteristics: in particular a figure with a horned head-dress and arms loaded with bracelets, squatting on a low seat, an evident prototype of Síva in his aspect of Lord of the Beasts.

It may well be asked why so well-organized and stable a civilization should have collapsed apparently so suddenly. The possibility should not be overlooked of an ecological upset sufficient to disturb irretrievably a finely balanced economy. There are many signs that in the Indus Valley, as on the highlands, rainfall was substantially higher when the civilization was taking shape during the third millennium than it has since been, and it is likely that the adverse effects of any decline in rainfall would have been magnified by deforestation brought about by the need for timber for the brick-kilns and other industrial purposes and by the effect of grazing by livestock. Any serious weakening of the rural economy would soon have brought down the urban superstructure in ruin. Yet there is no satisfactory evidence that the civilization was dying from the roots. The oft-cited evidence for civic disorganization during the final phase of Mohenjo-daro, the hovels and kilns encroaching on the streets, may well in fact relate to more barbarous peoples camping in the city after its fall and it is worthy of note that many of the best works of art came from the upper levels. While it is possible that resistance was weakened by some underlying ecological cause, it seems certain that the Indus Valley civilization, essentially civilian in character, was toppled over by assault on the part of barbarous but militarily effective invaders; vivid evidence of massacre is provided by the skeletons of men, women and children, some bearing clear marks of sword-cuts on their skulls, lying unburied in the streets of Mohenjo-daro.

The Aryans

There are many indications that the opening centuries of the second millennium were a period of widespread folk movement over much of temperate Europe and western Asia, and it may well be that it was through this movement that climatic change exerted its most powerful influence. Even a slight reduction of rainfall among peoples living close to the margin of subsistence in the confined valleys of Baluchistan and the contiguous highland zone may well have been enough to trigger off a series of movements of people, and it is doubtless in such a context that we must view the burning of Baluchi villages and possibly, even at some remove, the fall of the Indus Valley civilization. The suggestion has often been made that the agents of at least some of this destruction may have been Aryans or refugees displaced by their incursions. As we know them from the Rigveda—a collection of upwards of a thousand hymns, spells, prayers and epic-chants, first committed to writing in the late eighteenth or early nineteenth centuries, but composed by the Aryan priests during the latter half of the second millennium B.C.—the Aryans were barbarians who lived in houses of timber and thatch; worked bronze, but were not yet acquainted with iron; and gained a livelihood by stock-raising and cereal farming. Their leaders were hard-drinking cattle-raiders whose horse-drawn chariots, used for war and sport, closely resembled those of the Hittites, Mitannians and Mycenaeans, and their priests, who composed the Vedic hymns, ministered to a pantheon of gods headed by Indra, an apotheosis of the war-leader. Attempts to identify the intruders described in the literature with specific archaeological material are bound in the absence of coins or inscriptions to rest on conjecture, and this is likely to be particularly hazardous for the initial period when the warriors travelled light and brought peoples of higher culture into subjection.

Until recently very little indeed was known archaeologically of the long period during which the Aryans first consolidated their hold on the Upper Indus basin, established a main base in the Bramavata, expanded into the Gangetic basin and laid the foundations for the dynasties of the historical period. Latterly research has been concentrated on this gap, in many respects the most formative phase of Indian prehistory, and this has led to the recognition at a number of sites between the Sutlej and the Upper Ganges and Jumna rivers of a culture defined by a grey ware made from well-levigated clay, having a smooth surface and decorated in matt black paint with dotted and linear patterns. The fact that this painted grey ware overlies Harappa ware, occurs at many traditional sites and occupies approximately the area of the Bramavata, has suggested that it relates in some way to the Aryans, though it is important to note that there is as yet no firm indication of its absolute age. Of the fact of the Aryan conquests and of the general lines of their advance traditional sources leave no doubt, but it seems certain that these were much less disruptive of continuity than the composers of the epics would have us believe. One reason for this view lies in the pre-Aryan elements in Hindu religion, elements which we encountered in the Indus Valley civilization and which include phallicism, ritual cleansing by bathing, reverence for animals and the attributes of Síva. The ancient emphasis on kinship between animals and men, for example, which may well go back to a pre-Harappan stage in India, contributed to ideas concerning re-incarnation in the guise of animals, which in turn led to abstention from their flesh, concepts in marked contrast with beliefs about personal immortality and the future life entertained by the Aryans and with the emphasis on meat-eating in the Vedic tradition. No doubt the conquerors consorted far more with the despised peoples of the Indus Valley than their panegyrists allowed, even if it should prove that this admixture was more pronounced in marginal territories.

Chalcolithic of the Ganges and the northern Deccan

While there is no evidence that the Harappans were able to withdraw in compact units and colonize territories to the south or east, there is a distinct possibility that refugees may have contributed to the culture of such regions and in this way have helped perpetuate some of the old traditions. In this connection mention should be made of hoards of copper objects from the Gangetic basin found in two main groups, one in the Upper Ganges and Jumna valleys, the other centering on the Ranchi plateau of Bihar and extending south into Orissa, and each corresponding to early centres of copper production. Although clearly stemming from the Harappan school of metallurgy, the Gangetic types show considerable differences: flat axes, for instance, having more constricted butts and expanded cutting-edges, as well as entirely new forms like harpoon-heads barbed on either edge which were doubtless suggested by ones made by the hunter-fisher peoples of the Ganges from more perishable substances. Unfortunately little is known of the age of these hoards, except that they appear to be associated with ochre-coloured pottery like that found stratified below painted grey ware at Hastinapur.

Again, communities occupying the region between the Upper Chambal and Godavari basins in Malwan and the western part of the northern Deccan seem to have shared in a devolved form certain attributes of the Harappan culture, though living at a humbler standard much more equivalent to that of the hill-villages of Baluchistan. Recent radio-carbon determinations from the Maheswar settlement in the Narbada Valley suggests that this Chalcolithic culture may have begun in this region around 1500 B.C.; and it appears to have been brought to an end by the spread of iron technology around 400 to 500 B.C. The people lived close to the soil in houses of wood, wattle and daub. Their flint industry resembled that of the Harappans in that it was based on the production of blades from carefully prepared cores and included some simple forms of microlith; they made use of copper, though more sparingly; their pottery, red in colour and painted in black with geometric patterns and floral, animal and human representations, was turned on the wheel; and their personal ornaments significantly included beads of faience, as well as of agate and carnelian.

Stone-axe cultures of the Kistna-Cauvery area

Further south one encounters cultures at successively lower levels of complexity. From the Kistna to the Kaveri basins there flourished the South Indian Stone-axe culture first found clearly stratified at Brahmagiri. The stone axes, which generally had pointed butts and lozenge sections and were manufactured at factory-sites located close to the sources of raw material, were presumably used first and foremost by comparatively primitive agriculturists, unable to afford metal axes, for clearing forest and working timber. Copper was very rare, and the pottery was hand-made rather than turned on the wheel. On the other hand the blade technique of the Stone-axe people, the prepared cores and simple forms of microlith, all match closely the flint inventory of the marginal Chalcolithic and Harappan culture areas. To judge from the rock-engravings clustering round the stone-axe sites in certain localities and presumably related to the same culture, hunting was carried on as well as the keeping of long-horned cattle, terracotta figurines of which have also been found at Piklihal. The Stone-axe cultures occupied the marginal zone of farming that encroached on the hunter-fisher economy practised by the mesolithic aborigines of the sub-continent, and in turn persisted down to the spread of iron-technology during the closing centuries of the first millennium B.C.

Hunter-fishers of the extreme south and Ceylon

Lastly, in the extremity of the sub-continent, and notably in Ceylon, the hunter-fishers maintained their old way of life into the historic period, continuing to arm their arrows with microliths chipped from quartz and other materials. Although polished axes failed to penetrate this zone, some of the 'Mesolithic' people in this area acquired the art of potting, for instance those who left the midden of Bellan Bändi Palässa in Ceylon, dated by C^{14} analysis to around the beginning of the Christian era.

Spread of iron-working

The use of iron, by whatever means it was introduced, spread rapidly over the sub-continent during the latter half of the first millennium B.C. and incorporated within one technology agricultural communities relying hitherto on copper or stone. At the same time new classes of pottery made their appearance: Northern Black Polished ware from the Gangetic plain to the Godavari and Black-and-Red ware over much of the rest of the Deccan. Moreover, megalithic tombs came into use over large tracts of southern India: the chambers, designed to receive the long bones and skulls of up to half a dozen bodies, from which the fleshy parts had decayed, were partly sunk in the ground, frequently had a port-hole entrance through one slab and were protected by dry-stone walling that might be supplemented by a circle of undressed boulders. With these changes the prehistory of all but the most backward parts of India was ended, even if the beginnings of recorded history are still very obscure.

The Mauryan Empire

It is possible to infer the existence during the later Vedic period of numerous warring kingdoms in the northern part of the country, and it was no doubt this that made it comparatively easy for the invader. The conquest of the northern Punjab by Darius in 516 B.C. and its incorporation as a satrapy within the Persian Empire seems to have had no wider repercussions in India. The impact of Alexander the Great, who entered the country by the Kabul river in 327 B.C. and pressed down the length of the Indus basin, proved to be much greater: by playing off one petty king against another he succeeded not only in conquering a remote province, but in arousing strong centralizing forces. Alexander's death at Babylon in 323 B.C. was the signal for something like a national rising and led to the establishment by Chandragupta Maurya of a dynasty that marks the true beginning of an Indian history. As we know from the report of the Greek Megasthenes at the Mauryan court, even in Chandragupta's lifetime northern India was administered by an elaborately organized bureaucracy. By adding the Gangetic plain to that of the Indus, Chandragupta laid a firm basis from which his grandson Aśoka was able to extend the Mauryan Empire to the limits of the wide territories over which a farming economy prevailed, as far south as the northern limits of Mysore. One of the main forces that impelled Aśoka was his conversion to the teaching of Buddha (c. 560–480 B.C.) and, indeed, it is propaganda for his faith cut into rock-surfaces in Brāhmī script (incidentally the earliest inscriptions to survive in India since the eclipse of the Indus Valley civilization) that most clearly defines the extent of his realms. Yet as an organized religion Buddhism failed to endure in India. It needed the invasion and conquest of the north by Arabs, Afghans, Pathans and others of Moslem faith between the tenth and twelfth centuries A.D. to detach any substantial part of the sub-continent from the ways of Hinduism, based as these were on the Aryan conquest, but stemming in part from Harappan and possibly even more ancient sources.

CHINA

Chinese civilization originated and took the form destined to endure in essentials down to modern times in the basin of the Hwango-ho, and it was not until the period of the Han dynasty (202 B.C.–A.D. 9) that its centre of gravity shifted south to the Yangtze river. Among the factors favouring the north were its situation and its soil: geographically it formed part of the vast temperate zone of East Asia, extending southward from the Amur basin, and at the same time was accessible, albeit remotely, by routes skirting north of the Tibetan plateau, to influences from early centres of Old World civilization; and geologically the loess, that blanketed high ground in Shansi, Shensi and Kansu and spread over much of the North China plain in the form of alluvium brought down by the Yellow River, endowed it with a soil at once fertile and easily worked. Yet, though the northern part of the country enjoyed certain advantages over the south during the initial formative stages, the whole of China was relatively remote from the focal area of Old World civilization, and the appearance of settled life based on farming was correspondingly retarded.

Hunter-fishers

The extent to which China was occupied by hunter-fisher peoples during early Neothermal times is still uncertain, and it has even been suggested that there was a break at this time in the human settlement of what was destined to be the cradle of Chinese civilization. The probability remains that the Late Pleistocene hunters of the Ordos desert and Choukoutien represent a population that survived into the Neothermal period and that future research will reveal their presence. North of the Great Wall in the Gobi and the highlands of Manchuria, marginal areas in which hunter-fishers in fact maintained their mode of life throughout the prehistoric and early historic periods of the Hwang-ho basin, there are flint industries with microlithic blades like those used as insets for slotted bone tools in the Advanced Palaeolithic, Mesolithic and Sub-neolithic industries of Siberia. Further south, traces of crude pebble industries, that stem ultimately from a tradition going back to Middle Pleistocene time, have been found on the surface in the old forested areas of Szechwan on the Upper Yangtze and in lime-stone caves at Kwei-lin and Wu-ming in Kwangsi, associated with pebbles with hour-glass perforation and tools of antler and bone. Although there is thus evidence for the occupation of different parts of China by hunter-fishers during the Neothermal period, there is nothing to suggest the existence of conditions likely to have given rise to the independent invention of farming in the Hwang-ho basin, and the mere fact that the earliest evidence for this comes from the part of China most accessible to influences from the west goes to emphasize that the Neolithic way of life was intrusive.

Neolithic peasants of North China

The material equipment of the Neolithic peoples of North China, notably the hand-made pottery with textured surface and the extensive use of polished stone for wood-working equipment, knives and projectile-heads, falls broadly speaking into the same category as that associated with Sub-neolithic groups over a large part of the circumpolar zone. On the other hand one can hardly look to the north as a source of domestication, and it seems that to account for this and for such cultural innovations as painting pottery and in due course bronze metallurgy it is necessary to turn to the west. The most likely route linking the Hwang-ho basin with early centres of farming in west-central Asia is that later followed by the silk route, skirting south of the Gobi and traversing Sinkiang by way of the Tarim basin and Kashgar.

The probability is that while the earliest farmers of North China were laying the foundations of settled life the loess still carried forest vegetation, and that, like the Danubians of central Europe, they practised 'slash and burn' agriculture while maintaining livestock largely on forest products. Their main crop was millet and their most important domestic animals the pig and the dog. It is evident that the peasants lived in substantial village communities—the settlement of Pan Po near Sian in Shensi seems to have covered about 2½ acres—but the nature of their economy involved movement at fairly frequent intervals; and though they seem, like their analogues on the European loess, to have resettled the same site several times over, they never stayed long enough to accumulate tells like those of the Near East. This, and the fact that the loess soil has been intensively dug over and cultivated, has made it difficult to recover detailed information about the nature of the settlements and above all about their history. Although, as we shall see, different groups can be distinguished by their pottery, the Neolithic peasants shared in other respects the same basic culture. Their houses, which might be round, or rectangular with rounded corners, and were sometimes sunk into the subsoil, were built of wattle and daub, the roof being carried on timber posts. The floors and inner faces of the walls of the Pan Po houses were plastered. Partition walls joining the front roof uprights to either side of the entrance formed a kind of internal porch, the roof of which was no doubt raised to allow easy access, and a clay oven set in the middle of the house between the roof posts helped to keep the interior warm in winter as well as providing for cooking. Crops were stored in beehive pits sunk into the loess, the walls being undercut to reduce the size of the aperture. Burial was by inhumation; children were often placed in pots among the houses; but adults were buried in cemeteries away from the settlement, sometimes in plank-lined graves and as a rule accompanied by rich grave goods that might include a dozen pots as well as other things. The skeletal remains suggest that Neolithic peasants were already of essentially the same racial type as that predominant in North China at the present day.

Important light is thrown both on their mode of life and their affiliations by the minor artifacts. The widely distributed stone axes, pecked out of hard rock and polished at the edges, point to forest clearance, as do the bevelled adze-blades to the working of timber. That hunting continued to play an important role is suggested by the wealth of leaf-shaped and tanged arrow-heads, commonly made from polished stone or bone and more rarely of shell or bifacially flaked stone. Among the more frequent artifacts were the stone knife-blades of lunate or oblong form, polished on either face and along the edge and perforated to secure the handle, tools which find ready analogies in north-east Asia and even in the Eskimo territories of North America. Another trait widely spread over northern Eurasia and North America is the bone handle slotted to receive flint flakes, examples of which have been met with, though rarely, in Kansu. Of more significance is the general emphasis on polishing rather than flaking stone artifacts and the use of bone for a wide range of tools and projectile heads.

Grey, Yang-shao and Lung-shan wares

Into this same context fits the hand-made grey pottery with textured surface that is predominant in North China, occurring both separately and alongside each of the other leading wares and surviving to provide the bulk of the pottery used under the Shang dynasty. The roughening of the surface was done by impressing basketwork, cords and toothed combs, as was the case over vast tracts of Russia from Karelia to Lake Baikal and the Lena River and from the Pontic steppes to Turkestan; but during the Shang period a similar effect was produced by a wooden beater or paddle with a grooved surface or wrapped with cord or textile, a technique which seems to have spread from South China.

The shapes of the grey ware pots in North China conformed to those of the red and black wares next to be described (Map 6). The red ware, often named after the site of Yang-shao in western Honan, extends over the loess territories of northern Honan, southern Shansi, a zone across Shensi and much of the southern half of Kansu, where it reached across the frontier almost to the Kuku Nor; indeed, traces of red ware, some of it painted, have been found in Sinkiang, for instance at Miao-erh-ku some 50 miles east-south-east of Hami and at several sites in the Turfan oasis. From a technical point of view this pottery falls into the context of painted wares found in many parts of western Asia and contiguous areas and it is tempting to view it as a product of some degree of western influence; however, it must be admitted that nothing certain has yet been established about where it was first made in China or about the direction in which it spread. The fine red ware, which despite some earlier reports seems to have been substantially hand-made, was characteristically flat-based and included bowls, flat dishes and various kinds of jar, that might be provided with perforated lug handles. The decoration of the funerary pottery was on the whole richer than that of domestic wares, as little as 8 per cent of which might be painted. The decoration was mostly abstract, composed of simple patterns like bands and triangles, but

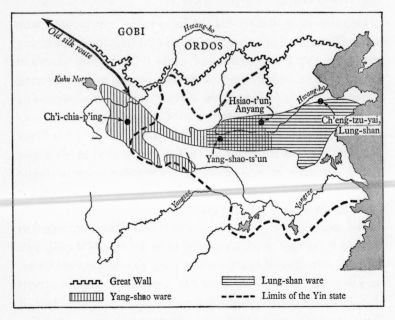

6. China: the prehistoric core of the earliest state

in Kansu spirals were employed as well as zoomorphic and even on occasion anthropomorphic designs.

The black ware, named after Lung-shan in the province of Shantung, was distributed widely over the flood-plain of the lower Hwang-ho. Geographically the black and red wares were largely complementary and the fact that the red ware underlay the black at certain sites in Honan does not of course prove any broad succession in time. Until the chronology and true epicentres of the two wares have been worked out, no valid estimate of their historical relationship can be made, but it is pertinent to note that the makers of the painted pottery of the Tripolje culture of the Ukraine, on the other side of the Russian steppes, seem to have turned over about the same time to the production of black polished ware without any apparent cultural break. Technically the fine black Lung-shan ware was more advanced than the others because it was made on the potter's wheel and its thin polished walls and fine finish lend it an air of sophistication wanting from other prehistoric wares in China. On the other hand the bulk of the pottery, and particularly of cooking vessels, was made of grey or dark brown ware already described and it was this, rather than the black ware, that dominated the overlying early historic levels. Among the pottery used for cooking, special interest attaches to various forms of tripod that form evident prototypes for the bronze ones of the following period, namely the *t'ing* with solid feet, the *li* with hollow ones, the *hsien*, comprising a *li* with an upper pot for steaming having a perforated base, and the *kuei* with hollow feet and spout. Another feature pointing ahead to the early historic period was the practice of scapulomancy: although as yet there were no indications of actual inscriptions in the form of petitions, there is no doubt that bones, notably ox scapulae, were scorched in order to provide clues in the form of cracks, a clear forerunner of the oracle bones that provided the earliest Chinese inscriptions.

Shang, Chou and Han dynasties

The contrast between the peasant communities just described and those of the Shang dynasty, the earliest attested by archaeology, is so pronounced that it almost certainly points to a major gap in our knowledge, which the recent excavations at Chêng-chou have only partly filled. The first insight into society as it existed under the Shang dynasty was provided by the exploration of a number of sites in the neighbourhood of An-yang, northern Honan, to which the capital was moved by King P'an-Kêng, probably about 1300 B.C.; but recent excavations at Chêng-chou carry the story back to the earlier phase, thought to have begun around 1520 B.C. At An-yang we are confronted with a veritable city laid out in zones, with palace and artisan quarters and rectangular wooden houses set on terraces of beaten earth and with gabled roofs supported on rows of pillars resting on stone or even bronze bases. From this city the kings of the Yin or later Shang dynasty ruled a stable and to some degree literate state, in which the art of the bronze worker had reached a high pitch of perfection and in which the leaders rode to war and the chase in chariots mounted on spoked wheels and drawn by pairs of yoked horses, vehicles recalling those of Mitannian and Mycenaean princes far away to the west.

Although the more elaborate pieces and notably the ritual vessels from the earliest Shang levels were already specifically Chinese in style, it seems highly unlikely that bronze metallurgy was invented independently in the valley of the Hwang-ho and the probability is that this, like the basic elements of farming and possibly the painting of pottery, spread to the area from much earlier centres in western Asia. Many of the leading bronze forms, also, including knives with incurving edge, certain types of dagger and socketed axe and leaf-shaped spearheads with a small loop near the base of the socket, are widely distributed over the steppe and forest zones from Baikal to the heart of European Russia. Detailed analogies between finds from places as far apart as Seima on the Upper Oka, Turbino and Gorbunovo on either side of the Mid-Urals, Minusinsk and Karasuk on the Upper Yenisei and Anyang itself suggest that lively trade contacts were maintained at some time during the period from the fifteenth to the eleventh centuries B.C. over a zone covering some 100 degrees of latitude: indeed, links can be detected as far west as Borodino near the Black Sea coast of Bessarabia, which itself seems to have been in touch with the central Caucasus and the Mycenaean world, and further north with the Arctic hunter-fishers of Finland and Middle Sweden. The rapidity of movement over such wide territories even in prehistoric times makes it difficult to assess the historical meaning of such analogies. Certain features, like the modelling of animal heads as terminals for dagger hilts, knife- and ladle-handles and the heads of axes and maces seem to have been a common inspiration of the peoples of northern Eurasia, whether carried out in bronze, stone or wood. On the other hand certain elaborations of the beast style at this early period were the product of the richer cultural environment of the Shangs. Again, it seems likely that some at least of the leading types mentioned above were first produced in Shang workshops and from there diffused among the metal-workers of the poorer societies of hunters, nomads and part-time farmers of the northern steppes and forests.

The splendid bronze vessels made by the Shang smiths provide one source of inscriptions, but a much more prolific one is afforded by the pieces of bone or tortoise-shell, on which questions were inscribed to ancestors or gods in the hope of obtaining answers by applying heat and watching the course of the ensuing cracks. From An-yang alone upwards of 100,000 such inscribed pieces have been examined and this has shown that the diviners made use of some 3500 characters, of which around a third can be read in the light of existing Chinese characters. The fact that inscribed oracle bones have been found in the earlier levels at Chêng-chou emphasizes that the Shang civilization was already Chinese in character as far back as it can be traced, and it will be recalled that the practice of scapulomancy, though not of writing, can be traced back to the 'Neolithic' Lung-shan culture.

As was to happen so often in the future, the reigning dynasty was overthrown by another less highly civilized without destroying the continuity of Chinese culture. In this case it was the Chous, issuing from the borderlands of Shensi, who overthrew the Shangs and destroyed their capital around 1030 B.C. Even at this early stage Chinese civilization was sufficiently robust to absorb relatively barbarous intruders and it was under the Chou dynasty that Chinese manners and customs largely took the form they were to retain down to modern times. Politically the period was one of expansion, and during it the Chinese state extended its boundaries north to Manchuria, east to the neck of the Shantung peninsula and south to the Hwai valley. In the course of this expansion many outlying parts of northern China, where, during Shang times, the old 'Neolithic' peasant cultures had continued very largely in their ancient ways, were brought for the first time within the sphere of civilization. To the south of the Shang territories, in an area on which the Chous began to encroach, there is evidence from the lower Yangtze basin of communities living at a Neolithic level of culture comparable with, though poorer than, those of the Hwang-ho. The Yangtze valley people made their cooking pots mainly by hand, occasionally employing the paddle to shape the vessel and apply cord-impressed decoration; but most of them used the wheel for their finer wares and some made highly burnished black ware in a devolved Lung-shan tradition. Likewise they finished their stone tools and weapons mainly by polishing in the northern fashion. Remoter areas in the upper Yangtze valley and in South China (see p. 204) remained prehistoric down to the last centuries before Christ.

The last five hundred years of nominal Chou rule, though they witnessed the rise of Chinese philosophy, and notably of Confucius and his pupil Mencius, and saw the introduction of iron-working, were notable in the political sphere for the disintegration of the central power, the growth of feudalism and the prevalence of warfare between minor states. This state of affairs was first brought to an end, though temporarily, by the Ch'ins, a clan from the steppe border who gained and for a brief time held the imperial power. It was under this dynasty that the Great Wall was built on the north and that the Empire was extended as far south as the Canton delta and even the northern part of Annam. Although some advances were lost during the years of anarchy that followed the death of the first Ch'in king in 210 B.C., these were more than regained during the Han dynasty (202 B.C.–A.D. 220) under whom the centre of gravity of the Empire shifted south from the Hwang-ho to the Yangtze basin. At the height of this dynasty the Chinese Empire covered almost the whole of the mainland of East Asia from Manchuria to northern Annam with an extension from Inner Mongolia to the Pamirs at the western frontier of Sinkiang. It was at this time that the development of the silk trade linked China to the Roman world: two distinct routes were followed, an overland one subject to interruption by the Parthians and a maritime by way of the Indian Ocean, the Coimbatore gap across the extreme south of India, and the Malacca straits.

SOUTH-EAST ASIA, INDONESIA AND THE PHILIPPINES

Origins of rice cultivation

One of the main reasons why the mainland of south-east Asia merits study is that it forms a kind of funnel through which peoples have spread over Indonesia, Melanesia and farther afield. Another is its intermediate position between the two main foci of culture in India and China respectively. Claims that it was in itself the cradle of an early civilization based on the cultivation of rice are not substantiated by the archaeological evidence; indeed, although regional sub-groups can be detected, which no doubt correspond to the beginning of settled life in the several areas, the indications are that the fundamental arts of pottery-making and the manufacture of finely polished stone tools spread down from China. As regards the origins of rice cultivation, which has made possible the dense populations of parts of India, south-east Asia and China, very little is yet known, except that on botanical grounds this must have occurred within the tropical zone of south-east Asia. According to the Greek Theophrastus, active during the latter half of the fourth and the early third centuries B.C., rice had been cultivated in the Ganges basin since time immemorial, but the earliest traces so far revealed by archaeology in India are the carbonized spikelets of cultivated rice from the painted grey ware site of Hastinapura, dating most probably from early in the first millennium B.C. As it happens, the oldest trace so far discovered comes from the opposite end of the zone of ancient rice-cultivation, in the form of impressions of husks on a sherd from Yang-shao Tsun, the classic site of the Honan painted pottery and dating in all probability from the middle or earliest half of the second millennium B.C.; the presence of cultivated rice as far north as the valley of the Hwang-ho means that it must already have been cultivated by the Neolithic peasants of the Lower Yangtze which in due course became the centre of gravity of the Chinese Empire.

Hoabinhian culture

So far from south-east Asia being an early focus of settled life, the indications are that Neolithic culture arrived there somewhat belatedly. Cultures of Mesolithic character were correspondingly well developed. On the mainland and in part of Sumatra plant food evidently played a leading part in the subsistence of the Bacsonian or Hoabinhian culture, so called from sites in Tonkin, Indo-China, where it was first explored; and it was presumably the bearers of this culture who discovered and then began to improve the properties of wild rice. Doubtless the heavy axe-like tools flaked from stone pebbles in a manner reminiscent of the Palaeolithic pebble tool tradition, though in some cases ground smooth at one end, were used in clearing wild vegetation, and the grinding-stones and pounders found in some abundance testify to the preparation of plant food. The Hoabinhian culture has since been recognized to the north in the Chinese provinces of Kwangsi and of Szechwan, also remotely situated on the upper course of the Yangtze, and to the south in Malaya and Sumatra; moreover to judge from preliminary accounts of the excavations in the Niah Cave, it spread as far east as Borneo. The Hoabinhians were fond of sheltering under overhanging rocks or in the mouths of caves, and the bones of animals which they hunted to supplement their plant food have therefore survived, including the mud turtle and various kinds of oxen, deer and swine; the cave and shelter deposits have also yielded shells of fresh-water molluscs, pointing to another gathering activity, for which the shell-middens on the north-east coast of Sumatra offer more impressive evidence. The human skeletal material recovered from the caves suggests that the bearers of the Hoabinhian culture were of the same basic stock as that represented to-day by the Melanesians and Papuans.

Microlithic industries

Contrasting with this heavy equipment are the industries, based on the utilization of small flakes and blades and relating to hunters depending primarily on the bow, found on a number of the main islands of Indonesia. Among these are obsidian industries from caves in the Djambi district of inner Sumatra, from sites bordering a former lake at Bandoeng in western Java and from the Manilla district of Luzon in the Philippines, each of which feature microliths with steep retouch. An industry of broadly similar character, but using triangular hollow-based arrowheads as well, has been recovered from caves in the south-west Celebes with remains of animals, which apart from the dog were exclusively of wild species. It may well be, as some authorities believe, that these industries came to be identified with hunting peoples of Negrito stock, but there seems little doubt that culturally they represent a drift south from the general area extending from Manchuria to Japan.

Lozenge and quadrangular polished adzes

Two main spreads of Neolithic culture have sometimes been distinguished in south-east Asia and Indonesia according to whether axes and adzes were made with lozenge or quadrangular sections. Geographically the two are to some extent complementary in distribution, though in places overlapping, the lozenge-sectioned or lentoid type making little impact on Malaya or West Indonesia, though abounding in the Philippines, Borneo, the

Celebes, New Guinea and Melanesia. Yet it must be remembered that the lentoid celt is after all the basic form over a large part of the world and is hardly in itself a trait of much diagnostic value.

The quadrangular adze on the other hand is much more clearly defined. Although present alongside ones of lentoid and ovoid section in the Hwang-ho basin, the type was particularly characteristic of Formosa and the coastal region of South China, where it was often highly finished. The indications are that it spread south in two main waves, one penetrating Indo-China, north-east India, Malaya and western Indonesia, overlying Hoabinhian levels where these were present, the other by way of the Philippines to North Borneo and the Celebes. Such a diffusion clearly implies sea-transport, and indeed boat-making was probably one of the main crafts for which the quadrangular adze was employed. The quadrangular adze people depended for their livelihood mainly on swine-keeping and the growing of rice and yams. They made pottery by hand, often with the help of a pad and beater, the latter frequently being wrapped with cord to give a characteristic cord-textured finish to the outer surface of the vessel. Over a territory which is as extensive as the continent of Europe it is not surprising that local variations should have occurred in the form of the adzes. In Malaya, where, if the radio-carbon date for Lengong in Perak is accepted, they were present already by the middle of the second millennium B.C., the quadrangular adzes were generally of simple type, the frequently bevelled cutting-edge being slightly wider than the butt; on the other hand a local beaked form, bevelled obliquely from two directions, was also present. Particularly fine quadrangular adzes were made in Java from such materials as jasper and agate, and here again a special form emerged in the pick-adze, having a keel on one face. In other areas the shouldered or tanged adze, constricted at the butt in various ways to facilitate hafting, played a leading role, a type which in Fukien and Kwan-tung and on Formosa flourished mainly during the Chou period and would seem to indicate a diffusion during the earlier half of the first millennium B.C. Adzes of this type were common in northern Indo-China and it was presumably thence, if ultimately from South China, that they spread over Burma and north-east India, where they are confined to regions with the strongest Mongoloid racial element, mainly in Assam, Bengal, Orissa and the eastern margins of the Central Provinces.

Dongson bronzes

Neither south-east Asia, Indonesia nor the Philippines experienced a phase of technology fully comparable with the Bronze Age in the more advanced parts of the Old World. Yet, while stone tools continued in general use into the Christian era, a certain number of bronze artifacts, named after the rich settlement and cemetery of Dong So'n in northern Annam, found their way over these territories during the latter half of the first millennium B.C. and in the richer graves of Annam these were sometimes accompanied by objects made of iron. The leading types of Dongson bronze, which as a rule was a lead alloy, included daggers, socketed axes, hoes and spear-heads, and kettledrums of a kind used by the Karens of Burma and western Siam down to modern times for calling up spirits, rain-making, casting spells on enemies and similar purposes. Scenes of horsemen wearing costume of Late Chou character point to the north as a likely source: it has been suggested that the Dongson style and industry was introduced from the north by barbarians from the steppe, forming part of the movement that overwhelmed the Western Chou dynasty; and even that certain decorative elements may be linked remotely with those employed by peoples far away in the Caucasus and the Thraco-Cimmerian zone of the Pontic steppes. However this may be, the Dongson bronzes affected only a small segment of the population, which remained as a whole in a basically Neolithic stage until the general use of iron was spread by Hindu merchants trading as far afield as Sumatra, Java, Bali and parts of Borneo during the early part of the Christian era.

Melanesia

The Melanesian islanders, beyond the range both of the Dongson bronzes and of the Hindu traders who introduced iron tools to Indonesia, remained in the Stone Age down to the European period, so that as recently as the second world war communities could be found in the interior of New Guinea in a 'Neolithic' state of culture. Rice was not eaten in Melanesia until modern times, and the natives lived mainly by cultivating such things as bananas, breadfruit, coconuts, tara and yams by the slash and burn method, helped out by raising pigs, dogs and chickens and by sea-food. For felling and working timber for boats and houses the Melanesians used adzes and axes of polished stone. They made all their pottery by hand, using two different techniques: coil-building, which probably came down from the north, and shaping by anvil and paddle, the immediate source of which was Malaya. Melanesian prehistory must remain obscure until sequences have been established in the various islands and the age of suitable samples correctly determined by radio-carbon dating, but already it seems to be established that a culture resembling the earlier Neolithic of the Philippines had reached New Caledonia at the latest by the middle of the first millennium B.C.

JAPAN

Earliest occupation

Although Japanese civilization was a late development and depended largely on infusions from the continental mainland, notably from Korea, its very insularity favoured the growth of distinctive features and a tenacity of cultural tradition which has enabled it to survive in some measure the impact of modern industrial society. Very little can yet be said of the earliest traces of human activity on the islands. There is no indication that Honsu was occupied earlier than Neothermal times: no reliable associations have been proved between stone implements and Pleistocene fauna; nor does the surface of the Kanto loams from which the implements come show signs of any marked erosion or other changes indicating a high antiquity. Finds made in the Gumma prefecture include pebble tools flaked on one surface which recall industries from Java and Sumatra and like them stem ultimately from the Palaeolithic tradition of East Asia. On the other hand the northern island, Hokkaido, could have been reached during the Ice Age by dry land from the mainland by way of Sakhalin and it may be that the earliest level recognized there and defined by a blade industry with some burins represents an extension of the Advanced Palaeolithic of Siberia.

Jōmon hunter-fishers

The first phase of Japanese prehistory about which much is known is represented by the Jōmon culture named after the cord-markings commonly imprinted on the outer surface of the pottery, a ware common to Korea and Manchuria and which provided the common background to the ceramic history of North China. Although generally described as 'Neolithic', there is no evidence that the Jōmon people practised farming, at least until the closing phases of their culture. Economically they belong to the same Sub-neolithic category as many other predominantly hunter-fisher peoples of the circumpolar zone. For the greater part of their history their only domestic animal was the dog, and it was only latterly that they began to cultivate millet, buckwheat and beans. As a rule Jōmon man preferred to live within reach of the sea to take advantage of a wide range of sea-foods: clusters of middens around Tokyo Bay and many other localities have yielded vast quantities of discarded shells of mussels, oysters and other shellfish and in addition plenty of fish-bones. Most of the fish taken for food were of kinds like mullet and perch that could be taken from inlets at high tide, but remains of shark, sting-ray and tunny show that boats, dug-out varieties of which have survived, must also have been used for angling. Jōmon fishing-gear includes fish-hooks with plain or externally barbed tip and harpoon or detachable spear-heads, perforated for attachment to a line. In addition inland game, including deer and wild pig, was hunted by arrows tipped with hollow-based triangular flint heads flaked on either face, and wild plants were prepared for food by grinding stones and mortars. The Jōmon people lived in settlements of trapeziform or circular houses, having floors lowered below ground-level and central fire-places, around which were set timber uprights for carrying the thatched roof. Like other Sub-neolithic peoples the Jōmon hunter-fishers made pottery by hand, and this they decorated with simple geometric patterns imprinted with cords or shells or executed with grooves: in form the earliest pots were conoid, but flat bases soon appeared and as time went on handles and spouts were successively added; and from the beginning human figurines were also made from fired clay. Their flint-work, as seen in the arrowheads and numerous scrapers, was of a relatively high standard, but the stone axes were generally crude—to begin with, hardly more than natural pebbles lightly ground at one end.

Yayoi farmers

An altogether more advanced economy, one that laid an adequate foundation for the relatively wealthy society of the Protohistoric period, was introduced to northern Kyushu from Korea along with other elements of the Yayoi culture some time during the third century B.C., probably as an indirect result of the expansion of the power of the Han dynasty of China. Although initially the Yayoi culture spread rapidly into western Honshu, reaching the Yamato Plain by around 200 B.C., its momentum slowed down, and it was not until A.D. 100 that it penetrated Tohoku. The interrelations between the Yayoi and older Jōmon cultures were quite complex and it would seem that in some parts of the country there was some real continuity between them. The most important single innovation was probably the introduction of rice-cultivation, which by middle Yayoi times had created in the western part of the country a predominantly agrarian society. Tangible evidence of the new economy includes traces of paddy fields and irrigation channels; carbonized grains and also impressions of rice; and granaries raised on timber piles and approached by ladders. Stone continued to be used for axes, adzes and arrowheads, but bronze weapons and mirrors were first imported from the mainland and then in due course cast in Japan itself, or alternatively copied in stone; and many tools began to be made of iron. As a further symbol of the sub-division of labour, it may be added that at this time the potter's wheel came into use.

Protohistoric Japan

Around A.D. 400 Japan entered on the Protohistoric phase that only ended with the introduction of Buddhism towards the end of the sixth century A.D. and the committal to writing between A.D. 712 and 720 of traditional claims surrounding the imperial dynasty. The main information about this intermediate period is derived from very numerous tombs, often of monumental construction and occasionally occupying areas, including surrounding moats, of as many as eighty acres. These testify to increasing wealth and technical skill, a growing density of population and a feudal organization of society with numerous clans owing allegiance to the imperial clan. Clay models buried with the dead indicate not merely the differentiation of town and country houses, but the emergence of palaces and shrines. Already during this period, coinciding more or less with that of the barbarian migrations into the European territories of the Roman Empire, the main social institutions of recent Japanese history were in being. As if to emphasize the continuity, wooden Shinto shrines have continued to be rebuilt on the same site and after the same pattern as examples first erected during the Protohistoric period. Again, though it seems likely that Shintoism itself was first institutionalized in competition with Buddhism, its basic belief in the need to offer thank-offerings and sacrifices to a multitude of natural spirits, inhabiting such places as groves, mountain tops, sources of water or stones of unusual size, must surely stretch far back into the prehistoric past.

NORTH-EAST ASIA

Hunter-fishers

The vast funnel-shaped territory of Siberia east of the Yenisei and north of the Amur owes its interest largely to its position in relation to the New World. Doubtless it was through this region that the first immigrants must have passed on their way to America, presumably at a time when the land-connection was still intact, and doubtless, also, when means of communication had been developed during Neothermal times, it provided a main avenue for cultural movements, not necessarily always in one direction, between the Old World and the New. On the other hand the climate of Siberia must throughout prehistoric times have imposed narrow limits on the possibility of local cultural development: even in modern times agriculture has been confined to the uppermost Yenisei and to the Angara Valley and hunting, gathering and fishing have provided the main and for most of the region the sole source of food-supply. Yet, if the possibility of sharing fully in the kind of life permitted to peasant farmers, still less of progressing towards urban civilization, was denied to the prehistoric inhabitants of Siberia, this did not prevent them developing effective cultures based on various forms of catching activity or of acquiring elements of technique, such as potting, originally developed among communities based to a greater or less degree on food-production.

The best sequence of Sub-neolithic cultures in Siberia is that established in the Angara Valley and Lake Baikal regions. Pottery first appeared in the Isakovo stage and comprised conoid jars with straight sides ornamented by net-impressions. Among the hunting-gear were bone spearheads armed by flint micro-blades inset in slots, a type found with a number of burials in the region lacking pottery and assigned on not very conclusive evidence to a distinct Khini phase of settlement. The device is also interesting because of its occurrence over northern Eurasia as far west as the Atlantic coast of Norway and as far south as Mongolia and Kansu; and because it turns up in North America in the context of the Denbigh culture of Alaska and the younger Dorset culture of the Hudson's Bay area. Other and more specifically Sub-neolithic elements to appear in the Isakovo culture include partially polished adzes, polished stone knives and bifacially flaked arrowheads. In the later Serovo and Kitoi stages a greater emphasis seems to have been placed on fishing, for which lures, barbed spears and fish-hooks were used. In the Glaskovo stage, contemporary with the Bronze Age in south-west Siberia and probably with the Shang dynasty, the pottery shows signs of contact with North China.

Abundant traces of Sub-neolithic people at the level of those of the Baikal area are known from the Lena Valley and even from as far east as the Kolyma. Over all this territory the hunter-fishers continued to combine the use of burins and bone tools inset with micro-blades with coarse, hand-made pottery, a sherd of which from a late site in the Lena Valley was found, significantly, to have had fish-scales mixed with the clay as tempering. Further east there are indications of well-developed maritime cultures. The Old Bering Sea culture probably grew up during the centuries immediately B.C. on either side of the strait and it occupied the coast of the Chukchi peninsula as far west as the Bear Islands on the north. Middens at the mouth of the Amur river suggest that coastal settlement may have begun there as far back as the middle of the second millennium B.C. and in this context it is worth recalling that the Jōmon people who occupied the main island of Japan possibly as far back as the fifth millennium B.C. were primarily coastal midden-dwellers. Whether or not the modern Ainu are remnants of the Jōmon people as was once thought, it is certain that they retreated before the Yayoi cultivators until by the end of the first millennium B.C. they were concentrated on Hokkaido; it was probably about this time and doubtless under the same pressure that they spread northward into Kamchatka and the Kurile Islands. The native peoples of north-east Siberia remained prehistoric down to the Russian colonization of the first half of the seventeenth century.

CHAPTER 9

THE NEW WORLD

The first immigrants

By comparison with most of the Old World the Americas were settled quite recently: no traces of human occupation have ever been found truly stratified in deposits of Early or Middle Pleistocene age, and it is significant that all hominid remains from the New World are of recent *Homo sapiens* type. Although recent discoveries have shown that the first immigration took place rather earlier than had previously been regarded as probable, there is still no valid evidence that it preceded a comparatively advanced stage of the Late Pleistocene. Whenever they came the first Americans must have been hunter-fishers, since they had to traverse nearly four thousand miles beyond the range of farming across territories ill-provided with wild vegetable food.

One may reasonably assume the earliest immigrants to have taken the same route as a number of the larger mammals, including the bison and the mammoth—two of those most keenly sought after by prehistoric man—namely the route across the Bering Sea. Precisely when and where and under what conditions the first crossing from Asia was made is still uncertain: a drop in sea-level of only 150 feet, such as could easily be envisaged for an advanced stage of the Late Pleistocene, would be sufficient to ensure a landbridge between the continents, and the probability is that it was during an interstadial of the last Ice Age that the immigration took place. What we do know for certain is that Palaeoindian hunters were active on the High Plains of North America by a period assessed by radio-carbon analysis at the tenth millennium B.C.: immediately prior, that is, to the final glacial episode of major importance. How much, if at all, earlier they may have arrived is still obscure. From what is known of the physiographic development of the territories through which the migration must have passed it seems clear that the movement can hardly have taken place at the height of a major glacial onset: at such a time north-east Siberia was blocked by a great ice-sheet, and though north-west Alaska was mainly free of ice, access to the High Plains would have been barred by the conjunction of the Laurentide ice-sheet, spreading from the Hudson's Bay region to the Rocky mountains. The probability is that the migration took place before the eustatic rise of sea-level was sufficient to breach the land-bridge between Asia and North America, but after the ice-sheets had retreated sufficiently to leave a free passage at either end. Such conditions may have obtained during the stage represented by the forest-bed at Two Creeks in Wisconsin, which according to radio-carbon dating dates from the tenth millennium B.C. and so is equivalent in age to the Allerød oscillation of north-west Europe, and possibly also during earlier warm phases towards the end of the Wisconsin glaciation.

Hunters on the High Plains: Folsom, Sandia, Clovis and other groups

It was the discovery by a party of palaeontologists in 1926 of two pieces of worked flint in apparent association with bones of extinct bison at Folsom in New Mexico that first opened up wider perspectives in New World prehistory (Map 7). Within the next two years systematic digging had established beyond reasonable doubt that bison of an extinct species (*Bison taylori*) had been hunted by projectiles tipped by flint heads of a very particular type. These 'Folsom points' had been carefully flaked on both faces to a rather obtuse point, and longitudinal flakes had been struck on either face of the concave base, presumably to facilitate mounting on a shaft. Similar points from near Lipscomb, Texas, were found alongside scrapers and utilized flakes with the remains of numerous bison, including nine skulls and the articulated remains of fourteen

animals, suggesting the sites of an actual butchery. Exploration of
an actual settlement site at Lindermeier in north-east Colorado
confirmed that the makers of these fluted points were hunting on

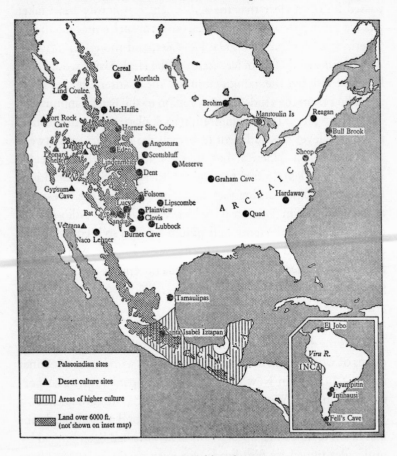

7. New World prehistory

the High Plains at a time when the fauna differed profoundly from
that found in the same territory in recent times. Yet there was still
no indication of precisely when the various fossil forms became
extinct. Nor did the archaeological material itself give any indication of high antiquity: it differed markedly from the Advanced

Palaeolithic industries of the Old World, notably in the complete absence of true burins, and on the other hand showed some affinities with industries of Sub-neolithic character in northern Eurasia; and, moreover, the characteristic Folsom fluted point has not been found in the Old World, a fact which caused it to be dismissed by some as a marginal and probably retarded development. In parenthesis, it may be added that this last objection has lost much of its force in the light of what is now known about the character of the Late Pleistocene industries of Siberia which stand closest to those of the New World: the Siberian industries in fact have a strong 'Mousterian' element, one which by analogy with the Szeletian of central Europe might almost have been expected to give rise to bifacially flaked points.

Whatever doubts may have been entertained about its age, the Folsom find was immensely stimulating and soon fresh discoveries were made. New types of chipped projectile-head were found with remains of extinct animals, and on two occasions these were overlaid by deposits containing Folsom material. The significance of these and other finds was only emphasized when the results of radio-carbon analysis of samples from a Folsom site at Lubbock, Texas, were published in 1949, establishing its age as somewhere in the eighth millennium B.C. The Palaeoindians were not only established on the High Plains near the beginning of the Anathermal or earliest phase of the Neothermal period, but were seen to have appeared even earlier.

Since the original Folsom discoveries two types of projectile-head have been found at still older levels. One may begin by mentioning the one first identified at the Sandia Cave, New Mexico, in association with extinct forms of horse, bison, camel, mastodon and mammoth. The Sandia point is typically asymmetrical in outline, having a shouldered tang; and stray specimens have been found over a fairly wide area. Precisely how far back in time the Sandia point extends is not yet known: the radio-carbon date of 20,000 + for the pre-Folsom level at Sandia itself is discounted;

but two specimens, distinguished by short flakes struck longitudinally from the base of the tang, were recovered at Lucy, in the same state, from a deposit immediately preceding the last major glacial phase and dating therefore from around 8500 to 10,000 B.C. The second variety was first identified at Clovis, also in New Mexico, where it was separated by two disconformities and an intervening bed of brown sand from an overlying Folsom level. Clovis points are characteristically heavy, run to three inches or more in length, as a rule are more tapered than Folsom points and are fluted for only about half their length. At the same site they were found with traces of mammoth, and a number of similar associations have been noted in this part of North America; no less than eight Clovis points were found with a single mammoth skeleton at Naco in Arizona; a single one accompanied an articulated skeleton at Dent, Colorado; and at Lehner, Arizona, an industry of Clovis type occurred with mammoth, bison, tapir and possibly horse. As in the case of the Sandia points, dating remains inconclusive. The geological evidence at Naco, where the archaeological level rested on pebbly sand deposited by a stream, and was directly covered by laminated water-laid beds, only to be succeeded by deposits indicating progressively more arid conditions, suggests that the Clovis hunters lived during a pluvial period. On the other hand the radio-carbon dates from Lehner and from the lower level at Burnet Cave point to a survival well into the Anathermal period. The fact that Clovis points have been found stratified below Folsom ones on more than one occasion is not inconsistent with their persistence into later periods: indeed, it may well prove that the distinction between Folsom and Clovis points is functional rather than cultural; and in this connection the persistent association of Clovis points with mammoths and Folsom ones with bison is at least suggestive.

There is good evidence that on the High Plains the specialized hunting economy lasted from Late Glacial down to well into the Neothermal period. Many distinct forms of projectile head, mostly associated with bison-hunting, have been recognized. Thus points of the Portales group—comparatively small, with parallel sides and obtuse points—have been found stratified above ones of Folsom type, and radio-carbon dates indicate a span from Anathermal to well into Altithermal times. Again, lanceolate points with slightly concave base and parallel oblique flake-scars (Brown's Valley and Angostura points) seem to have lasted down to the sixth millennium B.C. Lastly, the tanged or stemmed forms with parallel transverse flaking of the Cody group—thin-sectioned ones named after the bison-hunters' station of Scottsbluff, Nebraska, and thicker ones after Eden Valley, Wyoming—appear to date from the fifth millennium B.C. Incidentally, the type station of this group, the Horner site near Cody, Wyoming, yielded flint scrapers, a special type of asymmetrical tanged knife and remains of upwards of 180 bison, of which the tops of the skulls had in many cases been removed.

Expansion of the Palaeoindians east and south

That the High Plains should have been a main focus of early settlement is fully consistent with the hypothesis that the Palaeoindian hunters pressed south through a gap between the Laurentide and Cordilleran ice-sheets and along the eastern margin of the Rocky Mountains. It must be remembered that the High Plains, now an arid region, enjoyed Pluvial conditions during the Late Glacial period, and the evidence suggests that it was around lakes and ponds that the hunters of bison and mammoth habitually camped. On the other hand it is hardly surprising that they should have spread widely into the virgin hunting grounds that surrounded them. The precise significance of stray finds in northwest Canada and Alaska will only be known when more systematic excavations have been made, but in the case of fluted points, admittedly an American invention, it can only be supposed that examples from Alberta and Saskatchewan represent a movement from the south facilitated by the eastward contraction of the

Larentide ice-sheet. Much more important was the expansion to the east. Fluted points, often having a more pronounced concavity at the base than the classic Folsom type, are known from Alabama, east Tennessee, North Carolina and Virginia and up to Massachusetts and north Vermont. As the Palaeoindians pushed into more broken and forested ground they seem to have broadened the basis of their subsistence to include the gathering of shell-fish and plants, and in this way to have entered upon a new phase of culture, the Archaic of eastern North America. Equally, when they turned west, the Palaeoindians entered an environment ill-adapted to a way of life based on specialized hunting. The arid conditions of the Great Basin region necessitated heavy reliance on plant food and the capture of even the smallest animals, the basis of a distinctive Desert culture. More will be said later about both the Archaic and Desert cultures. Meanwhile it remains to consider the southward expansion of the Paleoindians.

This is marked in Mexico and in parts of South America by projectile heads of laurel-leaf form, the so-called Lerma Points, associated with mammoth skeletons. These include two skeletons of *Mammuthus* (*archidiskodon*) *imperator* showing clear signs of having been butchered—the base of one of the skulls had been smashed open, probably to facilitate the extraction of the brain, and many bones had been cut or grooved by stone tools—found at a distance of half a mile in the bed of an old lake at Santa Isabel Iztapan, near Tepexpan in the Valley of Mexico, accompanied in one instance by a Lerma point with slightly serrated edge and a lanceolate point with a squared base and in the other by a point with a weakly defined tang, a convex scraper and a spokeshave. The deposit in which the deposits lay formed part of the Upper Becerra formation assigned by geologists to the tenth millennium B.C., and radio-carbon analyses have given dates ranging from 9050 ± 300 to 14,000 + B.C. Another Lerma point from Tamaulipas in northeast Mexico has been radiocarbon-dated to the eighth millennium B.C. Further south the Palaeoindian trail is marked by laurel-leaf points at El Jobo in Venezuela and at Intihausi and Ayampitín in central Argentine, where bifacially flaked projectile heads have been dated by radio-carbon analysis of associated organic traces to the end of the seventh millennium B.C. Indeed it would seem from the finds at Fell's Cave and from numerous middens that by this time, if not before, the Palaeoindians had reached the north shore of the Strait of Magellan—impressive testimony, as was the spread to the Atlantic shore of North America, to man's inborn drive to explore his environment.

The culture developed by the Palaeoindians on the High Plains during the closing phases of the Wisconsin glaciation was based on the hunting of big-game, notably bison and mammoth. Indeed most of the finds relate to the places where the game was actually killed and dismembered, though Lindenmeier and a few other sites have provided us with a broader range of settlement material. The abundance of flint scrapers argues for the use of skin clothing, but burins are conspicuously absent, and it is worthy of note that by comparison with many Upper Palaeolithic cultures relatively little use was made of bone and antler. The impression remains of a highly specialized hunting culture in which projectiles, in this case darts tipped with flint heads and propelled by spear-throwers (atlatls), played a leading part. Although there is no evidence that the Palaeoindians practised art, as did the Advanced Palaeolithic hunters of parts of the Old World, it is certainly true that they fabricated their projectile heads to a standard well beyond what was functionally necessary, and perhaps we can see in the perfection and multiplicity of form of the various bifacially flaked points some counterpart to the engraving and painting through which the hunters of the Dordogne relaxed their tension.

Desert culture

West of the High Plains in the Great Basin area, from the Rockies to the Pacific the Palaeoindians encountered a desert environment, which called for a diligent quest for all available sources of food, rather than for the specialized hunting of particular kinds of big game. Where opportunity offered, indeed, the Desert culture people killed their bison, antelope or mountain sheep, but often they had to be content with lesser game, carnivores like desert fox, bobcat, coyote or skunk or rodents such as desert wood-rat, bushy tail rat, gopher or kangaroo rat. In catching these and any other animals they could get, they used nets, snares and traps as well as darts tipped with chipped heads (lanceolate or stemmed and notched, sometimes with indented base) and propelled by wooden atlatls or throwers. Further, considerable reliance was placed on plant food, particularly seeds and rhizomes, the former of which seem to have been parched, abraded on grinding-stones and eaten as a kind of mush or gruel. The necessity to exploit every source of wild food in an inhospitable land meant that the Desert people must have lived in small groups and moved over considerable territories in the course of a year. Fortunately they were in the habit of sheltering at some periods in caves and under rock-shelters and the exploration of some of these—notably Danger Cave, Utah; Roaring Springs and Fort Rock Caves, Oregon; Leonard Shelter near Lovelock and Gypsum Cave, Nevada; and Ventana Cave, Arizona—has given us a remarkably complete picture of their equipment. The relatively small size of the shelters and the intermittent character of their occupation confirm the impression that they lived in small, nomadic groups. Their equipment was easily carried; they used baskets—at first twined, later supplemented by coiled—and a variety of nets, cordage and matting; their digging-sticks, fire-drills, darts and atlatls were easily carried; and even their milling-stones were portable. A depressing feature of their way of life is that the food-quest can have left them but little leisure and it is hardly surprising to find no evidence for decorative art—no sign of contrasting colours in their basket-work, no fringes to their leather garments and but few signs of personal ornaments. By the same token, though the Desert culture appeared with most of its basic traits already by around 7000 B.C., there were few signs of progress over much of the territory; the adjustment to an unfavourable environment once made, there was small inducement to change. Yet, even though in some parts of California a similar way of life has lasted down to the present day, the Desert culture was by no means wholly a backwater; it was apparently Indians of this foraging-stage economy who in the southern zone of their territories—in New Mexico and in the Valley of Mexico—initiated the domestication of maize, on which the higher cultures of Mesoamerica and the Andean region alike were reared.

The origins of Mesoamerican and Andean civilizations

When the material productions of Aztec, Maya and Inca were first brought to light by archaeology, the tendency of European scholars was to seek their inspiration in the Old World: leaving aside those who were mesmerized by the supposed journeys of the Egyptian Children of the Sun, sober scholars looked with more discrimination across the Pacific to south-east Asia and even to China for sources of these civilizations, for which they could see no convincing native origins. Against this, American scholars have by and large maintained that the higher cultures of the New World represented no more than intensifications of the indigenous American Indian cultures with which they shared a basically common style; that though more elaborate they were nevertheless subject to many of the same basic limitations vis à vis the Old World as were the lowlier ones—for example in the lack of the plough and the wheel; and that they were grounded on the cultivation of distinctively New World crops, such as maize, squash and potato, rather than on the cereal grains on which the Old World civilizations depended. This does not exclude the possibility of trans-Pacific contacts in comparatively early times—many authorities for instance have found it difficult to believe that such a specialized process as tie-dying, by which patterns were produced on textiles by folding the material and tying it so as to prevent certain parts coming into contact with the dye, can have been practised independently in Pre-Incan Peru and Indonesia—but it does reduce the importance of these contacts in the process of building the higher cultures of the New World. The findings of modern archaeology have already strongly confirmed that by and large the higher civilizations of the Americas were indigenous growths, for not only do we now know that parts of each continent had been occupied from some thousands of years before the first appearance of these civilizations, but we can now view them as the climax of a long period of progressive development in time.

Cultivation of maize

Both the Mesoamerican and Andean civilizations rested in the final resort on the cultivation of maize. Precisely when and where maize was domesticated is still uncertain, but as we have seen there seems little doubt that this grew out of the foraging type of economy practised over so wide a territory by the peoples of the Desert culture. Traces of an extremely primitive form of maize in analogous contexts at Tamaulipas in north-east Mexico and at the Bat Cave, New Mexico, have both been dated by radio-carbon analysis to the mid-third millennium B.C., but it was not until a thousand years later that there is evidence from the Valley of Mexico for settled maize agriculture. This was accompanied not only by pottery vessels and figurines, but more notably by stepped pyramids presaging those of the higher civilizations of Meso-america. In fact by the middle of the second millennium B.C. Meso-american civilization had entered upon its Formative Stage, in which the main lines of future development were already defined.

Chicama, Chavin and Classic cultures of Peru

South of the Isthmus of Panama a stage of culture broadly com-parable with that of the Desert cultures of North America has been revealed rather more fully during the exploration of middens at Huaco Prèta in the Chicama Valley of the northern coastal district of Peru. Here, between the mid-third millennium and about 1200 B.C., there lived people who depended in large measure on sea-food: gathering shell-fish, catching fish in seine nets weighted by stone sinkers and supported by gourd floats, and hunting porpoises. They supplemented their diet by gathering wild roots, tubers and fruits and by cultivating beans, gourds, squash and presumably cotton, but noticeably they were not growing maize. They occupied subterranean one-roomed dwellings roofed by whale-bones or timber beams. They used cotton and bast-fibre to make bags, nets and fabrics, and they twined mats and baskets, for some of which activities there is evidence from much earlier cave-deposits as far north as New Mexico, Nevada and Utah; and like their northern fellows they got along without pottery.

The Formative Stage in Peru, particularly well documented in the Virú Valley settlements of the Chavin culture, was, as in the Valley of Mexico, marked by the appearance in embryo of many of the basic features of the civilization that was ultimately to develop in the region. The Chavin people, who lived in rect-angular gabled houses, cultivated maize as well as manioc, squash and, for industrial purposes, cotton, and kept dogs and, almost certainly, llamas. Ceremonial pottery elaborately moulded into animal and human forms, and stone-faced terraced pyramids, em-bellished with reliefs featuring felines, serpents and humans, point to the growing elaboration of religious practice. Furthermore the beginning of irrigation during the closing phase of the culture argues for an increase in the density of population and in the degree of social integration. The fact that the Chavin Culture appeared in Peru several hundred years later than a comparable one in Mexico, taken in conjunction with the presence in both areas of such specialized traits as stirrup-spouted jars, the preoccupation with felines in decorative designs, the terraced pyramid and the practice of cranial deformation, suggests that the Peruvians of the Forma-tive Stage owed much to impulses from the north during the broad period 1200–600 B.C. Indeed, the antiquity of maize in the north and its absence from the Preformative in Peru would alone suggest that Mexico was the main originative focus at this stage.

In both regions cultural development reached a climax during a so-called Classic or Florescent Stage, following the long period of incubation: at this time we recognize fully-formed and distinct civilizations each equipped with a technology sufficient for its needs and each having its own individual style. Once the civilizations of Mesoamerica and the Andes had achieved their Classic form, technical progress, though it did not cease, was much slower, and change took the form in the main of political vicissitudes within an established cultural framework up to the time when Spanish intervention and conquest brought to an end the independent histories of the higher civilizations of the New World. Modern research, notably the application of radiocarbon analysis, suggests that the Classic stage began substantially earlier than some recent authorities have been willing to admit, though confirming in the case of the Maya Old Empire with curious exactitude some earlier estimates based on study of the ancient calendars carved on stelae.

Early civilization in Mexico Valley

Mesoamerican civilization found classic expression both on the high plateau of Mexico, where at Teotihuacán in the Valley of Mexico there flourished a city of some 50,000 people equipped with ceremonial pyramids and monumental buildings as early as the sixth century A.D. and, by contrast, in the tropical rain-forests of Northern Guatemala and Honduras, where under the Old Empire the Maya civilization passed through its most creative period between the third and the seventh centuries A.D.

The Post-Classic phase in Mexico was marked less by significant advances in technology than by the successive rise to dominance of different peoples. It is noteworthy that stone continued to provide the main material for tools and weapons, and indeed it was only in the south-west coastal area, most accessible to influences from Ecuador, that metallurgy played a role of any importance and then

IX   Stone carving of bearded man from Mohenjo-daro, Pakistan

(facing p. 224)

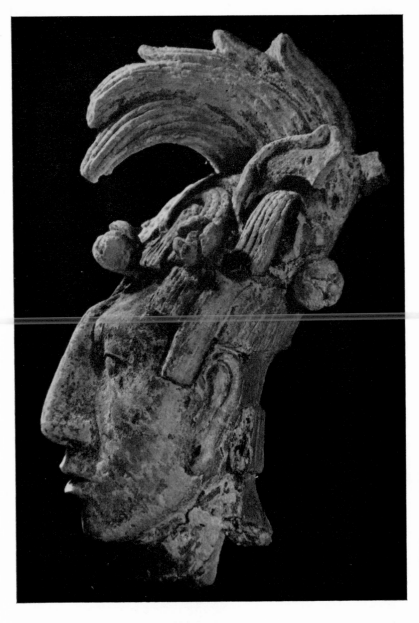

X   Model of Maya youth's head, Palenque, Mexico

only from late Post-Classic times. Among the first conspicuous groups of which we have knowledge were the Toltecs of Tula and the Chichimecs who overthrew them in the twelfth century, peoples who subscribed to a comparatively mild religion symbolized by the plumed serpent Quetzalcoatl carved on the columns of many of the public buildings. The Aztecs, from whom the Spaniards were to wrest the sovereignty of Mexico, first began to move into the Valley of Mexico from the north during the twelfth century, and it was not until around 1325 that they founded their capital city and ceremonial centre of Tenochtitlán on two islands in Lake Texcoco. By contrast with their predecessors and with the Maya the Aztecs were a fierce and cruel people: their social structure was hierarchical, comprising serfs, freemen, officials, nobles, priests and over all a semi-divine king; they worshipped a god Huitzilopochtli who demanded human sacrifice on a grand scale for his propitiation; and they exercised a ruthless domination over weaker neighbours, Huaxtecs, Mixtecs, Zapotecs and the like. In the long run it was some of their less amiable qualities that led to their downfall. Excessive veneration of their ruler Montezuma II made them incredulous of his seizure by Hernando Cortés and it was hatred of their Aztec overlords that prevented the peoples of Mexico from rallying against the Spanish invader. Thus it became possible for Hernando and his followers to topple over a populous empire in the full pride of power and growth within a period of two or three years (1519–21).

The Mayas

The classic Maya civilization, memorialized at such sites as Uaxactum, Tikal, Copan and Palenque (Pl. X) by stone buildings and inscribed stone stelae, and boasting a priestly caste learned in astronomy and mathematics, likewise made do with a technology based on the use of stone tools; copper tools did not appear until late Classic times and then only as foreign imports. The most prominent structures were temples, set on terraced pyramids with flights of steps for access, and dwellings for priests and rulers set round courts. Although outwardly imposing, these buildings were in fact archaic in character; their mode of construction with rubble core and ashlar facing and the lack of any such device as the true arch meant that within their massive walls the chambers were narrow and dark. The Maya religion, though having features in common with the Mexican, was milder in its requirements. Likewise the Maya state seems to have been a relatively pacific confederation of cities, dominated to a large degree by a priestly caste. One of the main preoccupations of the priests was the measurement and recording of time by observing the heavenly bodies and constructing an intricate calendrical system. To do this they employed a vigesimal system of numeration. Furthermore, they made use of hieroglyphs for recording outstanding events which they were careful to date by reference to their calendar, though as far as we know writing was restricted to this particular function in Maya society. For some reason not yet definitely established, but which may well have been connected with the limited possibilities of the soil in a tropical rain-forest habitat, the Old Empire seems to have died out in its original territories. By around A.D. 700 the focus of settlement had shifted to the limestone plateau of Yucatán, where the city of Chichén Itzá had been among the first to be founded. Around the tenth century the New Empire became involved in warfare and in the long run, after recourse to Mexican mercenaries, fell under Toltec influence. The Post-Classic Maya culture, having lost its autonomy, entered upon a period of sharp decline during the thirteenth century, and by the end of the fifteenth had virtually ceased to exist as a viable entity. In this particular instance the demise of a New World civilization can hardly be set at the door of the Spanish conquerors.

Peruvian civilization

The Classic stage of the Andean civilization, represented on the coast of Peru by the Mochica culture in the north and the Nazca in

the south and on the southern highlands by such sites as Tiahuanaco and Pucara, is tentatively dated to the period from the beginning of the Christian era to around A.D. 650. It was marked by the
full development of technical processes, a flourishing period of art
and the establishment of highly organized and aggressive states in
each of several regions. The basis of subsistence was enlarged by
the cultivation of the potato, sweet potato and pineapple. Metallurgy was now practised on a substantial scale and copper was used
for such things as the blades of digging-sticks, mace-heads and
lance-points as well as for ornaments. The fine, polished polychrome pottery included in its repertoire of design representations
of pumas, condors and humans. Textiles of both cotton and wool
were outstanding and represented practically the entire range of
aboriginal American techniques of weaving. Many different products, including tapestry, brocades and gauzes, were produced to a
very high standard of fineness. This fine quality was due in part to
the standard of selection and spinning of the fibres and in part to a
traditional dexterity in weaving for which belt looms were employed, but in which the hands played a main part. The effect was
heightened by the use of vegetable dyes—indigo, red and yellow to
orange brown. Some indication of the rivalry between regional
units characteristic of the age is given by the marked differentiation
of local art styles and by the emphasis laid in vase painting on
warriors and by such scenes as the execution of prisoners of war.

The immediate Post-Classic age was characterized by the
expansion of highland and specifically of Tiahuanaco influence to
the coastal regions. After this episode, which is thought to have
lasted for some three centuries, there followed a period during
which the population of the coastal tract tended to concentrate in
large cities organized in three states, of which Chimú in the north,
stretching from Timbea to the region of Lima in the south, was the
largest and most powerful. The capital city of Chimú, Chan-Chan,
was approximately eleven square miles in area and comprised ten or
more large rectangular enclosures averaging 1300 × 650 feet and

having powerful walls up to 40 feet high. The concentration of population implied by such cities was made possible by combining irrigation schemes in two or more neighbouring valleys and it was probably at this time that roads were constructed up and down the coast. In the highlands of Peru broken topography and multiple sources of water militated against large concentrations of population, yet it was from small beginnings in the Cuzco Valley that there issued the imperial race of the Incas.

Like the Aztecs, the Incas of Peru (Pl. XI) established and enlarged their empire with great rapidity, only to be cut down in full career by the Spaniards. A decisive factor in their rise was a succession of exceptionally able rulers. Between his accession in c. 1438 and 1460 Pachocuti had conquered the highlands of Peru. From this base, aided by his son Topaluca (1471–93), he incorporated first much of Ecuador and the empire of Chimú and later the south coastal region of Peru, the highlands of Bolivia, northern Argentine and Chile north of the Maule river. Over this considerable empire, rounded off under Huayna Capac (1493–1527) by the acquisition of the rest of Ecuador, presided a divine ruler, assisted by a hereditary nobility related to him by blood, by a priestly hierarchy and by an army of appointed officials, who between them controlled every aspect of the lives of the hapless people. The Incan state, indeed, with its minute regulation of economic and social life, forecast some of the worst features of modern collectivist societies: a completely regulated economy was associated with a relentless system of taxation exacted in the form of labour for agricultural works, mining, road-making and the army; marriages were arranged by appointed officials; and conquered populations were forcibly transferred to distant provinces. The empire was knit together on a material plane by an extensive system of narrow but well-built roads embracing the sometimes precipitous highlands as well as the easier coastal regions, a system equipped at intervals with rest- and store-houses and traversed by llamas and human runners; and on a spiritual one

by means of a religious system administered by a priestly hierarchy. Worship of a lord of creation and of the heavenly bodies
was carried on in stone temples decked with gold. Further, the
religion of the day called for sacrifices, on normal occasions of
such things as llamas and maize beer, but at moments of crisis,
such as the illness or death of the ruler, of the lives of women and
children. Yet the empire, though by far the most extensive and
the best organized in the New World, was much too weak to
withstand the impact of a small but resolute body of Spanish
adventurers. By comparison with that of sixteenth-century
Europe, the technology of the Incan civilization was miserably
defective: ahead of the rest of the New World in the ability to
make bronze tools and weapons, its lack of iron and gunpowder
was yet decisive; again, the Incas, though possessing a decimal
system of numeration, lacked any form of writing; and there were
inherent weaknesses in its constitution which made the state
exceptionally vulnerable on the death of a ruler—power was
excessively centralized in the person of the Emperor, but, the
Emperor having many wives, the succession, though passing to a
son, was not fixed on any particular one. As ill luck would have
it the Spaniards under the leadership of Pizarro reached the
country during precisely such a crisis of succession: Atahuallpa
had no sooner staged a successful revolt against his half-brother,
the new emperor Huascar, than he was seized by the Spanish
conqueror (1532). The Incan Empire fell at the height of its vigour
and glory, only local resistance surviving to remind the conquerors
of their victory.

Basket-maker and Pueblo cultures of the North American south-west

Beyond the comparatively restricted zone of indigenous higher
civilization in the Americas there were vast tracts over which the
intruding white man encountered a varied but everywhere less
advanced level of culture; indeed, there were only two regions
north of Mesoamerica in which maize agriculture was practised

during Pre-Columban times, namely the South-West and the East. The most clearly defined and vital focus of culture in the South-West was centred on the present-day junction of the four states of Utah, Colorado, Arizona and New Mexico. Here, in the centuries around the beginning of the Christian era, there developed from a Desert culture basis a type of settled economy that has managed to retain its essential pattern down to the present day. Within this area ethnologists distinguish three main cultures, exploiting rather different environments, laying a different emphasis on various aspects of the quest for food and displaying individual styles: at the juncture of the four states the Anasazi people, who for descriptive purposes we shall take as typical, occupied a predominantly plateau region (4000–7000 feet); by contrast, the Hohokam people to the south-west were desert-dwellers, whose economy depended to an important degree on irrigated maize-cultivation; and to the south-east the Mogollon-Mimbres people, occupying a more mountainous territory with forest and scrub, laid a greater emphasis on plant-gathering.

The Anasazi people emerged, probably in the second century A.D., from a generalized Desert culture background. They depended for food on maize, which they cultivated by digging-sticks and ground on saddle-querns, and on pumpkins, as well as on gathering wild seeds and hunting mainly small game, in which they used spears armed with stemmed and notched flint heads and propelled by atlatls. They grew tobacco which they smoked in tubular pipes. They had no domestic animals other than dogs. Although practising agriculture, the earliest Anasazi people relied for containers on bags made from vegetable fibres and on twined and coiled baskets, for which reason they are often referred to as Basket-Makers (second century A.D.–500 A.D.). They buried their dead in caves, wrapped in skin blankets and cloaks and provided with plaited sandals and with objects used in daily life. They lived in small hamlets, commonly of two or three houses, which were rounded in plan, had floors sunk below ground-level, and were provided with storage-pits for food. During the thousand years that ensued before the first intrusion of the Spaniards, the basic pattern of the Anasazi culture persisted, though subject to a number of important modifications. The so-called Modified Culture Stage (500–700 A.D.) was marked by the introduction of bean cultivation and turkey-keeping, by the substitution of the bow and arrow for the spear and atlatl, by the adoption of potting, at first moulded in baskets, later modelled by hand, by the aggregation of dwellings to form villages and by the construction of *Kivas*, the men's club-houses or ceremonial centres that played a leading part in later phases of the culture. The main trend in the Pueblo stages of the Anasazi culture (Pueblo I, 700–900; II, 900–1050; III, 1050–1300) was a progressive enlargement in the size of settlements, culminating in great cliff-house settlements and hill-top towns, compact masses of up to a thousand rooms of well-built masonry from one to four stories high. During the reign of Pueblo IV (1300–1700), while the Indians were still limited by a Stone Age technology, the Spaniards appeared for the first time in New Mexico (1540) and by the end of the period European influence had spread over the whole region. Yet, although no longer free to move their settlements, the Pueblo V Indians of the present day still retain a considerable control over their affairs and the painted pottery they sell to motorists carries on recognizably an ancient tradition.

Archaic culture of eastern North America

The second area in which maize agriculture was practised during prehistoric times to the north of Mesoamerica, was the Mississippi Valley and the territories to the east, where it seems to have appeared during the first millennium B.C. Initially the region bounded by the St Lawrence and the Atlantic seaboard had been penetrated by Palaeoindian hunters, but, as we have seen, the broken country and the spread of forests during Neothermal times combined to promote a widening of the food quest to include fishing, the gathering of shell-fish and wild plants, and also hunting. On such a basis there arose the Archaic culture of eastern North America, parallel in many respects with the Desert culture of the West, but recalling rather, because of the simi- larity in environment, the Mesolithic of northern Europe. Specific features which support this European analogy include among others: the domestication of the dog, the absence of pottery, the utilization of antler and bone as materials for such things as harpoon-heads, the heads of fish-spears and fish-hooks, and in the later stages the polishing of stone for such purposes as axes, spear-thrower weights, bowls and plummets. A feature of the Archaic stage which is surprising at first sight is the working of copper on a considerable scale for tools and weapons rather than ornaments; but the industry was of course based on the exploitation of outcrops of native metal in the southern region of Lake Superior and of detached fragments carried by glacial action over wide areas of Wisconsin, Minnesota and neighbouring states. It implied no knowledge of metallurgy, any more than did a similar utilization of native copper in more recent times by the Indians of the Copper River district of Alaska or by the Eskimo and Indians of the Coppermine River of northern Canada: as we are told by Samuel Hearne, who travelled in the latter area between 1769 and 1772, 'with the help of a fire and two stones, the Indians could beat a piece of copper into any shape they wished'. From such native copper the Indians of the Archaic period beat out awls, tanged knives, projectile heads with wrapped-over sockets and broad spud blades similarly wrapped over at either side to grip the wooden handle. The products of this industry, though con- centrated more densely in the area of production, were distri- buted by trade to the Laurentian area, New England and New York and as far south as the shell-heaps of the middle South. There is indeed plenty of other evidence for widespread trade in objects made of exotic materials among the Archaic people: for example, bowls of Appalachian steatite were traded as far as Florida and the lower Mississippi and objects made of shell were extensively traded from the south-east. The dead were cremated or buried flexed or seated and in either event might be scattered over with red ochre. Antler head-dresses of copper recall ones made from natural antler in the early Mesolithic of northern Europe.

Woodland culture

Over a large part of the eastern area the Archaic was transformed into the Woodland stage, mainly during the broad period 500 B.C.–A.D. 500, under impulses from two main directions. From the north came pottery-making and mound-building, the two most prominent traits in the purely archaeological record, but the practice of maize-cultivation, which doubtless helped to sustain the elaboration of mortuary and ceremonial practices with their attendant monuments so characteristic of the Woodland stage, must have come from the south-west—most probably from Mexico. Other innovations introduced from outside included tobacco-smoking in tubular pipes and weaving. Two distinct intensifications have been noted: the Adena, centred on south Ohio, south-east Indiana, north Kentucky, north-west West Virginia and south-east Pennsylvania; and the Hopewell, which seems to have appeared somewhat later and to have been centred on the south Ohio, Illinois and Mississippi area, with extensions down to Louisiana and Florida and across from Oklahoma to New York. In both cultures the burial mounds and associated monuments testify to a pronounced degree of social stratification. Thus, whereas the ordinary Adena individual was cremated without much ado, people of higher status were given an elaborate form of burial that took quite a long time to reach completion. First the dead man was placed in a log tomb erected on the floor of his house, together with suitable grave goods and the corpses of other people, probably retainers slaughtered for the purpose. After a while their bones were disinterred, painted and placed once again in the tomb which was now heaped over by a small mound. Finally a gigantic mound up to 70 feet high was erected to cover both the grave and the burnt-out remains of the house.

Middle Mississippi culture

A final step in the development of the eastern tradition occurred somewhere around 1000 A.D. with the emergence of the Middle Mississippi culture. Centred on a track from north-central Georgia through north Alabama and Mississippi to west Tennessee, Kentucky, south Illinois and south-east Missouri, it radiated influence over a much wider area. Even so, it had not everywhere brought Woodland cultures to an end at the time of European contact: when De Soto traversed the south-east in the middle of the seventeenth century he encountered Indians with a Middle Mississippi culture, but the English colonists of Virginia and the Carolinas found the Algonquin and Siouan peoples still preserving their Woodland heritage. The Middle Mississippi culture was not marked by technical innovations of any note, but rather by an intensification of the ceremonial aspect of social life. The larger village centres were built round plazas or squares and were marked by rectangular temple mounds, frequently built in tiers as though several times reconstructed to a greater height. One of the largest—at East St Louis in Illinois—covered an area of no less than 16 acres, was 1080 feet long, 710 feet broad and around 100 feet tall. Although the temples themselves were only enlarged versions of the ordinary domestic buildings, made of timber, lath and plaster and provided with a gabled roof, the whole arrangement recalls that found on a more elaborate scale in Mesoamerica. Several new art motives executed in clay, carved stone, shell and sheet copper—winged snakes, dancing bird-men with speech-scrolls and human skulls—point in the same direction, even if it is only fair to state that no precise source has been detected. Probably we should think in terms of inspiration, perhaps through a very few individuals, rather than of any movement of ethnic significance; indeed, as we have emphasized in this section, there was a very real continuity in the cultural history of the eastern United States from Archaic and even Palaeoindian times up to the moment of European penetration.

Hunting, fishing and gathering communities

Over the rest of North America, as well as over the inhospitable regions of the extreme South, communities subsisting exclusively on hunting, fishing and gathering prevailed down to modern times and in some instances still survive. Subject to this limitation, there was scope for considerable variation according to ecological conditions and to the nature of the response made by different societies. Thus among the Indians of central and southern California a pattern of subsistence formed at latest in the Anathermal period in the sphere of the Desert culture persisted throughout the prehistoric period well into the nineteenth century. A leading part was played by wild seeds, among which the acorn was of predominating importance, and these were prepared by grinding-stones, supplemented in due course by pestles reminiscent of those used so much earlier by the Natufians of Mount Carmel. That hunting still had a certain role is shown by the occurrence at each stage of chipped flint spearheads, at first leaf-shaped or squared at one end, and later stemmed, and by the introduction towards the end of the prehistoric period of the bow. On the coast fishing and the gathering of shell-fish were often leading sources of food. The prehistoric Californians depended throughout on flint and stone and on such materials as antler and bone from which they made fish-hooks and barbed spearheads. Pottery was strictly local in occurrence and well-twined and coiled baskets served for containing food and liquid, as well as cooking.

Coastal culture of the North-West

The aboriginal culture of the north-west coastal region was first brought into effective contact with European civilization at the time of Captain Cook's visit in 1778 and has survived, though with modifications, down to the present day. To judge from the small amount of material excavated, no change of note seems to have occurred in the equipment of the coastal Indians of British Columbia during the last five or six hundred years. Subsistence was based on exploitation of the resources of rivers and the sea: sea-fish and sea-mammals, like whales, seals, sea-lions and sea-otters, were significant sources of food, but it was the plentiful harvest of salmon, easily caught on their seasonal runs upstream, that made possible the elaboration of culture exemplified for instance by the historical Nootka and Kwatuitl. Although they undertook some seasonal movements in the quest for food, the assured supply of salmon made it possible to occupy permanent villages and live in comparatively large communities. Their villages might comprise upwards of thirty houses. These were built on massive timber frames with shells of wooden planking and might be as large as 520 feet long and 60 feet broad, providing accommodation for more than 100 people. The material culture included some elements, like twined basketry containers, derived ultimately from the ancient Desert culture, but many items of specialized coastal equipment show significant agreements with analogous ones from the Aleut and Eskimo areas. On the other hand the social system was highly complex: society was organized on a hierarchical principle with noble or chiefly families, commoners and slaves; and surplus wealth was dissipated in ceremonial feasting and competitive display.

Denbigh and Dorset cultures of the Arctic

The Arctic territories of North America seem to have been settled mainly by successive migrations from west to east, movements that stemmed ultimately from Siberia, and which represent no doubt only the latest of a series, the earliest of which brought the first men into the New World. No certain trace of the earliest migrations has yet been recognized in Alaska, and the oldest assemblage of material yet recovered there, that from the Denbigh

River, relates not to the great southern migrations but to the peopling of the Arctic Zone; indeed, Denbigh material has since been traced across the Hudson's Bay region to the Sarquaq area of West Greenland. The precise age of the Denbigh finds in western Alaska is still uncertain, but there seems no good reason for doubting the radio-carbon dates of up to *c.* 4000 B.C. already obtained. The Denbigh people were skilled at knapping materials like flint and turned out miniature burins, delicately flaked projectile-heads and side-blades for mounting in handles, and regular micro-blades, which at Trail Creek, Seward Peninsula, were found set in slotted bone projectile heads. The burins are in every respect similar to those made by the Advanced Palaeolithic and Mesolithic peoples in Eurasia, but also by the Sub-neolithic people of the Lena Valley of north-east Siberia; and the slotted bone projectile points extend right across northern Eurasia to western Norway. The lithic tradition of the Denbigh culture seems to have contributed to the formation of the first well-defined culture based on the Hudson's Bay region, that named after Cape Dorset on the south-west of Baffin Island. Although possessing marked characteristics of its own, notably the delicacy with which bone and ivory were worked and the art, comprising incised geometric designs and carved animal and human figurines, the emphasis on chipped stone and the presence of burins and micro-blades both point to Denbigh influence; on the other hand ground slate tools were also used and the culture shows some affinities with the early Eskimo cultures developing farther to the west.

Old Bering Sea, Thule and recent Eskimo cultures

The earliest specifically Eskimo group yet recognized is the Old Bering Sea culture of Alaska, St Lawrence Island and north-east Siberia, which on the evidence of radio-carbon analysis seems to go back to the last centuries before Christ. The people were adapted to a coastal way of life and lived in semi-subterranean houses, rectangular in plan and approached by narrow passages, a type of dwelling that goes back to Upper Palaeolithic times in Siberia. Their basic implements were made of chipped stone and ground slate and they used pottery cooking vessels and lamps. In course of time regional groups seem to have developed on this basis, for instance the Punuk culture of St Lawrence Island and the Birnik culture of Point Barrow and the Arctic coast of Alaska. The last of these is of basic importance as the immediate source of the widespread Thule culture centred on Hudson's Bay, but once covering a large part of northern Canada, including Labrador, and extending to Greenland. The Thule people, who spread east from northern Alaska, evidently came into contact both with the Dorset culture, occupying the heart of their new territories, and with the Norse settlers who had reached south-west Greenland already during the tenth century. Their basic economy and the type of houses in which they lived resembled those of their forebears in Alaska and Siberia, but their technology now depended on the iron borrowed from the Norse, rather than upon stone. In some parts of Canada the Thule culture has persisted in modified form down to the present day, but elsewhere it has been replaced by that of the existing Eskimos: there is evidence for a certain backwash of culture from the central regions to northern Alaska, and on the west coast of Greenland a distinctive Inugsuk culture grew up on the Thule basis. Since the Eskimo were the first people in the New World to encounter Europeans, and since they must always have been thinly spread—today barely 40,000 of them occupy more than 6000 miles of coast—their survival might at first sight seem surprising until we remember that their way of life marks one of the most effective adaptations to an environment of exceptional severity.

Yahgan, Ona and Alacu peoples of Tierra del Fuego

At the other end of the New World in Tierra del Fuego the Yahgan and their neighbours the Ona and Alacu maintained down to modern times the most southerly settlements of mankind. Isolation and an adverse environment combined to preserve a way of life that seems hardly to have differed from that revealed in the middens on the Beagle Channel which began to form at least eight or nine thousand years ago. These lowly denizens of a miserable land, as they were viewed by Charles Darwin, lived on a diet of shell-fish, supplemented by fish, birds, seals, whales, otters and wild vegetable food. Their dwellings were caves, windbreaks or primitive huts and they wore little beyond a skin mantle thrown over the shoulders in cold weather. Like many early Americans they were ignorant of pottery and used coiled baskets as containers. Their chipped stone projectile-heads, both stemmed and hollow-based, recall Palaeoindian ones in many different parts of America, and their harpoon and barbed spearheads of bone recall in a general way those of many North American groups, Archaic, North-western and Circumpolar. Unlike the Eskimo, who were comparatively recent intruders, the Tierra del Fuegians were survivors, in a modified and possibly even degenerate form, of the early Palaeoindians who found their way right down both the American continents. The contrast they offer to the sophisticated citizens of Mexico and Peru at the time of the Spanish conquests is a testimony to the achievements of the aboriginal Americans in Mesoamerica and on the Andean highlands.

CHAPTER 10

AUSTRALASIA AND THE PACIFIC

AUSTRALIA AND TASMANIA

Wallace Divide

Australasia, refuge of an archaic flora, recalling that of the Secondary era of geological time, and of a fauna of monotremes and marsupials, the most primitive and next most primitive of the three groups into which the mammals are divided, was the last continent to be settled by man. The barrier that sheltered these living fossils and at the same time prevented the spread of the earliest types of hominid was the trough in the ocean bed between Borneo and Celebes, known among biologists as the Wallace Divide (see Map 1). Since this would have been at least thirty miles wide, even when sea-levels were at their lowest during the maximum of glacial phases, the first men to reach Australia from south-east Asia can only have crossed by means of boats and this no doubt is why neither *Pithecanthropus* nor the Neanderthaloid species known from Late Pleistocene terrace deposits of the Solo river in Java *Homo soloensis* was able to do so.

Tasmanians

The least advanced of the inhabitants of Australasia at the time of its discovery by white men were the Tasmanians, who failed to withstand the impact for even three generations and were exterminated before any complete record of their culture was made. It would of course be quite wrong to interpret their culture as though it was a mere fossil preserving primitive Palaeolithic characteristics, but it remains true that they were subject to the same limitations as the men of the Old Stone Age.

XI   Inca figurines of gold (male) and silver (female)

(*facing p.* 240)

XII   Aboriginal hunter, Australia

They were restricted for their food-supply to what they could gather or hunt, and their equipment was very limited; they lacked bows, and at the time of their discovery depended very largely on wooden clubs and on spears of which the tips had been hardened by fire. As a result they lived in small bands widely distributed over the country and rarely settled in any one place for more than a brief time. Although Tasmania was not lacking in resources and extended over some 26,000 square miles, the aboriginal population at the time of the white occupation is not thought to have amounted to more than from two to four thousand. Individual hunting bands rarely exceeded fifty souls and much of the year was passed in smaller groups. Wind-breaks of tree-branches and bark provided rudimentary shelter. There was little scope for the sub-division of labour beyond that between the sexes, and technology was correspondingly simple. Like the men of the Old Stone Age the Tasmanians were ignorant of pottery and depended on chipped stones for their basic implements. This does not mean that their stone industries can usefully be compared with ones of Pleistocene antiquity from Europe, as has sometimes been done, since there can hardly have been any close historical connection between them. Moreover, as yet we know neither the sequence of Tasmanian industries nor their absolute age, beyond the fact that the youngest of them were still flourishing in the nineteenth century. What can be said is that they are limited to flake tools and unifacial pieces with edge-trimming and that the younger Australian types dating from the third millennium B.C. and later are conspicuously absent. No doubt the archaic aspect of Tasmanian culture resulted above all from the absence of stimulus that followed from its isolated position.

Racially the Tasmanians combined a tendency to the round-headedness and woolly hair of the Negrito peoples of New Guinea, the Celebes, the Philippines, Malaya and the Andaman Islands, with basic Australoid characteristics. Some anthropologists have been inclined to interpret the Tasmanians as evidence that the Negritos were the first people to colonize Australasia, surviving on their island refuge when this was severed from the mainland by the rise of sea-level at the close of the Pleistocene ice-age: in support of this they cite pockets or enclaves of Tasmanoid stock on the continental mainland, for example on Atherton Tableland at the extreme south-west of West Australia, and also on Melville Island. Others prefer to stress the Australoid character of the Tasmanians and attribute their Negrito elements to admixture by a later sea-borne strain.

Australoid migrations

The Australoids, with wavy hair plentifully distributed on their brown bodies, long heads with low foreheads and prominent brow-ridges, noses with low and broad roots, prognathous jaws, large palates and teeth and small chins, preserve a stage in the evolution of *Homo sapiens* probably anterior to the emergence of Negroids, Mongoloids, Whites and American Indians. It seems likely that they came from South Asia and it is significant that pockets of Australoids are found, though mixed with other strains, in Ceylon and possibly in South India. The route followed by the migration from south-east Asia passed through Indonesia and is marked by the fossil skulls from Wadjak in Java and by still living people on some of the Lesser Sunda Islands. Further it would appear that some of the Australoids, instead of pushing south, continued north of New Guinea to Melanesia, where they are still to be recognized in the Bismarck Archipelago and in New Caledonia. The high degree of homogeneity observed in all but a few enclaves of the aboriginal population—all the more notable in view of the extent of the territory and its varying ecology—and the fact that the known fossil skeletal remains, and most notably the cranium from a river terrace at Keilor a few miles north-west of Melbourne, are Australoid in type confirms the view that prior to the European colonization Australia was mainly peopled by a single stock.

Like the Tasmanians, the Australian aborigines (Pl. XII) were limited by the possibilities of food-gathering and hunting, though possessing highly complex social institutions. The population at the time of the discovery is estimated to have amounted to some 250,000 to 300,000, giving an average density about the same as that estimated for Tasmania. On the other hand people were very unevenly distributed over the 2,948,366 square miles of continental territory; much of the western and central parts was either desert or too arid to support more than very sparse settlement. Recent aboriginal habitation has been concentrated in the far north, along the extensive coastal territories, in the forested area of the south-east and in the valley of the Darling and Murray Rivers, but it has to be remembered that the main climatic and vegetational zones, and by consequence the distribution of population, must have shifted considerably within the probable span of human settlements: for instance at the height of the Pleistocene Ice Age the arid zone must have been much further north and the rain-belt in the south correspondingly more extensive, whereas at the climax of Neothermal times the arid belt would have been further south than to-day and tropical rain-forest must have spread over Arnhem Land and south of the Cape York Peninsula. Of some importance, also, as providing a chronological horizon for dating coastal and riverine sites, were eustatic changes of sea-level, more particularly the so-called Woakwine submergence that coincided with the climatic optimum around five thousand years ago.

Earliest traces of settlement

Although an immense amount of collecting has been done, the scientific pursuit of prehistory is still in its infancy over large areas of the vast Australian territories, and the account of prehistoric settlement which follows is necessarily sketchy. It may first be said that there is no convincing evidence for the immigration of man into Australia before Neothermal times. Various claims have been made for the occurrence of traces of man in deposits of Pleistocene age, but none of those so far published carries conviction: for instance the silt deposits of Lake Colongulac in West Victoria, which yield remains of giant extinct marsupials, were said to have produced the jaw of a dingo, a species of dog originally introduced from Asia, and a metatarsal of a giant kangaroo cut by man; but fluorine tests have since shown that the former was younger than the marsupial bones with which it was supposed to have been associated and the latter turns out not to have been found in position in the fossiliferous beds.

The oldest physical trace of the Australian aborigines yet recovered is the cranium from Keilor already mentioned. This came from a terrace antedating the Neothermal arid phase in south-east Australia. Fluorine tests have shown that it is of the same age as animal remains from the same deposit, and it may therefore prove significant that radio-carbon analysis of charcoal from the terrace dates from around the middle of the seventh millennium B.C.

It is only in the south-east of the continent that even the barest cultural succession has yet been established on the basis of stratigraphy. The best sequence to begin with is that first established in a rock-shelter at Devon Downs overlooking the river Murray some 60 miles east-north-east of Adelaide, where twelve layers have been recognized in 6·2 metres of deposit. The lowermost layers (XII–XI) yielded no more than stone chips and a bowl awl and the first definable cultural assemblage came from the succeeding three levels (X–VIII). These were characterized above all by chipped stone points, known by the aboriginal term *pirri* points and comprising leaf-shaped flakes from 1½ to 7½ cm. long, which retain the bulbar surface on one face and on the other have secondary flaking, directed from either side and round the butt, that meets at a keel formed by the intersection of primary flake scars. Together with these points, which served as small but strong spear-heads, the Pirrian levels yielded stout point bone

awls and remains of large mammals, including kangaroo, bandi-
coot and wallaby. Next in succession were layers (VII–V)
marked by double-ended bone points, known by the recent
Marundian aborigines as *muduk* and which provided the tips and
barbs of spearheads as well perhaps as gorges for fishing; in
addition these layers yielded flakes known as *tula* flakes, resembling scrapers but with the butt trimmed as well as the thin
edge, that were mounted in resin on wooden handles and intended
to serve as the blades of adzes or chisels. Over these Mudukian
layers were others (IV–I) containing traces of the Marundians and
their immediate predecessors.

Radio-carbon analysis of shells from layer IX at Devon Downs
gave a date of *c.* 2540 ± 140 B.C. and this was confirmed by investigations at Fromm's Landing some ten miles downstream, where a
date a few hundred years earlier was obtained for the basal deposit
with *pirri* points and various forms of microlith. Evidence for
earlier periods is still slight, but a radio-carbon date of *c.* 4280 ±
120 B.C. has been obtained for a deposit mid-way in the sequence of
Tartanga beds exposed on a long island in the Murray river a few
miles east of Devon Downs. The beds have also yielded human
skeletons of Australian type and remains of opossum, two kinds
of kangaroo, tortoises, fish and molluscs, as well as broken bone
points and rough stone tools made by trimming the edges of
struck flakes and rough discs.

Microlithic cultures

During the third millennium, south-east Australia seems to
have been occupied by hunters who tipped and barbed their
weapons with armatures made from small flakes of stone. In the
corner of South Australia south of the Murray river and in Victoria
and eastern New South Wales these were shaped by the steep retouch characteristic of microlithic work in many parts of the Old
World. One of the most widely recognized forms consists of the
Bondi point, named after a site at Port Jackson near Sydney, a

simple type retouched obliquely or down one side; but frequently these are associated, as at Singleton and Bathurst in eastern New South Wales, with geometric microliths including triangles, trapezoids and crescents. North of the Murray river on the other hand and in western New South Wales the normal type of stone head was the *pirri* point. That there was at least an overlap in time between the two groups is indicated by the occurrence of *pirri* points alongside numerous microliths in the lower levels at Fromm's Landing on the Murray river, the divide between the two provinces, but how big this overlap was has still to be established.

Muduk-eloura *industries*

In the south-east these microlithic industries were succeeded by ones in which the bone *muduk* served to arm hunting weapons in place of *pirri* points and microliths, and the leading stone tools were scraper-like stone blades, originally inset in resin and mounted on wooden handles for use as adzes. The distribution of *muduk* points suggests that the idea of making them spread into Australia by way of Cape York from New Guinea and ultimately from Indonesia, where they formed an element in the Toalian culture of the Celebes and south Java. To judge from the radio-carbon date (c. 1290 ± 80 B.C.) from a deposit immediately overlying a Mudukian level at Fromm's Landing, they had reached the Murray river well before the end of the second millennium B.C. Adze-flakes of *tula* type have already been described from Mudukian levels at Devon Downs. An alternative variety, termed an *eloura* flake by the aborigines and made from a crescentic flake the convex edge of which had been steeply blunted, was represented in a level overlying one with Bondi points in the rock-shelter at Lapstone Creek in eastern New South Wales. Elouran flakes have a wide distribution from surface-sites, rock-shelters and middens from the coastal region of New South Wales to West Australia and from South Australia to Arnhem

Land, where a specimen hafted as an adze-blade was recovered from Shelter 2 on Oenpelli Hill with its mounting still intact.

Over a territory as vast as Australia, first settled only a few thousand years ago and which remained at a hunter-fisher stage of economic development until the colonization by Europeans, it is only to be expected that all but the older types should have survived in one locality or another down to recent times. Indeed most types, other than Bondi points and microliths, were sufficiently familiar to the aborigines for them to be able to supply native names for them, and it need cause no surprise that the Tandandjal cave and the Oenpelli rock-shelter in Arnhem Land should have yielded *pirri* points in the same deposit as types that first appeared more recently, like the bifacially flaked point and the *leilira* blades. The bifacial point, which was mounted in resin at the blunt end and often had a finely serrated edge, seems to have been manufactured by especially skilled knappers in the Kimberley Hills and to have been traded thence over a substantial part of the Northern Territories. In the same way the *leilira* blades, observed in use by Spencer and Gillen, were mostly made from close-grained quartzite at quarry sites in the northern part of Central Australia. Another form of stone tool in recent use over much of Australia, and which in the south-east seems to have appeared in the local Murundian stage, is the edge-ground axe or adze made from pebbles or from quarried stone and shaped by pecking or flaking according to the rock: knowledge of this type of tool probably reached Australia from Hoabinhian sources in south-east Asia.

Recent Australian aboriginal culture

It is only for the brief period during which they have come under the scrutiny of competent observers that we have any full information about the non-material aspects of aboriginal life. From the writings of Spencer and Gillen and their successors, it is evident that, though economically and technically still at a level comparable with that of the Mesolithic peoples occupying much of north-western Europe between 5000 and 10,000 years ago, the Australian aborigines had developed one of the most complex kinship systems in the world as well as an elaborate ceremonial for initiating adolescents into adult society. Their religion was equally intricate, centring on myths concerned with the doings of more or less remote ancestors and on totemism, a multitude of beliefs based on a supposed intimate relationship between individuals, but more especially between classes of men, such as members of the same clan or sex, and specific animals, plants or natural forces like the sun or rain. Among the overt expressions of such beliefs were tabus on the killing or eating of the totem, ceremonies aimed at its increase and representations in art. These latter, which might be crudely naturalistic or symbolic in style, were commonly engraved or painted on rocks, stone cult objects, wooden shields, boomerangs and spear-throwers or pillars and trees marking burial or other ceremonial places. Of such art very little beyond rock-engravings and, less frequently, paintings might be expected to survive for very long.

As to how far back in prehistory the Australian aboriginal art goes, it has been pointed out that many of the rock-engravings in widely separated parts of the continent, for instance in the Flinders Range of South Australia, at Port Hedland on the north coast of West Australia and on the courses of the Flinders and Burnett rivers of Queensland, are unknown to the existing aborigines. This need not of itself imply a high antiquity, but it has further been pointed out that the pecked areas of some engravings are covered by surface films which must have taken some time to form and that others are on rocks that have fallen as a result of weathering since the execution of the art; again, engravings sometimes depict animals no longer found in the same locality. The early engravings were frequently merely outlined, but sometimes the area of the representation was pecked all over. In addition to abstract patterns, the engravings include representations of human beings, their foot-prints and their hunting equipment and above all animals and their tracks, notably emu, kangaroo, lizards, turtles and fish. Although it seems evident that some of the rock-art is ancient, it is not yet possible to attach specific works of art, still less specific styles, to individual prehistoric cultures. The fact that rock-engravings have been found in Tasmania makes it likely that some of them belong to one of the earliest spreads into Australia, and a number of rock-shelters in eastern New South Wales with red ochre drawings, paintings and stencils of human hands, weapons and culture-heroes have yielded lithic industries with Bondi points. We may feel reasonably sure that the rock art goes far back in Australian prehistory, a reminder of the many other elements in the spiritual life of the early aborigines that we have lost.

The Australian continent was first drawn within the purview of history as a by-product of Dutch enterprise in the East Indies during the early seventeenth century. By the middle of the century the north, west and south coasts of Australia and that of Tasmania had been explored, but it was not until 1770, when Captain Cook sailed north from New Zealand, that the east coast was sighted. Real progress in bringing Australian prehistory to an end was not however initiated till the founding of a penal colony at Sydney in 1788 and the appointment of the first governor of New South Wales in 1810. During the second quarter of the nineteenth century rapid progress was made in exploring the interior. Although it has been possible to undertake important field studies in remote parts of the country down to very recent times, aboriginal culture only continues to survive, like many forms of wild life in much of the world to-day, because it is consciously protected.

THE PACIFIC

It is hardly to be wondered at that the Pacific islands, spread out over vast tracts of ocean, should have been occupied later than the larger island groups of Indonesia, the Philippines and

Melanesia, that stood so much closer to south-east Asia, or even than the Australian mainland and Tasmania. They were not only more remote, but their very discovery and colonization implied a high standard of boat-building, social cohesion and navigation. Indeed the peopling of Micronesia east of the Marianas, which like the Philippines seem to have been occupied as early as the second millennium B.C., and of Polynesia was not accomplished until towards the end of the first millennium A.D. Despite claims to the contrary there is no real doubt that the migrations stemmed predominantly from East Asia. The discovery of Ecuadoran pottery dating from around A.D. 500 on the Galápagos islands some 500 miles from the American coast shows, it is true, that occasional voyages were made in a contrary direction and by means of these the diffusion of any New World elements, such as the sweet potato, should be explained. The broad fact remains that the livestock and almost all of the cultivated plants of the Polynesians, as of the Melanesians, stem from Asiatic sources. The same applies to their material equipment. Certain elements were left behind—pottery for instance failed to spread into Polynesia, or even into Micronesia beyond the Marianas, and the islanders made do with bark cloth in place of textiles—and despite the late date of their migrations the Polynesians used no metal until the European period. On the other hand their fishing gear and the quadrangular polished stone adzes with butts shaped for hafting, both vital elements in their culture and often reaching a high standard of workmanship, stem ultimately from Eurasiatic sources. The discovery and settlement of the Pacific islands was accomplished in double canoes hewn out of great trunks by stone adzes, vessels capable of sailing rapidly before the wind, but which had to be paddled against it. Moreover apart from their families and supplies of food and drink for the voyage, the navigators had to take with them livestock and plant tubers to stock their new homelands, for the Polynesians no less than the Melanesians depended largely on raising species which they themselves introduced. On the other hand their environment provided important additional resources: generally these were in the form of sea-food, but in the case of the earliest settlers of New Zealand they included the moa, a giant ostrich-like, flightless bird. The courage and skill of the Polynesian navigators can be gauged from the fact that without compasses or other scientific aids they sought out small, often widely separated islands distributed over a third of the globe's circumference. The Pacific was first crossed by Europeans in 1521, when Magellan sailed round South America and traversed the whole ocean before hitting the Marianas, but it was not until Captain Cook's explorations between 1768 and 1779 that the brief prehistory of Oceania was brought within immediate sight of its end.

RETROSPECT

The story of mankind reflected in prehistory may be viewed most simply as one of biological progress, of life lived more abundantly and, however one defines this, more fully. It was, as we have seen, as hunters that the Pithecanthropians—and conceivably certain Australopithecines before them—emerged from their basically vegetarian Primate relatives as the ancestors of Man. For by far the greater part of their prehistory, a period to be measured in hundreds of thousands of years, the progress of the hominids was restricted by their abilities as hunters; and the Advanced Palaeolithic cultures that flourished in restricted zones of western Asia, northern Africa and Europe between some thirty-five and ten thousand years ago, were characterized above all by specialized hunting-gear, by the fuller utilization of animal skeletal material and by a graphic art in which fertility and the chase provided the main themes. Conversely, when man first began to advance, around ten thousand years ago, towards the threshold of civilization, he did so by extending his dominance over wild animals and plants up to the point at which he was able to control their breeding and genetic composition so as to elicit new domesticated varieties in accordance with his own needs.

Another sign of growing biological effectiveness was enlargement of the area of settlement. It was not until Late Pleistocene times that man extended beyond the territories of his fossil forebears. Throughout the Early and Middle Pleistocene he was confined to those parts of the Old World free from winter frost and which could be reached on foot. These included the greater part of continental Africa; southern Asia from Syria to Indonesia, which during periods of low ocean levels must have formed a south-eastern extension of the continent; and on the other hand south-western Europe, extending as far north as lowland England and the Elbe. There is no certain evidence that the colonization of any part of the Soviet Union was undertaken until well into the Late Pleistocene, when the Mousterian culture intruded into territories marginal to the north-east of the Black Sea and further east into restricted parts of central Asia, notably western Turkmenia and south-eastern Uzbekistan. The remainder of the southern parts of European Russia as far north as the river Oka, together with extensive tracts of Siberia from the Upper Ob to the Lena Valley, were first occupied by bearers of Advanced Palaeolithic culture equipped with skin clothing and accustomed to erect artificial dwellings in the open. Again, it was presumably at an advanced stage of Late Pleistocene times that groups of hardy hunters pressed through the funnel of north-east Siberia into Alaska and down the foothills of the eastern Rockies to initiate the first or Palaeoindian phase of New World prehistory. Large areas of the globe were first settled during Neothermal times, due partly to new territories becoming available as a result of the melting of Pleistocene ice-sheets, notably in northern Europe, but in large measure to the development of improved means of communication; thus boats, however primitive, were needed before the Wallace line could be crossed and the colonization of Australia begun; again, the settling of most of Micronesia and of Polynesia required navigation of a relatively advanced order; and in our own times long-distance aircraft have served to open up some of the few remaining lands hitherto inaccessible.

As man grew more successful he not only spread farther afield, but multiplied in numbers, and in due course was able to lead a more settled existence in groups sufficiently nucleated to make possible the development of civilization. So long as he was limited to hunting and gathering the animals and plants naturally available in the wild state, he was, with few exceptions, constrained to exist in small groups and move over more or less extensive territories to gain his food in the course of each year. One of the few sources of animal protein obtainable with comparatively slight effort and expenditure of time were certain kinds of fish: as we know from the Indians of the American North-west and as we suspect may have been the case in the Dordogne during the Late Glacial period, it was possible to settle comparatively densely and to enjoy relative security on the banks of rivers having a strong seasonal run of salmon; or, again, those who at a relatively advanced stage of Neothermal times were first willing to venture on the sea and fish from boats, were able to live in permanent coastal settlements. On the other hand most land-bound peoples were more restricted and it was only when advanced hunters were confronted by altogether exceptional circumstances, like those prevailing during the initial dry phase of Neothermal times round the spring of Jericho, that it was feasible to live in settled groups of any size while depending on a hunting and gathering mode of life; and, as we have seen, at Jericho itself the big expansion in population came with the establishment between men and animals of a special form of relationship amounting to primitive domestication. It was the adoption of farming that alone provided the assured basis of subsistence needed before men generally speaking could live permanently in large groups; and it was life in cities which first made possible the sub-division of labour and the social integration needed to ensure rapid and far-reaching advances in the subjugation of natural forces, advances on which the origins, expansion and intensification of civilization itself depended.

In the nature of things it is traces of the intensification and spread of human settlement and of the advances in technology which accompanied them that survive most palpably in the archaeological record, but it would be a great mistake to suppose that these are more than aspects of man's success in the struggle for dominance. No less important are the social, intellectual and spiritual advances which leave fewer material clues behind them. Dependence on social cohesion for such purposes as winning a livelihood, erecting shelters against the elements, ensuring continuity and so on are common to the whole animal world and are frequently carried much further in insect than in human society. The special characteristic of human society, or rather, to express it another way, the reason which causes one to describe a society as human rather than animal, resides in the degree to which its patterns of behaviour are artificial, institutional and traditional, rather than instinctive; and it is because human society is artificial that it is subject to an evolution far more rapid and striking than that of animal societies. Social evolution proceeds by means of culture, the possession of which beyond a certain level itself provides the only valid criterion for distinguishing man and his immediate hominid forebears from the other Primates. The possibility of developing culture, by which one means the patterns of behaviour and thought inherited by virtue of belonging to society rather than through genetical inheritance, depended on the possession of an adequate brain; but conversely, as we have pointed out (p. 26), there are reasons for supposing that the ability to acquire culture was adaptive, in the sense that the strains most capable of doing so were those whose genotypes were propagated most abundantly in the course of natural selection. At least it is true that the period that witnessed the first essays in cultural development was marked by unprecedented advances in the growth of the brain. Equally, though, the physical evolution of *Homo sapiens* in his modern form was already complete with the first appearance of Advanced Palaeolithic culture, with which indeed it seems to have been intimately connected. Quite clearly the immense and accelerating advances in social evolution of the last 50,000 years must, though conferring biological advantages in the sense of permitting greater fullness and security of life, have been independent of organic evolution; indeed it could be argued that in certain respects cultural evolution may have been achieved at some cost to man's purely physical endowment.

The ability to learn, on which culture depends, is widespread in the natural world. In man this ability is not only more developed, but, thanks to speech, social institutions and, beyond the stage of complexity termed civilization, to writing, advances made by individuals can be absorbed into the traditional lore transmitted from one generation to another. The cultural endowment of humanity thus persistently grows. This occurs even though the centre of cultural advance may shift and certain areas undergo more or less pronounced cultural regression. Moreover, the advance is not merely cumulative but tends to gain in momentum, so that the advances of the last five thousand years exceed those of the previous fifty thousand and are in turn eclipsed in many respects by those of the last fifty. All this goes to emphasize the immense importance of transmission or of what in modern society we would speak of as the educational process.

Much of the mounting weight of knowledge transmitted to successive generations can be viewed as no more than the accompaniment of economic and technological advance, part of the cultural apparatus by which men made themselves more effective as biological organisms. There remain spheres of knowledge or awareness which, though not immediately concerned with making life more abundant for mankind in general, have been of supreme importance to individual men and as a matter of fact, through their influence on social life have ultimately served to enhance biological effectiveness. I refer to self-knowledge, awareness of limitations in relation to others and apprehension of unseen powers, qualities that differentiate human personality from those of organisms wholly regulated by instinctive appetites and drives. A crucial moment in the growth of personal awareness was reached with the symbolic recognition of death as the fate of the individual, and for this there is no evidence before the onset of the last major glaciation, when Neanderthaloid people began to give careful burial to the dead and deposited objects with them for use after death. The first sign of aesthetic awareness, evidenced by personal adornment and graphic art, two of the leading features of Advanced Palaeolithic culture, was delayed until the appearance of *Homo sapiens* in his fully developed form. Advanced Palaeolithic art, particularly that applied to the walls and ceilings of caves, is further revealing for the clear indications it gives of a belief in magic, a belief that by going through prescribed motions it is possible automatically to activate supernatural forces for the accomplishing of human desires. It is in the Advanced Palaeolithic art that we first encounter representations of human beings, representations which though primarily intended as symbols of fertility were nevertheless endowed with genuine human feelings (frontispiece). The first portrayals of definite individuals are those modelled in clay on human skulls from the earlier Proto-Neolithic level at Jericho (Pl. II). This is particularly appropriate because it was precisely at this critical juncture in human history that men were beginning to enter an era marked by a progressive widening of the range of social choice, a factor which together with the adoption of settled life made for an increasing variation of cultural style and expression.

The growth of urban civilizations involved a progressive elaboration of social organization, an ever greater subdivision of economic and social functions and an increasingly complex nexus of rights and obligations or, to put it another way, a growing burden of ethical demands. Although individuals were nominally free to reject these, they were under strong pressure to conform; indeed, a certain standard of conformity was necessary if societies were to cohere and survive in the face of internal stresses and external competition, and it must be supposed that those societies were favoured in the struggle for survival which most effectively harnessed the energies of outstanding individuals to the overriding social purpose of maintaining cultural continuity. Customary constraints operated in part through family upbringing and the complex net-work of social institutions and in part through historical lore enshrined for most of human history in oral traditions; but behind all these was the force of supernatural sanctions embodied in religion.

Speculations about the origins and earliest history of religion based solely on what ethnologists have been able to discover about the peoples of simpler culture living in our own time are no longer held of much account, since the primitive stages must have been passed through thousands of years ago under quite different historical circumstances. On the other hand the archaeological traces relate solely to overt manifestations. As a working hypothesis it may be assumed that awareness of superhuman powers and of the need to establish some relation with them formed part and parcel of the emergence of something that we can recognize as human personality: the more consciously aware prehistoric man became of his predicament, the more anxious he would have been to resolve it. The most pressing anxiety, or at least the one which elicited the first overt response, seems as we have already emphasized to have been the full realization of death as a personal fate. The careful disposal of the dead by Neanderthal man initiated funeral rituals which down to our own day have served to reassure the living: the material settings of these rituals varied according to the economic level reached, from shallow graves scooped out of earlier cave deposits to the Pyramids of Egypt, the royal graves of Ur or Mycenae, or the timber-lined shaft-graves of the Altai; but their purpose remained fundamentally the same. Others of the main anxieties, those relating to subsistence and reproduction, found their first expression in the figurines of pregnant women and the representations of game animals accompanied by weapons and other signs on the walls and ceilings of caves, attributable to various groups of Advanced Palaeolithic hunters in Europe. The cult of the generative forces embodied in various symbols of the male and female principles was a persisting element in prehistoric culture that in due course became embodied in the religious traditions of the great literate civilizations of mankind. In the same way subsistence continued to form the object of religious preoccupation. Among agricultural peoples the vegetative principle and forces powerfully affecting this, such as the sun, grew increasingly important and, together with fertility and death, contributed most powerfully to the organized religions that first grew up in the earliest civilizations of western Asia.

Archaeology of itself can hardly answer the question, so often raised, whether the concept of an overall, supreme power or god appeared relatively late as the final outcome of a long evolution or whether, as Wilhelm Schmidt and his followers have maintained, the notion of a transcendent deity was apprehended by primitive man. Even if it were possible to study the oral traditions of the pre-literate societies of remote antiquity, it is doubtful how explicit an answer would be forthcoming, since it was of the essence of primitive religion to be nebulous; clarification had to wait on abstract formulation of speculative thought of the kind first achieved by the philosophical schools of advanced literate societies. The realities of religion among primitive peoples must surely have resided in the ritual by which they assuaged their more pressing anxieties and in the acts of worship by which they sought to establish relations with supernatural forces; and these, whether recognized as stemming from a deity or not, certainly manifested themselves in a multiplicity of outward appearances. Of the existence of ritual practices as far back as the middle of the Late Pleistocene archaeology offers abounding evidence, more particularly of those concerning burial of the dead. Traces of the earliest worship are more elusive, partly because at a certain level religions can hardly be separated from magical practices and partly because of the difficulty of distinguishing for example between sacred and profane structures or between votive offerings and hoards buried for security. The first certain evidence for domestic shrines and public temples comes from the earliest fixed settlements of western Asia. In this region it can be said that the earliest cities grew up with temples at their cores and that the earliest citizens conceived themselves to be subjects of gods and members of temple communities. Indeed it seems to have been for the purpose of maintaining temple records that writing was first devised, as if

17-2

to emphasize that the earliest civilizations were as much the products of religion as of technology; each in its own way served to enhance the biological effectiveness of society, the former by relieving tensions that would otherwise impede its smooth working, the latter by improving the degree of control over physical environments.

To the individuals who comprise human societies the effect of social evolution has been to enrich the quality of their lives. The cultural endowment of mankind has become more variegated, both in respect of the range of potential functions within individual societies and on account of wider divergencies between the form and style of different communities; and this occurred at a time when men were becoming more keenly aware, both aesthetically and intellectually, of the nature and possibilities of their surroundings. One of the most significant lines of progress in human evolution has been a growth in the appreciation of the past and the future. The whole possibility of economic advance has been bound up with the notion of deferring immediate satisfaction in the expectation of future benefits, as when seed corn was preserved even in times of famine to ensure the next crop; hard labour sunk in extensive workings in the hope of reaching ores; or when distant voyages were undertaken in the hope of trade or discovery. Indeed one can say that speculation or prediction, whether in the economic or purely intellectual fields, are among the most significant attributes of man, serving to differentiate him increasingly from the brutes. Again, the transmission of culture has been made possible by storing up experience of the past; much of this communal memory has in course of time been so to speak built into the structure of society, for example into the means of production, but a body of explicit tradition must also have been transmitted largely by word of mouth. Most peoples at a simple level of culture transmit mythological stories purporting to account for outstanding features of their social organization, technology and even physical surroundings. Stories of this kind served at once to invest the existing usages of the community with ancestral sanctions and to enhance the feelings of solidarity of those subscribing to them. In literate communities these functions are to a large degree performed by histories: indeed the major political and cultural units of the modern world owe their very existence to awareness of their common pasts. This is why prehistory, the only kind of history capable of being shared by men of all levels of cultural attainment, whether heirs of ancient literate traditions or only recently preliterate, is so peculiarly relevant to a world which from the standpoint of science and technology is already one.

FURTHER READING

Note. In compiling this list of references for further reading care has been taken to cite works in English wherever possible. References are mainly confined to books and monographs, most of which have more or less comprehensive bibliographies; communications in the periodical literature are as a rule only cited when these have not yet been assimilated in larger works.

CHAPTER I

Physical environment

Deevey, E. S. 'Biogeography of the Pleistocene', *Bull. Geol. Soc. Amer.* LX (1949), 1315–416.

Flint, R. F. *Glacial Geology and the Pleistocene Epoch.* 4th reprint, New York, 1953.

Godwin, H. *The History of the British Flora.* Cambridge, 1956.

Iversen, J. *Landnam i Danmarks Stenalder.* Copenhagen, 1941.

Zeuner, F. E. *The Pleistocene Period, its Climate, Chronology and Faunal Successions.* London, 1959.

Biological evolution

Boule, M. and Vallois, H. V. *Les Hommes Fossiles.* 3rd edn, Paris, 1946.

Breitinger, E. 'Zur frühesten Phase der Hominiden-Evolution', *Beiträge Österreichs zur Erforschung der Vergangenheit und Kulturgeschichte der Menschheit* (ed. E. Breitinger *et al.*), pp. 205–35. Wenner-Gren Foundation, New York, 1959.

Clark, W. le G. *The Fossil Evidence for Human Evolution.* Chicago, 1955.

—— *The Antecedents of Man.* Edinburgh, 1959.

Howell, F. C. 'The Age of the Australopithecines of Southern Africa', *Amer. J. Phys. Anthrop.* XIII (1955), 635–62.

—— 'Upper Pleistocene Men of the Southwest Asian Mousterian', *see below under* Koenigswald, pp. 185–98.

Koenigswald, G. H. R. von (ed.). *Hundert Jahre Neanderthaler.* Wenner-Gren Foundation, New York, 1958.

Oakley, K. P. 'Swanscombe Man', *Proc. Geol. Assoc. London,* LXIII (1952), 271–300.

Robinson, J. T. 'Meganthropus, Australopithecus and Hominids', *Amer. J. Phys. Anthrop.* XI (1953), 1–38.

—— 'Telanthropus and its Phylogenetic Significance', *ibid.* 445–501.

Weidenreich, F. *The Skull of Sinanthropus pekinensis.* Pal. Sinica, no. 127, Pekin, 1943.

CHAPTERS II AND III

Arkell, A. J. *The Old Stone Age in the Anglo-Egyptian Sudan*. Khartoum, 1949.

Balout, L. *Préhistoire de l'Afrique du Nord*. Paris, 1955.

Black, D. *et al*. *Fossil Man in China*. Mem. Geol. Survey China, Ser. A, vol. II, Pekin, 1933.

Boriskovskii, P. I. *Palaeolithic of the Ukraine*, Materialy i Issledovaniya po Arkheologii S.S.S.R. no. 40, Moscow, 1953.

Breuil, H. 'Le Paléolithique au Congo Belge d'après les recherches du Docteur Cabu', *Trans. Roy. Soc. S. Africa*, XXX (1944), 143–60.

—— *Four Hundred Centuries of Cave Art*. Montignac, Dordogne, 1952.

Burkitt, M. C. *South Africa's Past in Stone and Paint*. Cambridge, 1928.

—— *The Old Stone Age*. 3rd edn, London, 1955.

Clark, J. D. *The Prehistory of Southern Africa*. Pelican, London, 1959.

Clark, J. G. D. *The Mesolithic Settlement of Northern Europe*. Cambridge, 1935.

Clark, J. G. D. *et al*. *Excavations at Star Carr*. Cambridge, 1954.

Cole, S. *The Prehistory of East Africa*. Pelican, London, 1954.

Coon, C. S. *Seven Caves*. London, 1957.

De Sonneville-Bordes, D. *Le Paléolithique supérieur en Périgord*. Bordeaux, 1960.

Garrod, D. A. E. and Bate, D. M. A. *The Stone Age of Mount Carmel*. Oxford, 1937.

—— 'The Relations between South-west Asia and Europe in the Later Palaeolithic Age', *J. World History*, I (1953), 13–37.

Golomshtok, E. A. *The Old Stone Age in European Russia*. Trans. Am. Phil. Soc. n.s. XXIX, part 2, Philadelphia, 1938.

Grahmann, R. 'The Lower Palaeolithic Site of Markkleeberg and Other Contemporary Localities near Leipzig', *Trans. Amer. Phil. Soc.* n.s. XLV (1955), 509–687.

Graziosi, P. *L'Arte dell'Antica Eta della Pietra*. Florence, 1956.

Hayes, C. *The Ape in our House*. London, 1952.

Klima, B. 'Übersicht über die jüngsten paläolithischen Forschungen in Mähren', *Quartär*, IX (1957), 85–136.

Köhler, W. *The Mentality of Apes*. Pelican, London, 1952.

Laming, A. *Lascaux, Paintings and Engravings*. Pelican, London, 1959.

Leakey, L. S. B. *Stone Age Africa*. Oxford, 1936.

—— *Olduvai Gorge*. Cambridge, 1951.

—— *Adam's Ancestors*. 4th edn, London, 1953.

McBurney, C. B. M. 'The Geographical Study of the Older Palaeolithic Stages in Europe', *Proc. Prehist. Soc.* XVI (1950), 163–83.

McBurney, C. B. M. 'Evidence for the Distribution in Space and Time of Neanderthaloids and Allied Strains in Northern Africa', *Hundert Jahre Neanderthaler* (von Koenigswald ed.), pp. 253–64. New York, 1958.

Movius, H. L. *The Lower Palaeolithic Cultures of Southern and Eastern Asia.* Trans. Amer. Phil. Soc. n.s. XXXVIII, part 4. Philadelphia, 1948.

—— 'Palaeolithic and Mesolithic Sites in Soviet Central Asia', *Proc. Amer. Phil. Soc.* XCVII (1953), 383–421.

—— 'The Mousterian Cave of Teshik-Tash, Southeastern Uzbekistan, Central Asia', *Amer. School of Prehist. Res. Bull.* XVII (1953), 11–71.

—— 'Palaeolithic Archaeology in Southern and Eastern Asia, exclusive of India', *J. World History,* II (1955), 257–82, 525–53.

—— 'Radiocarbon Dates and Upper Palaeolithic Archaeology', *Current Anthropology,* I (1960), 355–91. Chicago.

Oakley, K. P. *Man the Tool-maker.* 2nd edn, B.M. (Nat. Hist.), London, 1952.

Obermaier, H. *Fossil Man in Spain.* Oxford, 1925.

Okladnikov, A. P. *Palaeolithic and Neolithic in the SSSR,* vol. III. Materialy i Issledovaniya po Arkheologiyi SSSR, no. 59, Moscow, 1957.

Pericot García, L. *La Cueva del Parpallo.* Madrid, 1942.

Robinson, J. T. and Mason, R. J. 'Occurrence of Stone Artefacts with Australopithecus at Sterkfontein', *Nature,* CLXXX (1957), 521–4.

Thorpe, W. H. *Learning and Instinct in Animals.* Cambridge, 1956.

Tobias, P. V. and Plotkin, R. (eds.). *The Leech, Raymond A. Dart Commemorative Number,* XXVIII, nos. 3–5. Witwatersrand, 1958.

Vértes, L. *et al. Die Höhle von Istállóskö.* Acta Arch. Hung. V. Budapest, 1955.

Yerkes, R. M. *Chimpanzees. A Laboratory Colony.* New Haven, 1943.

Zeuner, F. E. *Dating the Past.* 3rd edn, London, 1952.

CHAPTER IV

Blegen, C. W. *et al. Troy: General Introduction, the First and Second Settlements.* Princeton, 1950.

Braidwood, R. J. *The Near East and the Foundations for Civilization.* Eugene, 1952.

Braidwood, R. J. and L. 'The Earliest Village Communities of Southwestern Asia', *J. World History,* I (1953), 278–310.

Braidwood, R. J. and Reed, C. A. 'The Achievement and Early Consequences of Food-Production', *Cold Spring Harbor Symposium on Quantitative Biology,* XXII (1957), 19–31.

Braidwood, R. J. and L., Smith, J. G. and Leslie, C. 'Matarrah', *J. Near Eastern Studies,* XI (1952), 1–75.

Braidwood, R. V. and Howe, B. *Prehistoric Investigations in Iraqi Kurdistan.* Chicago, 1960.

Childe, V. G. 'The Urban Revolution', *The Town Planning Review*, XXI (1950), 3–17.

—— *New Light on the Most Ancient East.* 4th edn, London, 1952.

Frankfort, H. *The Birth of Civilization in the Near East.* London, 1951.

Garstang, J. *Prehistoric Mersin.* Oxford, 1953.

Ghirshman, R. *Fouilles de Sialk.* 2 vols., Paris, 1938–39.

Hall, H. R. and Woolley, L. *Ur Excavations I: al'Ubaid.* London, 1927.

Kenyon, K. M. *Digging up Jericho.* London, 1957.

Lamb, W. *The Excavations at Thermi in Lesbos.* Cambridge, 1936.

Lloyd, S., Safer, F. and Braidwood, R. J. 'Tell Hassuna', *J. Near Eastern Studies*, IV (1945), 255–89.

McCown, D. *The Comparative Stratigraphy of Early Iran.* Chicago, 1942.

Mallowan, M. E. L. and Rose, J. C. *Prehistoric Assyria: The Excavations at Tell Arpachiyah.* Oxford, 1935.

Mecquenem, R. de. 'Fouilles de Suse, 1933 et 1939', *Mém. de la Mission arch. en Iran*, XXIX (1943), 3–161.

Perkins, A. L. *The Comparative Archaeology of Early Mesopotamia.* Chicago, 1949.

Schmidt, H. *Tell Halaf.* Bd. I, Berlin, 1943.

Speiser, E. A. *Excavations at Tepe Gawra*, vol. I. Philadelphia, 1935.

Tobler, A. J. *Excavations at Tepe Gawra*, vol. II. Philadelphia, 1950.

Woolley, L. *Ur Excavations II: The Royal Cemetery.* London, 1934.

—— 'The Prehistoric Pottery of Carchemish', *Iraq*, I (1934) 146–62.

CHAPTER V

Ancient Egypt

Baumgärtel, E. *The Cultures of Prehistoric Egypt.* Oxford, 1947.

Brunton, G. and Caton-Thompson, G. *The Badarian Civilization.* London, 1928.

Childe, V. G. *New Light on the Most Ancient East*, 4th edn, chaps. III–V. London, 1952.

Capart, J. *Les Débuts de l'Art en Egypte.* Brussels, 1904.

Caton-Thompson, G. *The Desert Fayum.* London, 1935.

Edwards, I. E. S. *The Pyramids of Egypt.* London, 1947.

Frankfort, H. *The Birth of Civilization in the Near East.* London, 1951.

Glanville, S. R. K. (ed.). *The Legacy of Egypt.* Oxford, 1942.

Junker, H. 'Vorläufige Berichte über die Gräbung...auf der neolithischen Siedlung von Merimde-Benisalâme', *Anz. d. Akad. d. Wiss. Wien., phil.-hist. Kl.*, 1929, 1930, 1932 and 1940.

Menghin, O. and Amer, M. *The Excavations...in the Neolithic Site at Maadi: 1st Prel. Rep., Season 1930–1*. Cairo, 1932.

Petrie, W. M. F. *The Royal Tombs*. Parts I–II, London, 1900–1.

—— *Prehistoric Egypt*. London, 1920.

—— *The Making of Egypt*. London, 1939.

Quibell, J. E. and Green, F. W. *Hierakonpolis*. Vols. I–II, London, 1900–2.

Later prehistoric Africa

Balout, L. *Préhistoire de l'Afrique du Nord*, chap. x. Paris, 1955.

Arkell, A. J. *Early Khartoum*. Oxford, 1949.

—— *Shaheinab*. Oxford, 1953.

Caton-Thompson, G. *The Zimbabwe Culture*. Oxford, 1931.

Clarke, J. D. *The Prehistory of Southern Africa*, chaps. 8–10. Pelican, London, 1959.

Cole, S. *The Prehistory of East Africa*, chaps. 8–10. Pelican, London, 1954.

Fagg, B. 'New Discoveries from Ife...', *Man*, 1949, no. 79.

—— 'A Life-size Terra-cotta Head from Nok', *Man*, 1956, no. 95.

Leakey, M. D. 'Report on the Excavations at Hyrax Hill, Nakuru, Kenya Colony', *Trans. Roy. Soc. S. Africa*, xxx (1945), 271–406.

Lowe, C. van Riet. *The Distribution of Prehistoric Rock Engravings and Paintings in South Africa*. Pretoria, 1956.

Shaw, C. T. 'Report on Excavations carried out in the Cave known as "Bosumpra" at Abetifi, Kwahu, Gold Coast Colony', *Proc. Prehist. Soc.* x (1944), 1–67.

Summers, R. F. H. *Inyanga: Ancient Settlements in Southern Rhodesia*. Cambridge, 1958.

Vaufrey, R. *L'Art rupestre nord-africain*. Paris, 1939.

CHAPTERS VI AND VII

Arnal, J. and Burnez, C. 'Die Struktur des französischen Neolithikums auf Grund neuester stratigraphischer Beobachtungen', *Ber. Röm.-Germ. Komm.* 1956–7, 1–90.

Atkinson, R. J. C. *Stonehenge*. London, 1956.

Bailloud, G. and Mieg de Boofzheim, P. *Les Civilizations néolithiques de la France*. Paris, 1955.

Bloch, R. *Ancient Peoples and Places. The Etruscans*. London, 1958.

Brjussov, A. J. *Geschichte der neolithischen Stämme im europäischen Teil der USSR*. Berlin, 1952.

Brøndsted, J. *Danmarks Oldtid*. Bd. I–III, Copenhagen, 1957–9.

Buttler, W. *Der Donauländische und der westische Kulturkreis der jüngeren Steinzeit*. Berlin, 1938.

Childe, V. G. 'The Final Bronze Age in the Near East and in Temperate Europe', *Proc. Prehist. Soc.* XIV (1948), 177–95.

—— *Prehistoric Migrations in Europe*. Oslo, 1950.

—— 'The First Waggons and Carts—from the Tigris to the Severn', *Proc. Prehist. Soc.* XVII (1951), 177–94.

—— *The Dawn of European Civilization*. 6th edn, London, 1957.

Ciba Foundation Symposium on Medical Biology and Etruscan Origins. London, 1959.

Clark, J. G. D. *Prehistoric Europe: the Economic Basis*. London, 1952.

Daniel, G. E. *The Megalith Builders of Western Europe*. London, 1958.

Déchelette, J. *Manuel d'archéologie préhistorique*. Vols. I–III, Paris, 1924–7.

Dehn, W. 'Die Heuneburg beim Talhof...', *Fundber. aus Schwaben*, XIV (1957), 78–99. Stuttgart.

Diringer, D. *The Alphabet*. 2nd edn, London, 1949.

Dunbabin, T. J. *The Western Greeks*. Oxford, 1948.

Eggers, H. J. *Der Römische Import im Freien Germanien*. Berlin, 1951.

Evans, A. *The Palace of Minos*. London, 1921–8.

Evans, J. D. 'Two Phases of Prehistoric Settlement in the Western Mediterranean', *13th Ann. Rep. and Bull. London Univ. Inst. Arch.* pp. 49–70. Berlin, 1958.

Filip, J. *Keltové ve Střední Europě*. Prague, 1957.

Fox, C. F. C. *Pattern and Purpose. A Survey of Early Celtic Art in Britain*. Cardiff, 1958.

Gaul, J. H. *The Neolithic Period in Bulgaria*. Amer. School. Prehist. Res., Harvard Bull. XVI, 1948.

Gimbutas, M. *The Prehistory of Eastern Europe. I. Ibid.* XX. 1956.

—— 'Borodino, Seima and their Contemporaries: Key Sites for the Bronze Age Chronology of Eastern Europe', *Proc. Prehist. Soc.* XXII (1956).

Gjessing, G. *Norges Steinalder*. Oslo, 1945.

Guyan, W. U. (ed.). *Das Pfahlbauproblem*. Basel, 1955.

Hawkes, C. F. C. 'From Bronze Age to Iron Age: Middle Europe, Italy, and the North and West'. *Proc. Prehist. Soc.* XIV (1948), 196–218.

—— 'The ABC of the British Iron Age', *Antiquity*, XXXIII (1959), 170–88.

Hencken, H. *The Archaeology of Cornwall and Scilly*, chap. V. London, 1932.

—— *Indo-European Languages and Archaeology*. Am. Anthrop. Mem. 84, 1955.

—— 'Archaeological Evidence for the Origin of the Etruscans', *Ciba Symposium*, pp. 29–47. London, 1959.

Heurtley, W. A. *Prehistoric Macedonia*. Cambridge, 1939.

Holmqvist, W. *Germanic Art*. Stockholm, 1955.

Jacobsthal, P. *Early Celtic Art*. Oxford, 1944.

Joffroy, R. *Le Trésor de Vix*. Paris, 1954.

Karo, G. *Die Schachtgräber von Mykenai*. Munich, 1930.

Kimmig, W. 'Zur Urnenfelderkultur in Südwesteuropa', *Festschrift für Peter Goessler*, pp. 41–107. Stuttgart, 1954.

Lorimer, L. H. *Homer and the Monuments*. London, 1950.

Milojčić, V. *Chronologie der jüngeren Steinzeit Mittel- und Südosteuropas*. Berlin, 1949.

Minns, E. H. *Scythians and Greeks*. Cambridge, 1913.

—— *The Art of the Northern Nomads*. British Academy, London, 1942.

Mongait, A. *Archaeology in the U.S.S.R.* Moscow, 1959.

Muluquer de Motes, J. 'Pueblas Celtas', *Historia de España*, T. I, 3, 5–194. Madrid, 1954.

Navarro, J. M. de. *A Survey of Research on an Early Phase of Celtic Culture*. British Academy, London, 1936.

Nilsson, M. P. *The Minoan–Mycenaean Religion and its Survival in Greek Religion*. 2nd edn, Lund, 1950.

Pendlebury, J. D. S. *The Archaeology of Crete*. London, 1939.

Pericot García, L. *La España primitiva*. Barcelona, 1950.

Piggott, S. *The Neolithic Cultures of the British Isles*. Cambridge, 1954.

Pittioni, R. and Preuschen, E. *Untersuchungen im Bergbaugebiete Kelchalpe bei Kitzbühel, Tirol*. Vienna, 1937 and 1949.

—— *Urgeschichte des Österreichischen Raumes*. Vienna, 1954.

Powell, T. G. E. *Ancient Peoples and Places. The Celts*. London, 1958.

Rice, T. T. *Ancient Peoples and Places. The Scythians*. London, 1957.

Previté-Orton, C. W. *The Shorter Cambridge Medieval History*. Cambridge, 1952.

Rostovtzeff, M. *Iranians and Greeks in South Russia*. Oxford, 1922.

Rudenko, S. I. *Kulturnoe naselenie gornovo Altaya v Skifskoe vremia*. Moscow, 1953.

Sandars, N. K. *Bronze Age Cultures in France*. Cambridge, 1957.

Shetelig, H., Falk, H. and Gordon, E. V. *Scandinavian Archaeology*. Oxford, 1937.

Stone, J. F. S. and Thomas, L. C. 'The Use and Distribution of Faience in the Ancient East and Prehistoric Europe', *Proc. Prehist. Soc.* XXII (1956), 37–84.

Sulimirski, T. *Polska Przedhistoryczna*. London, 1957–9.

Taylour, Lord W. *Mycenaean Pottery in Italy and Adjacent Areas*. Cambridge, 1958.

Ventris, M. and Chadwick, J. *Documents in Mycenaean Greek*. Cambridge, 1956.

Vulpe, R., *Izvoare. Săpăturile din 1936–48*. Bucharest, 1957.

Wace, A. J. B. and Thompson, M. S. *Prehistoric Thessaly*. Cambridge, 1912.

Wace, A. J. B. *Mycenae. An Archaeological History and Guide*. Princeton, 1949.

Weinberg, S. S. (ed.). *The Aegean and the Near East*. New York, 1956.

CHAPTER VIII

India

Ancient India. Bulletin of the Archaeological Survey of India.

Childe, V. Gordon. *New Light on the Most Ancient East*, chap. IX. London, 1952.

Fairservis, W. A. *Excavations in the Quetta Valley, West Pakistan.* Amer. Mus. Nat. Hist., New York, 1956.

Ghosh, A. (ed.). *Ancient India*, no. 9. Special Jubilee Number. A Survey of Half a Century, 1953.

Gordon, D. H. *The Pre-historic Background of Indian Culture.* Bombay, 1958.

Krishnaswami, V. D. 'The Neolithic Pattern of India', *46th Indian Science Congress*, Delhi, 1959.

Lal, B. B. 'Excavations at Hastinapura and Other Explorations in the Upper Ganga and Sutlej Basins, 1950–2...', *Ancient India*, nos. 10–11 (1954–5), 1–151.

Mackay, E. J. H. *Further Excavations at Mohenjo-daro.* Delhi, 1938.

Marshall, Sir John *et al. Mohenjo-daro and the Indus Civilization.* London, 1931.

Piggott, Stuart. *Prehistoric India.* Pelican, London, 1950.

Sankalia, H. D., Subbarao, B. and Deo, S. B. 'The Archaeological Sequence of Central India', *Southwestern J. of Archaeology*, IX, 343–56. Albuquerque, New Mexico, 1953.

—— *The Excavations at Maheshwar and Navdatoli 1952–3.* Poona, 1958.

Subbarao, B. *The Personality of India.* 2nd edn, Baroda, 1958.

Vats, M. S. *Excavations at Harappā.* Delhi, 1940.

Wheeler, Sir R. E. M. 'Brahmagiri and Chandra-valli 1947: Megalithic and Other Cultures in the Chitaldrug District, Mysore State', *Ancient India*, no. 4, 180–310, 1948.

—— *The Indus Valley Civilization.* Cambridge, 1953.

China

Andersson, J. G. 'An Early Chinese Culture', *Bull. Geological Soc. of China*, no. 5. Peking, 1923.

—— *Children of the Yellow Earth.* London, 1934.

—— 'Researches into the Prehistory of the Chinese', *Bull. Museum Far Eastern Antiquities Stockholm*, no. 15 (1943).

—— 'The Site of Chu Chia Chai', *ibid.* no. 17 (1945).

Arne, T. J. 'Painted Stone Age Pottery from the Province of Honan, China', *Palaeontologia Sinica*, Ser. D, vol. I, fasc. 2. Peking, 1925.

Bishop, C. W. 'The Neolithic Age in Northern China', *Antiquity* (1933), 389–404.

—— 'Beginnings of Civilization in Eastern Asia', *Antiquity* (1940), 301 ff.

Bylin-Althin, M. 'The Sites of Ch'i Chia P'ing and Lo Han T'ang in Kansu', *Bull. Museum Far Eastern Antiquities, Stockholm*, no. 18 (1946), 383–498.

Chêng Tê-K'un. *Archaeological Studies in Szechwan*. Cambridge, 1957.

—— 'The Origin and Development of Shang Culture', *Asia Major*, vol. VI (1957), 80–98.

—— *Archaeology in China*, vol. I, *Prehistoric China*. Cambridge, 1958.

Childe, V. G. 'The Socketed Celt in Upper Eurasia', *Ann. Rep. Inst. Arch. London Univ. for 1953*, II, 25.

Creel, H. G. *The Birth of China*. London, 1936.

Finn, D. J. *Archaeological Finds on Lamma Island near Hong Kong*. Hong Kong, 1958.

Karlgren, B. 'Some Weapons and Tools of the Yin Dynasty', *Bull. Museum Far Eastern Antiquities*, no. 17 (1945), 101–45.

Li Chi *et al.* 'Ch'êng-tzŭ-yai, A Report of Excavations of the Proto-historic Site at Ch'êng-tzŭ-yai, Li-ch'eng Hsien, Shantung', *Archaeologica Sinica*, no. 1. Nanking, 1934.

Loehr, Max. 'Zur Ur- und Vorgeschichte Chinas', *Saeculum*, Bd. III (1952), 15–55.

Maglioni, R. 'Archaeology in South China', *J. East Asiatic Studies*, II (1952), 1–20.

Maringer, J. *Contribution to the Prehistory of Mongolia*. Stockholm, 1950.

Needham, J. *Science and Civilization in China*, vol. I, *Introductory Orientations*. Cambridge, 1954.

Nelson, N. C. 'The Dune Dwellers of the Gobi', *Natural History*, XXVI (1926), 246–51.

Pei Wên-Chung, 'On a Mesolithic (?) Industry in the Caves of Kwangsi', *Bull. Geological Soc. of China*, no. 14 (1935), 383–412.

Teilhard de Chardin, P. and Pei Wên-Chung. *Le Néolithique de la Chine*. Peking, 1944.

Tolstoy, P. 'Some Amerasian Pottery Traits in North Asian Prehistory', *American Antiquity*, XIX (1953–4), 25–39.

Torii, R. and K. 'Etudes Archéologiques et Ethnologiques. Populations Primitives de la Mongolie Orientale', *J. College of Science Imp. Univ. of Tokyo*, vol. XXXV, art. 4, 1–100. Tokyo, 1914.

Wu, G. D. *Prehistoric Pottery in China*. London, 1938.

South-east Asia, Indonesia and the Philippines

Beyer, H. O. 'Outline Review of Philippine Archaeology...', *Philippine J. of Science*, LXXVII (1947), 205–374.

Goloubew, V., 'L'Age du Bronze au Tonkin et dans le Nord-Annam', *Bull. de l'Ecole Franç. d'Extrême Orient*, XXIX, 1–46.

Harrisson, T. 'The Great Cave of Niah', *Man*, LVII (1957), no. 211.

Heekeren, M. R. van. *The Stone Age of Indonesia*. The Hague, 1956.
—— *The Bronze–Iron Age of Indonesia*. The Hague, 1958.
Heine-Geldern, R. von. 'Prehistoric Research in the Netherlands Indies', *Science and Scientists in the Netherlands Indies* (P. Honig and F. Verdoon eds.), pp. 129–67. New York, 1945.
Mansuy, H. 'Contribution a l'étude de la préhistoire de l'Indochine. IV. Stations préhistoriques dans les carènes du massif calcaire de Bac-Son (Tonkin)', *Mém. Serv. Géologique de l'Indochine*, XI, no. 2. Hanoi, 1924.
Mansuy, H. and Colani, M. *Ibid*. 'VIII. Néolithique inférieure (Bacsonien) et Néolithique supérieure dans le Haut-Tonkin', *op. cit.* XII, no. 3. Hanoi, 1925.
Sieveking, G. de G. 'Excavations at Gua Cha, Kelantan, 1954. Part I', *Federation Museums J.* (Malaya), I–II (1954–5), 75–138.
Solheim, W. G. 'Philippine Archaeology', *Archaeology*, VI (1953), 154–8.
Tweedie, M. W. F. 'The Stone Age in Malaya', *J. Malayan Branch Roy. Asiatic Soc.* XXVI, part 2 (1953), 1–90.
—— *Prehistoric Malaya*. Singapore, 1955.

Japan

Groot, G. J. *The Prehistory of Japan*. New York, 1951.
Kidder, J. E. *Ancient Peoples and Places*. *Japan*. London, 1959.
Maringer, J. 'A Core and Flake Industry of Palaeolithic Type from Central Japan', *Artibus Asiae*, XIX, part 2 (1956), 111–25.
—— 'Some Stone Tools of Early Hoabinhian Type from Central Japan', *Man*, 1957, no. 1.
Sugihara, S. *The Stone Age Remains Found at Iwajuku, Gumma Pref., Japan*. Tokyo, 1956.

North-east Asia

Chard, C. S. 'An Outline of the Prehistory of Siberia', *Southwestern J. of Anthropology*, XIV (1958), 1–33.

CHAPTER IX

Bird, J. B. 'Preceramic Cultures in Chicama and Viru', *Mem. Soc. Amer. Arch.* no. 4 (1948), 21–8.
—— 'Antiquity and Migrations of the Early Inhabitants of Patagonia', *Geogr. Rev.* XXVIII (1938), 250–75.
Bushnell, G. H. S. *Ancient Peoples and Places*. *Peru*. London, 1956.
Bushnell, G. H. S. and McBurney, C. 'New World Origins seen from the Old World', *Antiquity*, XXXIII (1959), 93–101.
Collins, H. B. 'Eskimo Archaeology and its Bearing on the Problem of Man's Antiquity in America', *Proc. Amer. Phil. Soc.* vol. LXXXVI, no. 2, 220–35.

Giddings, J. L. 'A Flint Site in Northernmost Manitoba', *Amer. Antiquity*, XXI (1951), 255–68.

Griffin, J. B. *Archaeology of Eastern United States*. Chicago, 1952.

Handbook of South American Indians. Smithsonian Institution, Bur. Amer. Ethnology, Bull. 143. Washington, 1946.

Jennings, J. D. *Danger Cave*. Utah, 1957.

Lothrop, S. K. *The Indians of Tierra del Fuego*. New York, 1928.

Kroeber, A. L. *Cultural and Natural Areas of Native North America*. Berkeley, 1939.

MacNeish, R. S. 'Preliminary Archaeological Investigations in the Sierra de Tamaulipas, Mexico', *Trans. Amer. Phil. Soc.* XLVIII (1958), part 6.

Martin, P. S., Quimby, G. L. and Collier, D. *Indians before Columbus*. Chicago, 1946.

Mathiassen, T. *Archaeology of the Central Eskimos*. Copenhagen, 1927.

Miles, S. W. 'A Revaluation of the Old Copper Industry', *Amer. Antiquity*, XVI (1951), 240–7.

Morley, S. G. *The Ancient Maya*. Stanford, 1946.

Rex Gonzalez, A. 'Antiguo horizonte precerámico en las Sierras Centrales de la Argentina', *Runa Arch. para las Ciencias del Hombre*, V, 110–33. Buenos Aires, 1952.

Thompson, J. E. S. *The Rise and Fall of Maya Civilization*. Oklahoma, 1954.

Vaillant, G. C. *The Aztecs of Mexico*. Pelican, 1951.

Willey, G. R. *Prehistoric Settlement Patterns in the New World*. New York, 1956.

Wormington, H. M. *Ancient Man in North America*. Denver, 1957.

CHAPTER X

Australia and Tasmania

Balfour, H. 'The Status of the Tasmanians among the Stone-age Peoples', *Proc. Prehist. Soc. East Anglia*, V (1925), 1–15.

Basedow, H. *The Australian Aboriginal*. Adelaide, 1925.

Campbell, T. D. and Noone, H. V. V. 'South Australian Microlithic Stone Implements', *Records S. Australian Mus.* VII (1943), 281–307.

Davidson, D. S. 'Archaeological Problems of Northern Australia', *J. Roy. Anthrop. Inst.* LXV (1935), 145–83.

—— *Aboriginal Australian and Tasmanian Rock Carvings and Paintings*. Mem. American Phil. Soc. V (1936).

Gill, E. D. 'Geological Evidence in Western Victoria Relative to the Antiquity of the Australian Aborigines', *Mem. Nat. Mus.* XVIII, 25–92. Melbourne, 1953.

Hale, H. M. and Tindale, N. B. 'Notes on Some Human Remains in the Lower Murray Valley, South Australia', *Records S. Australian Mus.* IV (1930), 145–218.

Howells, W. H. 'Anthropometry of the Natives of Arnhem Land and the Australian Race Problem', *Papers Peabody Mus. Amer. Arch. and Ethn. Harvard Univ.* XVI (1937), 1–97.

Keble, R. A. 'Notes on Australian Quaternary Climates and Migration', *Mem. Nat. Mus.* XV, 28–81. Melbourne, 1947.

McCarthy, F. D. 'Two Pebble Industry Sites of Hoabinhian I Type on the North Coast of New South Wales', *Records Australian Mus.* XXI (1941), 21–6. Sydney.

McCarthy, F. D. 'An Analysis of the Knapped Implements from Eight *eloura* Industry Stations on the South Coast of New South Wales', *Records Australian Mus.* XXI (1943), 127–53, Sydney.

—— *The Stone Implements of Australia.* Sydney, 1946.

—— 'The Lapstone Creek Excavation', *Records Australian Mus.* XXII (1948), 1–34.

—— 'Stone Implements from Tandandjal Cave—An Appendix', *Oceania,* XXI (1951), 205–13.

Macintosh, N. W. G. 'Archaeology of Tandandjal Cave, South-west Arnhem Land', *Oceania,* XXI (1951), 178–204.

Mahony, D. J. 'The Problem of Antiquity of Man in Australia', *Mem. Nat. Mus. Victoria,* XIII (1943), 7–56.

Mitchell, S. R. *Stone-Age Craftsmen. Stone Tools and Camping-Places of the Australian Aborigines.* Melbourne, 1949.

Mountford, C. P. *Arnhem Land. Art, Myth and Symbolism.* Melbourne, 1956.

Noone, H. V. V. 'Some Aboriginal Stone Implements of Western Australia', *Rec. South Australian Mus.* VII (1943), 271–80.

Pulleine, R. H. 'The Tasmanians and Their Stone Culture', *Rep. 19th Meeting Australian Assn. Adv. Science,* Hobart (1929), pp. 294–322.

Roth, H. L. *The Aborigines of Tasmania.* London, 1890.

Setzler, F. M. and McCarthy, F. D. 'A Unique Archaeological Specimen from Australia', *J. Washington Acad. of Sciences,* XL (1950), 1–5.

Spencer, B. and Gillen, F. J. *The Native Tribes of Central Australia.* London, 1899.

Thomson, D. F. *Economic Structure and the Ceremonial Exchange Cycle in Arnhem Land.* Melbourne, 1949.

Tindale, N. B. 'Culture Succession in South Eastern Australia from Late Pleistocene to the Present', *Rec. South Australian Mus.* XIII (1957).

Wunderly, J. 'The Origin of the Tasmanian Race', *Man,* XXXVIII (1938), no. 217.

The Pacific

Duff, R. *The Moa-hunter Period of Maori Culture.* Wellington, N.Z., 1956.

Gifford, E. W. and Shutler, D. 'Archaeological Excavations in New Caledonia', *Univ. of California Anthrop. Records,* XVIII (1956), no. 1.

Golson, J. 'Dating New Zealand's Prehistory', *J. Polynesian Soc.* LXIV (1955), 113–36.

—— 'New Zealand Archaeology, 1957', *J. Polynesian Soc.* LXVI (1957), 271–90.

Heyerdal, T. and Skjölsvold, A. *Archaeological Evidence of Pre-Spanish Visits to the Galápagos Islands.* Mem. Soc. Am. Arch. no. 12 (1956).

Métraux, A. *Easter Island. A Stone-age Civilization of the Pacific.* London, 1957.

Oliver, Douglas L. *The Pacific Islands.* Harvard, 1951.

Sauer, C. O. 'Agricultural Origins and Dispersals', *Am. Geogr. Soc. Bowman Memorial Lectures.* Ser. 2. 1952.

Sharp, A. *Ancient Voyages in the Pacific.* Pelican, London, 1957.

Solheim, W. G. 'Oceanian Pottery Manufacture', *J. East Asiatic Studies*, I (1951), no. 2, 1–39.

Spoehr, A. 'Marianas Prehistory. Archaeological Survey and Excavations on Saipan, Tinian and Rota', *Fieldiana: Anthropology*, XLVIII, 1–187. Chicago, 1957.

INDEX

Abbevillian culture 36, 38
Abyssinia 46
Acheulian culture 21, 36
Adalbert, St 177
Adena culture 233
Aegean 120, 123, 125, 135–8, 161, 162
Afghanistan 52, 80, 87, 106, 178
Afontova Gora, U.S.S.R. 61
Africa 12, 15, 17–20, 24 f., 31 f., 35 ff., 37,
    39 ff., 45 f., 48 f., 64, 77, 97, 99–118,
    135 ff., 148, 154, 161, 163 f., 166, 173,
    175, 178 ff., 252, 258
Agricola 173
agriculture 66 f., 72, 76–90, 99 ff., 113–
    16, 119–32, 139, 142 f., 156, 193,
    201 f., 204, 206, 208 ff., 221 f., 229 ff.,
    233
Ahrensburg culture 61
Ainu 211
Alacu 238 f.
Alaric 175
Alaska, U.S.A. 13, 62, 211, 217, 232, 236 ff.,
    253
Aleutian islands 236
Alexander the Great 98, 112, 164, 190
Algeria 20, 39, 46, 113
Algonquins 234
Allerød oscillation 12, 213
alphabet 161 f.
Altamira, Spain 59
Al Ubaid, Iraq 90 f.
amber 71, 132, 141, 145, 150 ff.
America, North 8, 13, 15, 62, 76, 211–26,
    230–9, 253 f.
America, South 218 f., 212 ff., 224–9, 238–9,
    250 f.
Ampurias, Spain 163
Amratian culture 103 ff.
Amri, Pakistan 182
Amur river 191, 211
Anasazi people 230 f.
Anau, Turkestan, U.S.S.R. 89
Andaman islands 24
Angara Valley 210
Angles-sur-Anglin, France 59
Anglo-Saxons 175 f.

Angola 37, 41
Anyang, China 197 f.
Apennine culture 158, 165
apes, anthropoid (Pongidae) 16, 27 f., 31,
    33
Arabs 116 ff.
Arcadius 175
Archaic (N. Am.) culture 218, 231 ff., 235,
    239
Arctic culture 143–6, 193, 198 f.
Argentine 219
Argissa, Greece 121
Arnhem Land, Australia 243, 246 f.
Arpachiya, Iraq 87, 91
art 43, 49, 54–60, 65, 67 f., 71, 107 f., 113,
    115, 135, 138 f., 146, 168, 171 f., 174,
    189, 199, 220, 223, 234, 237, 248 f.,
    252, 256 ff.
Aryans 186 f., 191
Asia 13, 15, 17–21, 23 ff., 31–5, 37, 41 ff.,
    45, 49–52, 60–7, 75, 77–98, 101, 105 f.,
    108, 112, 118, 129, 134–7, 147 f., 154 f.,
    160 f., 163 f., 166–9, 173, 177–213,
    215, 236 ff., 240 ff., 244, 246–50, 252 ff.,
    257 ff.
Aśoka 191
Assyrians 97, 112, 163
Aterian culture 46
Augustine, St 176
Aunjetitz culture 150 f., 155
Aurignacian culture 51 f., 55, 58
Australasia 13, 240–51
Australoids 242
Australopithecines 17 ff., 31, 252
Austria 52, 124, 133, 155 f., 169
axes, adzes 70 f., 82, 101, 105, 114 f., 120,
    125 ff., 130–4, 139, 141, 149, 156,
    188 f., 198 f., 202–6, 208, 211, 246 f.,
    250
Ayampitín, Argentine 219
Azilian culture 68, 73
Aztec civilization 221, 225

Babylon 97
Badarian culture 102 f.
Baden culture 133